THE REFERENCE SHELF (Continued)

Volume XII. $

Volume XI

Volume X. $4.20

THE REFERENCE SHELF

Vol. 15   No. 2

UNIVERSAL MILITARY SERVICE

Compiled by
ROBERT E. SUMMERS
and
HARRISON B. SUMMERS

NEW YORK
THE H. W. WILSON COMPANY
1941

7287

ACKNOWLEDGMENT

For their kindness in permitting the reproduction of copyright materials appearing in these pages or in making available other materials, the compilers are deeply indebted to Dr. Paul F. Lazarsfeld, Dr. Robert M. Hutchins, Mr. Frank E. Samuel, Mr. Frank A. Tichenor, Mr. R. E. Wood, Mr. Albert Shaw, Jr., the Funk & Wagnalls Company, the Foreign Policy Association, and the Civilian Military Education Fund; and also to the editors of *The American Magazine, The American Mercury, The Chicago Tribune, Christian Century, Education, Educational Record, Fortune, Liberty, The Nation, The New Republic, Newsweek, The New York Times, New York World-Telegram, PM, Reader's Digest, The Reserve Officer, Scholastic, School and Society, School Review, Science News-Letter, Scribner's Commentator, Survey, Thought,* and *Time.*

R. E. Summers
H. B. Summers

New York, N.Y.

September 15, 1941

BRIEF

No brief has been included in this volume, but an excellent one on this subject may be found in Julia E. Johnsen's *Compulsory Military Training,* The Reference Shelf, Volume 14, No. 6. H. W. Wilson Co.

CONTENTS

CONTENTS

INTRODUCTION

Universal military training as a permanent peacetime policy is still an unfamiliar idea to the people of the United States. We are not a militaristic nation; we have had no fears of invasion, and no desire to attack our neighbors or nations in other parts of the world. So we have been committed as a people to the policy of maintaining a small military establishment in peacetime, and of building up large armies only after war has been declared.

But the events of the past three years have changed our thinking with respect to military defense. The German march into Austria, the Munich Conference, the seizure of Czechoslovakia, the alliance of Germany, Italy and Japan, made us aware that another great war was threatening, one in which we might find ourselves involved. A large part of the population believed that larger armies were needed, even though the nation was still at peace. According to the Gallup poll of December 1938, 37 per cent of our people favored compulsory military training as a measure of preparedness for a possible emergency.

With the outbreak of war in 1939, that percentage began to climb. With the blitzkrieg in the spring of 1940, as Denmark, Norway, Holland, Belgium and finally France fell before the Nazi panzer divisions, the Gallup poll reported that 50 per cent of the American people favored compulsory military training. And in June 1940, after France had made peace with her conquerors and invasion of Britain seemed imminent, the figure had risen to 64 per cent. So Congress enacted the Selective Service Law of 1940, providing for the registration of men from 21 to 35 years of age, and the military training for 12-month periods of a million selectees each year.

The Selective Service Act is distinctly an emergency measure. It does not provide for compulsory training of young men as a part of our permanent peacetime military policy. But the months required to register, select, and train the first million draftees have made the American people conscious of the fact that if an emergency were to arise in which speed in arming was essential, the emergency training method would be too slow to provide us with an adequate defense force. So advocates of preparedness have advocated a drastic change in our military policy. They have suggested that our permanent peacetime policy should include universal military training for every American young man upon attaining military age, to keep available at all times a huge reservoir of manpower, trained in the fundamentals of warfare and prepared for action upon short notice.

The subject has become so important that it has been chosen by the National University Extension Association as the topic for debate in high schools throughout the nation. The question for debate, as stated by the Association, is:

RESOLVED, that every able-bodied male citizen in the United States should be required to have one year of full-time military training before attaining the present draft age.

Since the present draft age begins at 21 years, military training "before the present draft age" could be given during any year prior to the 21st birthday of the young man called for training.

The question does not, of course, refer only to the present emergency; it suggests military training as a permanent peacetime policy, after World War II has ended and peace has again been established. Likewise, it does not call for the training of selectees, a small percentage of the population chosen by lot, but for the training of *every able-bodied male*—in other words, *universal* military training.

Many questions arise which must be answered before such a policy of universal military training may be put into effect:

(1) Do we need a strong military force? The American Legion and other groups advocate preparedness at all times.

But opponents of universal service feel that with the end of this war, the United States will no longer have need for any army except that necessary to police our borders. Some of the anti-militarists such as Senator Burton K. Wheeler and Charles A. Lindbergh feel that even today we need no greatly expanded army, since armed invasion of American shores would not be possible.

On the other hand, if it is conceded that we need a strong military defense, both now and after the war,

(2) Can we or should we maintain a large standing army of professional soldiers? Here the arguments run mainly to cost, for a large standing army even approaching the size of our present establishment would cost untold billions of dollars. And if the army were to be built into the highly trained mechanized force of the Nazi war machine, opponents of the "big army" plan can easily envision an inflationary period which would bankrupt the entire nation. As to whether we *should* maintain a large professional army, there the arguments hinge upon the necessity for such an army, as well as upon the cost.

If we are not to maintain a large professional army, and a "citizen" army is to be trained,

(3) Should it be trained as the emergency arises, as we have done in the past, or should it be trained in advance? The American Legion, the Reserve Officers Corps and other military groups advocate advance training, both as a means of saving money and lives and as a means of having men trained and ready for action when an emergency comes. Church groups and other anti-militarists denounce compulsory training in peacetime as undemocratic and as marking a trend toward dictatorship.

But if we accept the peacetime "citizen army" philosophy of the American Legion and others, another question presents itself:

(4) Granting that men must be trained in advance, which form of service should be adopted to provide us with an adequately trained army: universal or selective service? A number of interpretations enter into our consideration of this

question. We have adopted selective service today because universal service would deprive industry of its trained personnel, of men who make the machines and weapons for our defense. In an emergency any draft plan must be selective, to send into the armed forces those men least essential to the national defense and to keep the defense workers in their civilian occupations. This principle, in time of emergency, is as firmly accepted as the entire conscription idea itself.

Yet proponents of universal military training counter the selective service argument with the reasoning that taking *all* young men before they reach present military age and thus before they have really completed their education, the selective principle will no longer be necessary. Every man, regardless of his status in later life, can be given the necessary military education.

But here another question presents itself:

(5) At what age should men be trained? The American Legion has long argued for training at the age of 18, though in the past few months they have adopted a more flexible plan to take men whenever they wish to serve, anytime between the ages of 18 and 21. Other plans have suggested training to begin with high school, at 15 or 16, and from there all the way up to and including 21.

But before any decision on the matter of age can be made, another question must be considered:

(6) What type of training should be given and how should it be administered? In other words, should this training be strictly in the manual of arms? Regular course work in military theory? Actual field instruction in practical warfare? Should it be taught the youth of America in the schools as a part of their regular education? In camps such as the CCC or the CMTC? Through a combination of both? Through the medium of extracurricular organizations as the National Guard? Or should it be taught in some other means?

These are just a few of the many questions which must be considered in any complete study of universal military training.

Universal service is significant because it *is* different, because it *is* strange to the American Way our fathers knew. But whether it is undemocratic, foreign to American institutions and ideals is yet to be proved.

In the following pages the various phases of the question are explained in greater detail. The statements of America's leaders and authorities should help to suggest a solution.

Almost parallel to the present situation in many respects was the state of affairs in 1917 when the United States entered World War I. An editorial in *The Outlook* for April 18, 1917,[1] might have appeared in any magazine published in 1940 or 1941:

> In calling the country to arms the President used the phrase, "universal liability to service."
>
> With these few words he has done what no one in any less exalted position could do. Because he has the ear of the country he has accomplished with a phrase more more than books, speeches, and articles by the score have been able to accomplish. For the first time a great many Americans are realizing that war brings a burden of duty upon the individual. . . .
>
> To recognize, however, that all citizens are liable to service is one thing. It is a very different thing to adopt a system of universal training. . . .
>
> Universal training is different from conscription . . . in that it means not waiting until a man's services are needed in war before calling upon him, but rather putting every man under discipline in order to fit him for his service when the time comes.
>
> In the present emergency this country has suddenly come to realize that it will have to call its citizens into military service without having given them military training. For such an emergency there is need for emergency measures. If we are to raise an army of five hundred thousand or a million or two million men, we cannot select them from trained citizen soldiers. We shall have to train our soldiers as we raise them.

[1] "Conscription and Training," an editorial. *The Outlook*. 115:68-9. April 18, 1917. Reprinted by permission.

For the raising of the forces needed this year or next the country may, and we believe should, depend upon the principle of universal liability to service, but it cannot depend . . . upon universal training. What the best measure is for meeting this particular emergency we do not here discuss. We simply suggest that that measure can rest upon a basis of universal liability, and yet at the same time call for volunteers. If, for instance, we had five million men trained and subject to call, there would be nothing inconsistent with the principle of universal service if the government from out of those five million should call for half a million volunteers for special service abroad. This is what Australia has done. What is true of a company of men serving out of compulsion in the trenches, from whom half a dozen men may offer their services for a specially hazardous enterprise, may be true of the nation at large. . . .

This emergency measure does not, however, and ought not to take the place of the universal compulsory military training that the country must have.

The danger is that we shall enter the war as we have entered other wars—on a hit-or-miss basis, without providing for the future.

Today the great majority of boys of military age who will be called upon to enter into military service have little or no military training. It will be a crime as well as a blunder if two years from now the boys who enter military service at that time should enter it with as little preparation as the boys who are enlisted this year.

Either we should provide for universal military training or we should abandon universal military liability. The nation cannot justly hold boys liable for a service for which the nation does not prepare them. The boy of seventeen will be the boy of nineteen two years from now. If he is as ignorant of his duties two years from now as he is today; it will be not only the nation's fault but the nation's crime against itself as well as against him.

For this reason such training camps as that at Fort Terry on Plum Island last summer,[2] for boys from fifteen or sixteen to eighteen, are if anything more important this year than they ever were before.

Military authorities intent on the raising of immediately needed forces may, as some of them do, say that the training of boys under military age is, under the circumstances, impossible. It may be impossible. That is not a reason for not doing it; it is simply a reason for making it possible. It is our business today to do the impossible. England has done a much more impossible task. We can do this task.

[2] 1916.

All of this sounds familiar and might have been written, with few modifications, anytime since 1939. But the facts it stresses form the basis for the entire argument in favor of universal military training, namely that it is the national duty to train men in advance if it must later require them to serve in the national army upon short notice.

This subject does not revolve around the Burke-Wadsworth bill which instituted the 1940 draft, nor is it affected by any other measure at present before Congress. The question of universal military training to be debated this year is an affair of the future, a program of national security built for permanent peacetime use.

In fact, the question cannot even be simply stated as to whether we *should* or *should not* have compulsory military training for all young men before reaching the present draft age. Even if compulsory service is accepted as essential and desirable, the form of such service and such training in peacetime is what concerns the student of universal training.

In brief, if we need a large army, and agree that a large professional force would be too costly to maintain, at what age should the youth of America be trained? Should training be received in army camps, through present educational institutions, or how?

But in any case, every discussion of this subject which is so important to the people of the United States today must leave no question unanswered, no argument unfinished. Universal military training for American youth is a principle which may be accepted before the end of the present war situation. Yet a full understanding of its implications and its problems is necessary before such a system should be established in a nation which has traditionally opposed it.

Should every young man in America today be required to spend one year receiving military training before he reaches the present draft age?

The question is one for you to decide!

A HISTORY OF
COMPULSORY MILITARY SERVICE

DISCUSSION

Compulsory military service has been an accepted philosophy of men and nations since the dawn of history. In wars between tribes among primitive peoples, every man was expected to lend his strength to the strength of the group. The ancient Egyptians conscripted men to make up professional armies. The great Persian armies of Darius and Xerxes were composed of conscripts; so were the armies with which Alexander conquered the then civilized world. In the days of the Roman Republic, and later the Roman Empire, the obligation of citizens to bear arms in the Roman legions was a basic principle of government. And during the Middle Ages, military service as well as payment of taxes was an obligation of every freeman to his manorial lord, and of every nobleman to his king or emperor. Even when professional armies were attached to the court of every baron, prince or king, the soldiers who made up these forces were often secured by a process of conscription, and the professional armies were augmented in time of war by levies of citizens, drafted for temporary service.

Except for members of the professional armies, however, these conscripted soldiers were given no systematic peacetime training in the use of arms. They were available as manpower in emergency; but the military procedures of the time did not call for intensive training in preparation for service. Not until the time of the French Revolution was the concept of *universal* service, for long periods, accepted; the French, in 1793, adopted the slogan of the "nation in arms," with all male citizens a part of the military forces. Modifying the French concept Prussia, in 1814, inaugurated a system of universal military service, with all males called to the colors for training and service. This in turn led to the practice common in most of the nations of Europe of requiring all young men, upon reaching the age of 18, to spend a term of from one to three years in the army, for military training. At the expiration of the training period, they were permitted to return to civil life, but remained a part of the organized reserve of the armed forces.

As a result of this system, World War I found most of the warring nations able to put in the field armies of millions of trained soldiers, at a few days' notice. England and the United States were conspicuous exceptions; neither had followed a policy of peacetime universal training, and months elapsed before they were able to train and equip armies of volunteers or emergency conscripts. England, indeed, was even unwilling to adopt conscription until long after the war had begun, depending through half of the war period on her small standing army and on men volunteering for service.

Since the close of the first World War, France, Italy, Russia and most of the smaller nations of Europe have followed policies of universal military service, training their young men as they came to military age, and retiring them after a year's or two years' training to the status of civilian reserves. Germany was prohibited by the Treaty of Versailles from continuing her pre-1914 universal training policy; however, by making frequent changes in personnel in the army of 100,000 allowed her by the treaty, and through organization of various unofficial uniformed "marching clubs," Germany was able to approximate universal training for her young men, until following the rise of Hitler to power, she openly discarded the treaty restrictions and resumed her former system of universal military service.

England alone of the major European nations did not accept the universal training principle; like the United States, England has long opposed compulsory service in peacetime, accepting it only in times of extreme need. While England finally did adopt, in 1939, a plan to train all British youth as they reached the age of 20, the war was upon her before the plan could produce any results. Immediately after the opening of hostilities in September 1939, England adopted conscription, registering all citizens in all occupations. Today her war economy is admittedly that of a fascist state, in practice if not in ideology. Every able-bodied man and woman in England has his or her assigned place in the defense effort. Britain today is the perfect example of a democratic nation engaged in "total war."

Switzerland has a system of universal service which is always taken as a model by proponents of peacetime military training. Fiercely democratic, the Swiss dislike military regimentation. So their method of training an armed militia has always seemed more "American," and acceptable to American military observers, than the system followed in Prussia. The article beginning on page 30 gives an excellent description of the Swiss training system as it is used today.

THE STONE AGE CONCEPT OF UNIVERSAL SERVICE [1]

The story of compulsory military training is as old as the story of the human animal's futile struggle for peace and social security. . . .

With monotonous regularity, from the misty beginnings of recorded history, it seems that every time two or more human beings got together in peace and attained even a modicum of security, there always was someone within grabbing distance who wanted to take it away from them.

Our earliest ancestors found the solution a rather simple one. A good stone axe, wielded with a degree of skill and ambidexterity, insured both peace and security, because it kept enemies at a distance and meat on the table. Thus did the rugged individualists of the stone age by skill at arms and ceaseless vigilance survive an era that knew but one law—"Eat or be eaten."

[1] By Major Ernest M. Culligan, United States Army, public relations officer for the Selective Service system. From *Selective Service*. Pamphlet reprint from *The Reserve Officer* for June, 1941.

However, this happy state was soon complicated by the discovery of metal and the invention of the plow. The hunting nomad, creaking with rheumatism, succumbed to the temptations of a life of ease and comfort and settled down. He picked out a cave, with all modern improvements and a southern exposure. He put his woman by the fireplace with a skillet, his sons in the field with a plow, and sat by the mouth of his cave to watch his food grow instead of chasing it all over the forest.

True, he did some hunting, during the open season, but he was essentially an agriculturist—the first of the landed gentry.

He made a new axe, first of bronze, then of iron. When he was not hunting or fighting off some marauder, he kept it reasonably handy, but it was no longer the ever-in-hand good-provider of food and protector of life.

As long as he kept it handy enough and could still swing it effectively, he lived, kept his cave, and had some groceries laid away in the pantry.

By this time the cave was becoming slightly over-crowded—particularly on rainy days, what with the whole family indoors, the stored-up groceries crowding one corner, domesticated animals underfoot and mama's pots and pans all over the place.

Becoming something of a sybarite and desiring a fitting edifice to attest his opulence, man built himself a home.

To build a home was easy, to hold onto it was something else again. The man with a home and a few groceries laid away had the standing and sporting offer to defend his home or give it up to the man with a bigger axe or a greater skill in its use.

Then as now, the price of life and security was eternal vigilance. The price of peace was skill at arms and a reputation that kept less peaceful and less prosperous men at a comfortable distance.

For mutual protection against roving marauders, peaceful men settled near each other and entered unwritten mutual assistance pacts to defend their peace and security.

The obligation to defend the common community was fundamental, universal, and unquestioned.

In recorded history, we find the first reference to compulsory military service in ancient Egypt as early as the 6th Dynasty, about 2500 B. C., with annual levies of young men called each year for military training. In the 18th Dynasty, about 1600 B. C., one of the titles held by the most important minister of state, Amenhotep, son of Hapu, was "Director of Recruiting in Charge of Conscription." . . .

The call to arms and compulsory military service takes many forms in the pages of history. . . . In the Fourth Book of Moses, First Chapter of Numbers, the Bible gives us this novel 1600 B. C. version:

> Jehovah spake unto Moses in the wilderness of Sinai in the second year after they were come out of the land of Egypt, saying, take ye the sum of all the congregation of the children of Israel by their families, by their father's houses, according to the numbers of the names, every male by their polls from twenty years old and upwards, all that are able to go forth to war in Israel, thou and Aaron shall number them by their hosts.

Nearly forty centuries later in 1927, sensing the evil eye of one Benito Mussolini upon him, Haile Selassie, the Lion of Judah, made this classic contribution to our collection of conscription proclamations:

> Everyone will now be mobilized and all boys old enough to carry a spear will be sent to Addis Ababa. Married men will take their wives to carry food and cook. Those without wives will take any women without husbands. Women with small babies need not go. The blind, those who cannot walk or for any reason cannot carry a spear are exempted. Anyone found at home after the receipt of this order will be hanged.

Today, America is answering a call to arms. We are not going "forth to war in Israel" nor will "anyone found at home . . . be hanged." We are building a democratic army to defend the democracy that was built for us by the blood, sweat and tears of those who cried for it, worked for it, and died for it.

MILITARY SERVICE IN GREAT BRITAIN [2]

In the earliest Anglo-Saxon days, every free man was obligated to respond to the summons to arms, and to furnish his own arms and equipment and maintain himself in the field at his own expense. . . . Military service was a personal obligation—the obligation of Freedom. The old English *fyrd* or militia was the nation in arms. Service was incumbent upon all able-bodied males between 16 and 60. This obligation had no relation to the feudal system; it was centuries older.

The Norman kings continued the ancient militia, and extended its liability to service on foreign soil. . . . In 1285 the great Edward I recognized it afresh and decreed that every man between 15 and 60 should keep in his house "harness for to keep peace after the ancient Assize." The temper of the armed militia was essentially defensive, and in 1352 Parliament, while sustaining the obligation of universal military service, decreed that only with consent of Parliament should any man be obliged to go beyond the realm. After the War of the Roses, the militia was the only military force which remained. It was the only army England had when the Spanish Armada in 1588 threatened a landing in force.

Thus until the accession of James I, England's traditional defense was the armed militia, the nation in arms. As a fighting force it was inefficient, ill-trained, undisciplined, incapable of prolonged campaigning, and constitutionally exempt from foreign service. This instrument of war was inherited by the United States in all its congenital weakness.

During the 300 years between the accession of James I and the World War, the militia gradually declined into a mere theory, and Britain came to rely upon professional troops.

[2] From "Military Service in Great Britain." *American Selective Service,* a pamphlet prepared by the Joint Army and Navy Selective Service Committee as a text for students of selective service extension courses. U. S. Gov. Ptg. Office. Washington. October, 1939. p. 2-5.

James I was a Scot, a foreigner from a traditionally hostile country, to whose dynasty the English militia was a latent threat. In the first year of his reign, he excused its members from the burden of providing their own weapons, and from this time the militia declined. It was hopelessly divided in the Civil War (1642-48). Cromwell created a disciplined standing army—significantly called The New Model—with which he won the war and thereafter ruled England. Cromwell's military rule is significant in American history, for it gave the English that profound distrust of standing armies, which has been one of our most deep-rooted traditions.

After the Stuart Restoration in 1660, the militia was formally reestablished, but England's island immunity from invasion deprived it of vigorous life, while the ever-growing demand for expeditionary forces and colonial garrisons put the emphasis increasingly on professional troops because the militia was exempt from such employment. The principle of universal obligation indeed survived; as late as 1803 there was a levee *en masse* of all men between 17 and 55 to meet an expected French invasion. But during the nineteenth century, while the continental nations of Europe developed the modern practices of universal military training, Britain fell ever further away from it, and concerned herself more and more with professional units for colonial warfare.

It was not until 1914 that Britain came face to face with a situation long familiar on the continent—she must organize "the nation in arms" for a long and exhausting war on foreign soil. The principle of universal service was a thousand years old in England, but its application had never extended to long periods of training nor to prolonged campaigns, and for over six hundred years it had been limited to service within the kingdom. In their insular safety, the British had developed a strong prejudice against conscription as it existed abroad. The government approached the inevitable with hesitation and timidity, clinging to its established system of voluntary enlistment with almost unreasonable tenacity.   In less than two months the first enthusiastic rush of volunteers was ended; thereafter the numbers of volunteers always ran far behind requirements.   The most drastic pressure was aroused to compel men to "volunteer."   The spirit of the volunteer principle was soon lost, yet from fear of political repercussions the government clung to the empty form, while it exerted every kind of moral compulsion and finally used the threat of conscription as a persuader.   As always happens, this threat was ineffective; the nation's manpower remained unwilling to enlist.

The National Registration Act, passed after a year of war, authorized a complete inventory of manpower.   It was not a law for compulsory service, but it was intended as a further means of "inducing" shirkers to volunteer.   The scheme in brief was that after the registration men would be asked to "attest" their willingness to go when needed.   The joker was that the need already existed.   Moreover, married men who attested were explicitly promised that none of them would be taken until *all* single men, whether attested or not, had been called up.

And so, six months after the attesting scheme was launched, Britain came in January 1916 to conscription of unmarried men, not on the broad and sound principle of obligation, but as a means to clean up the single men and thus get at the married men who had attested.   And finally, in May of the same year, new legislation gave Britain that complete control of her entire male strength which is essential in a major war.   (Ireland was excepted) This inevitable position had been reached by shifts, evasions, and piecemeal expedients which gravely hampered the national effort, and even now there were dangerous flaws.   Men were called into service solely by their years of age, a method of classification which never works in an industrial nation.   A selective balance between the needs of essential industries and of the armed forces is the only suitable process; this was not provided until great damage had been done.   A number of independent authorities could grant exemptions; this process also never works.

Unless a single authority has charge, nobody can make accurate calculations of the manpower situation. Moreover, when the power to exempt is given to authorities who are not responsible for recruitment of the armed forces, it always becomes a means of evading military service by favoritism. . . .

Facing in 1939 the threat of a world upheaval, the British government reluctantly fell in step with the practice of other European powers and adopted compulsory peacetime training. When war actually began, this innovation was still too recent to permit any conclusions; but the very fact that Britain took a step so repugnant to its national prejudice is significant. Modern conditions constantly shorten the time available for training after war has begun, and necessitate a constantly increasing degree of readiness on M-Day.

MILITARY TRAINING AND BRITISH LAW [3]

Voluntary enlistment existed in England in early times and its origin is closely linked to her constitutional history. The right to maintain a standing army under martial law, claimed by the Stuart kings, was first denied by Parliament and then condemned as illegal by the Bill of Rights itself. . . .

By 1689, the Mutiny Act declaring standing armies and courts martial unknown to the law of England, authorized them for the current year and on a regular yearly footing thereafter under the sanction of Parliament. But the historian says,

To have proceeded further and to have decreed that every Englishman must serve in that army would have seemed to our ancestors a surrender of their liberties.

Blackstone's famous *Commentaries on the Laws of England*, familiar to the framers of our Constitution, likewise inveighed against the practice of raising armies of conscripted men. He prescribes "enlistment" as the only alternative in a free government. "It (the army) ought to be enlisted for a short and

[3] By Senator Burton K. Wheeler of Montana. *Congressional Record*. Vol. 86. August 23, 1940. p. 16544.

limited time. . . . No separate camp, no barracks, no inland fortresses should be allowed."

Space forbids a detailed treatment of this historic struggle, but careful study will show that the military despotism of Cromwell left an indelible impression on the English people; that the maintenance of a standing army of 30,000 by King James, without consent of Parliament, was a major cause of his unpopularity; that while the Stuart kings sought to maintain, in peacetime, a considerable military force altogether subject to their control, the Parliament, on the other hand, developed a militia which they believed could never become inimical to the principle of free England, and insisted upon disbanding in time of peace the whole army of the king, except perhaps a bodyguard and garrisons for the forts. . . .

Throughout the Eighteenth Century, this struggle against a standing army in peacetime continued unabated. Most significant it is too that never, during this entire period was it contended by King, Parliament or people that Englishmen could be forced into the army against their will. Even in time of war, when press-gangs drafted suspected criminals or notorious characters for army service, the Act of Anne expressly restricted the practice to such able-bodied men as had no lawful calling or employment or visible means for their maintenance or livelihood.

Thus the draft, even when invoked in wartime, was a mark of disgrace upon the man conscripted—a method applied only against those who had no lawful or respected place in the society of their day. This, then, is the background of the English struggle, in the light of which the American struggle must be understood.

COMPULSORY TRAINING IN EUROPE [4]

. . . Up to the outbreak of the French revolution, European armies for some six hundred years had been maintained on a

[4] By Charles Callan Tansill. From "Historical Background of Compulsory Military Service." *Thought.* 15, no. 59:623-40. December, 1940. Reprinted by permission.

professional basis, and large numbers of mercenaries had been included in the military organizations of most nations. The stirring events in France subsequent to 1789 produced a striking departure from the established order of things military, and Europe soon witnessed what may be termed "the nation in arms." According to the French constitution of September 3, 1791, the "public force" of the Republic was "composed of the army and the navy, of troops especially intended for internal service, and subsidiarily of the active citizens and their children, in condition to bear arms, registered upon the roll of the national guard." . . .

In principle, therefore, every citizen was a soldier, albeit not a trained one. It was this indefinite state of affairs that led Dubois Crancé, during the debates of December 1789, to insist upon universal training and service. "It is necessary," he declared, "to establish a truly national conscription, which should include everyone from the second man in the Empire in rank, down to the last active citizen.

The Duc de Liancourt, Mirabeau, and others resisted this plea for national conscription as opposed to the principles of liberty and of the Rights of Man, and the Assembly voted in favor of voluntary enlistment for the regular army. But voluntary enlistment was not as successful as had been anticipated. Therefore, on July 8 and on July 11, 1792, the Assembly decreed that every able-bodied man should consider himself liable for active service, but left the execution of military measures to the communes and districts.

The results of this method were distinctly disappointing; so on February 24, 1793, the Convention issued a call for 300,000 new troops between the ages of 18 and 40. Quotas were assigned to each department and commune, but when it appeared that these requisitions would not be compiled with, "recourse was had to compulsion, all unmarried national guards between the ages of 18 and 40 being held liable. Thereupon thousands fled from their homes, and Vendée rose in open revolt."

Faced with the double peril of foreign invasion and of civil war, the Convention, on August 23, 1793, issued a new decree with a more limited application. The following excerpts indicate its general tenor:

1. From this moment until that in which the enemy shall have been driven from the soil of the Republic of France, all Frenchmen are in permament requisition for the service of the armies. The young men shall go to battle; the married men shall forge arms and transport provisions.

2. The levy shall be general. The unmarried citizens and widowers without children, from 18 to 25 years, shall march first.

. . . Although Bonaparte's success of 1796 was the "highest expression of the new French method thus developed," yet "a reaction against the severity of the conscription soon made itself felt. . . . To the political economists of the period it seems a deliberate waste of productive energy to take the young merchant or clerk from his work and force a musket into his hands, whilst other men already trained were willing to renew their contract and defend the state." [5] In order to regulate this question, the law of 1798 was finally passed. This law remained practically unaltered as the basis of French military organization down to 1870. It formally laid down the basis for military service, regulated the enrollment of volunteers, and with reference to conscription, fixed liability to compulsory service between 20 and 25 years.

As a result of the French system of conscription, the armies of Napoleon were more rapidly and efficiently mobilized than those of his opponents. This fact was soon recognized, and each in turn was compelled to follow the French example.

Prussia, however, alone pursued the idea to its logical conclusion. After the crushing defeats at Jena and other places, it was apparent to farseeing German leaders that the regeneration of Prussia could be effected only through wide-reaching reforms. To Baron von Stein belongs the chief credit for the important

[5] Encyclopædia Britannica. Vol. VI, p. 973.

administrative and social reforms of 1807 and 1808, but the important military reforms . . . were to a great extent the work of a talented Hanoverian, General Gerhard David Johann Scharnhorst. . . .

It was Scharnhorst's idea to make every able-bodied citizen an active defender of the state, through a system of universal military service. In 1808, 1809 and 1811, efforts were made to persuade the Prussian king formally to adopt this measure; but the time was not yet ripe for such a striking innovation. The great uprising of 1813, however, swept away the opposition which had hampered Scharnhorst in carrying out his plan. He was able to put an army into the field as national as the earlier revolutionary armies of France. The military triumphs of this new Prussian army augured well for the continuance of the system that had produced it.

On June 3, 1814, General Hermann von Boyen was appointed as the Minister of War for Prussia, and in a memoir prepared by him and General Grolman in August, 1814, the essential features of the new military organization were presented. After careful consideration, the plan was accepted by Frederick William III, and the law for universal military service was proclaimed September 3, 1814. . . .

The importance of Boyen's law is lucidly indicated by the following excerpt from an article by Professor Guy Stanton Ford: [6]

The historical importance of Boyen's law can escape no thinking mind today. . . . Universal military service and the law which embodied it made a new citizenship, and was in a truly Prussian-Hohenzollern sense, a constitution which was to knit together the areas called Prussia after 1815. . . . Through it, Prussia was prepared to enter on its twofold task of becoming a constitutional state and of unifying Germany.

Much of the history of the nineteenth century is occupied with the establishment of nationality. None is more important than that in Germany, made possible by the development of the Prussian army as Scharnhorst and Boyen conceived it.

[6] Guy Stanton Ford, "Boyen's Military Law." *American Historical Review.* April, 1915. p. 537-8.

Since 1870, every great power in Europe, except England, has adopted the Prussian universal military service.

THE SWISS PLAN [7]

Switzerland was the first nation in modern times to introduce compulsory military service. The Federal Constitution adopted in 1848 and revised in 1874, provides in its article 18: "Every Swiss is bound to do military service." The federal law concerning the organization of the Swiss Army of April 12, 1907, called the Military Constitution of the Swiss Confederation, amended in 1927 and subsequent dates, provides that the army shall consist of three classes, namely, the elite or first line: men from 20 to 32 years old; the Landwehr or second line: men from 33 to 40 years; and the Landsturm or territorial troops: men from the age of 41 to 48.

Every male Swiss, when reaching the age of 19, must submit to a mental and physical examination. The mental test includes reading, arithmetic, geography, history of the government, and composition. For physical examination he performs various gymnastic exercises. Some Cantons (states) compel the youths from 17 to 19 years of age to go to night school for 64 hours during winter to prepare for the examination.

When accepted in his twentieth year the infantry recruit enters the recruiting school of his territorial division, or, if he is to become an artilleryman, or a cavalryman, or a pilot, etc., he joins his respective school, of which there are several for each branch.

The length of time devoted to the first year's training of the recruit is for all branches of the army (infantry, artillery, sanitary troops, supply trains, etc.)—day of entrance and day of discharge included—116 days; for the cavalry, 130 days. The pilot has to undergo an additional training of six months.

[7] By C. Bruggmann, minister of Switzerland, quoted by Senator Rush D. Holt of West Virginia. *Congressional Record*, Vol. 86. August 22, 1940. p. 16441.

At the time the recruit reports for his service he is given a complete equipment and regulation rifle, all of which he takes home after finishing the course. For yearly inspection and active duty he must turn out with his full equipment, which finally becomes his private property upon his discharge from active duty at the age of 48.

The recruiting-school course is hard work, as each day means eight strenuous hours, with night work, such as patrolling, entrenching, and maneuvers probably twice a week.

The completion of the course promotes the recruit to a full-fledged soldier, assigned to a battalion in his home district, which is a unit of the division of which his Canton is a territorial part. As a member of his unit he serves each year a so-called repetition course of 19 days, until he is 26. He belongs to the first line for six years longer, until he is 32, but in these six years he is bound to serve only every second year for a period of three weeks. A private of the first-line troops must therefore undergo within a period of twelve years after completion of the recruiting school a military training of eight repetition courses of 19 days each.

The repetition courses of the first-line troops are so arranged that an adequate change in smaller tactical units with training in army units will take place.

From 32 to 40 years, the Swiss soldier belongs to the second line or Landwehr. In this capacity he serves two repetition courses of 19 days each. For the next eight years, until he is 48, he serves in the Landsturm or territorial troops and is called to the colors only under special orders. In addition, every Landwehr soldier presents himself for annual inspection, at which time he must account for the care of his uniform and arms.

A recent decree of the Swiss government extended the army age limit to 60 years, thus keeping every able-bodied man up to 60 years of age subject to military service in case of general mobilization.

The figures of the time of instruction for a Swiss infantry private are therefore:

	Days
Recruiting school at his twentieth year	116
First line or Auszug, up to his thirty-second year, 8 repetition courses at 19 days each	152
Second line, Landwehr, up to his fortieth year, 2 repetition courses of 19 days each	38
Plus annual inspection	6
Territorial troops or Landsturm up to his forty-eighth year, annual inspection and subject to service under special orders	8
Territorial troops from the age of 48-60, subject to special service only in case of general mobilization	..
Total	320

Specialists, as for instance gunsmiths, farriers, etc., receive their necessary professional training in special courses. Those belonging to the ambulance corps take besides the recruiting school a hospital training course.

Part of the military training of the Swiss soldier is the obligatory and voluntary rifle practice which he attends in civil life under the auspices of a rifle club. Every community is compelled by the federal government to build and maintain a rifle range in the open field. Enlisted men, and noncommissioned officers of the first line and the Landwehr armed with rifles or carbines, as well as subaltern officers of the troops, must pass a yearly rifle practice test. Such tests, as well as the rifle practices, are conducted by the rifle clubs according to the military regulations. Those who neglect this test must take a special course without pay. The federal government refunds the cost of the ammunition used to all those who pass the test and subsidizes the rifle clubs. The federal government encourages and aids financially any movement toward preparatory military training.

Those Swiss who are found physically unfit to serve in the regular army are assigned to certain of the auxiliary branches, as for instance, the ambulance corps, commissary department, information department, transportation department, and, more recently, are trained in the air defense of the civil population and as anti-parachutists, etc. Members assigned to the auxiliary service attend instruction services of much shorter periods than do the regular soldiers.

Citizens who for physical reasons are not serving personally in the army, as well as those incorporated in the auxiliary service, must pay an annual tax of exemption. Swiss citizens living in foreign countries are also obliged to pay this tax, and with few exceptions they do so.

The foregoing concerns privates in the Swiss army. The officers and noncommissioned officers naturally are subject to additional instruction and training. Every Swiss who has the ambition and possesses intelligence and ability, can become an officer in the army. After completing the 116, or as the case may be, 130 days in the regular recruiting school, if his conduct warrants the recommendation from his superiors, he will be called to attend a school for noncommissioned officers lasting three weeks for those in the artillery, or in the air corps, engineering, and fortress troops, four weeks, after which he receives the rank of a corporal. As such he attends another recruiting school a year later and the corporal with a good record and the ambition to become an officer enters the school for officers. The duration of this school varies between 60 and 120 days, according to the branch of service (for instance, infantry 88, artillery and air corps, 102 days). For practical and training purposes a school for noncommissioned officers is connected with the school for officers.

The newly appointed lieutenant must pass a recruiting school as instructor to qualify and thereafter he serves the regular annual repetition course of 19 days with his unit. If qualified, he will be promoted to the rank of first lieutenant after the completion of three or four repetition courses. To advance to the rank of captain he must take a 30-day course in the Central Military School No. 1, and attend several other special courses. Officers above the rank of captain devote a considerable part of their time to special courses in tactics, information, etc.

Furthermore, it should be mentioned that the Swiss military constitution provides for a small corps of instructors. They are professional or career officers and conduct the instruction of recruits and the training of noncommissioned and commissioned officers in the respective courses. A fixed number of instructors are assigned to each of the different branches of the army. The commanders of division and army corps are chosen from among the professional officers.

The military-training program is not coordinated with the educational institutions. There are projects to make preparatory training for boys of the age of 17 to 19 compulsory. This program would be conducted by educational institutions as well as by gymnastic societies.

UNIVERSAL MILITARY TRAINING ABROAD:

A SUMMARY

With the exception of Great Britain and the United States, no major power in the world has not adopted universal peacetime military service and training. The systems adopted have taken various forms, but usually have been based upon the Prussian plan of automatic enlistment upon the attainment of a specified military age.

Since the beginning of World War II, compulsory service plans have been adopted by Great Britain and the United States, as well as by many minor nations.

England adopted conscription April 27, 1939, for the duration of the war period. Service begins at the age of 20 and consists of six months' training, at the end of which the draftee may choose between the Regular Army Reserve forces, which are now in active service, and the Territorial Army, corresponding to the National Guard in the United States and requiring a three-and-one-half-year period of enlistment.

The Union of South Africa imposes the obligations of military service on every citizen of European descent between the ages of 17 and 60. Men between the ages of 17 and 25 are required to enter the Coast Garrison Force, the Active Citizen Force, the Royal Naval Volunteer Force, or a Rifle Association for a four-year period of training.

Between 1911 and 1929, Australia required military training of all men between 18 and 26 years of age; in 1929, however, a system of voluntary enlistment was adopted. This continued until 1940, when compulsory service was again introduced. Men drafted for training are required to be available for home defense service within Australia; all overseas forces are raised by the volunteer method from the group already trained for home service.

New Zealand requires military training for all men as they reach the age of 16, and conscripts men for foreign service in the 21 to 41 year age group.

Canada adopted military conscription in June 1940, for the first time since the first World War. All able-bodied men under 45 are liable for service, unless needed for defense industries. The training period for conscripted men is limited to 30 days, and overseas service is on a voluntary basis.

On the continent of Europe, most of the nations conquered by Germany had systems of universal military training up to the time of their conquest. Of course, such training is not permitted in countries now under German control.

Germany reintroduced compulsory universal training in 1935. The German system calls for one year of military training for all able-bodied Aryan Germans from 18 to 45 years of age. Active military service in the army begins at 20; following the completion of his period of full-time training, the German conscript is made a member of the organized reserve until he reaches the age of 35, and is then attached to the Landwehr for an additional ten-year period. The one year of active military training required before the outbreak of the war did not include service in govern-

ment labor camps, required of all German youth on reaching the
age of 18.

Italy makes all men subject to military service between the
ages of 18 and 55; the service required begins with an 18 months'
period of active training, at the end of which the conscript remains a member of the organized reserve until he reaches the
age of 55. All educational institutions offer courses in military
science which are required of all students.

Portugal requires military service of all men between the
ages of 17 and 45, the service including six years in the active
armed forces and 22 years in special and territorial troops.

Sweden requires military service of men between 20 and 45,
with a special universal service law requiring all Swedes to perform government designated non-military duties which may be
assigned to them in the interests of national defense.

Switzerland requires military service of men between 18 and
60 in a regulated national militia. Revisions in the national
military program have lowered the age at which militia training
begins from 20 to 19 years.

Military training is compulsory in Russia beginning at 19, or
for high school graduates, at 18. The conscript puts in the usual
period of training in the Regular Army, followed by assignment
to various organized reserves.

China, since the beginning of her war with Japan, has instituted a system of compulsory military service over a three-year
period. The Regular Army is made up of volunteers and con-
scriptees between the ages of 20 and 25.

In Japan, military service is compulsory and universal, beginning at 17 and including two years of service in the Regular
Army beginning at the age of 20. Men between 17 and 20, and
between 22 and 40, are enrolled as members of the Army Reserve
Corps.

In the Western Hemisphere, most of the Latin American
nations require military service of all able-bodied male citizens.
Argentina requires military service of all men from 20 to 45

years; most of them are expected to spend ten years in the Regular Army, ten additional years in the National Guard, and five years in the Territorial Guard, mobilized only in case of war. Brazil gives each man a year of active training at the age of 21, and requires him to spend eight additional years in the organized reserves. From 30 to 45, he is subject to call in case of war. In Chile, men from 19 to 45 are liable for military service. Service from 19 to 31 is with the Regular Army; from 31 to 45, the Chilean citizen is a member of the national reserve forces. Mexico requires one year of military service of all male citizens between the ages of 18 and 45.

Bolivia provides for compulsory military service in case of war for men from 19 to 50. Pre-age military instruction is also provided for boys between 12 and 19, and for girls between 15 and 20. Columbia requires one year of military service of all men between the ages of 21 and 30; Guatemala makes service compulsory between the ages of 18 and 50, in case of emergency. Paraguay requires military service of men between 18 and 22, and provides for the calling to service in case of war of all men up to 45 years of age.

Peru demands two years of compulsory military training of all men in the 18 to 20 year age group. On completion of the training period, the trainee is for ten years a member of the reserve; for an additional ten years a member of the National Guard; and from 39 to 45 a member of the Territorial Guard. Venezuela requires three years of training for all male citizens beginning at the age of 21; at the end of the active service period, the trainee is held liable for military service on call until he reaches the age of 45. Uruguay requires a short intensive period of military training of all men reaching the age of 21.

In most of the remaining Latin American nations, professional armies are maintained; however, the idea of universal service in time of emergency is accepted in practically every Latin American state.

In the Philippine Islands, military training is compulsory for all youth, both male and female, beginning at the age of 10. Service in time of emergency is obligatory until the age of 50. In August, 1941, the Philippine army was mobilized and approximately 140,000 reservists were called to the colors. The recently-adopted military training plan calls for the intensive training of 40,000 men a year, the training period beginning at the age of 20.

CONSCRIPTION IN THE UNITED STATES

DISCUSSION

Opposition to compulsory military service is an age-old American tradition. It has been a part of the basic thinking of Americans since early colonial times; it reflects a fear of all governmental power, a distrust of military establishments, a resistance to all interference with the personal liberties of individuals.

Our American constitution gives to the Congress the power "to raise and support armies," and to "provide for calling forth the militia," the word "militia" being interpreted by the Supreme Court as including all able-bodied male citizens. Yet attempts of our government to exercise this power have sometimes met with resistance, or at best have been given grudging acceptance by the people of the United States.

Many varied elements in our national life have probably combined to produce this opposition to compulsory service. First, there is the distrust and fear of all governmental authority which dates back to colonial days, when government represented a tyrannical English king and when armies were agencies not of defense, but of oppression. This fear of government accounted in large part for the demand of Anti-Federalists for decentralization of power in the early days of our nation; it certainly played a part in producing, in the years before the Civil War, the insistence on the principle of "states' rights"—a principle which, by the way, did not disappear with the defeat of the Confederacy.

A second factor was the effect of conditions of life on the American frontier. A large proportion of the men and women now living in the Mississippi valley or in the Western areas of our country are descendants, only a generation or two removed, from men who settled the Western frontier; much of the culture and many of the attitudes of the frontier still persist among them. And conditions on the American frontier were scarcely those which would produce a feeling of dependence on government. With the primitive methods of transportation and communication then existing, the government at Washington was literally months away; the men who settled the Western states neither asked nor expected protection from government agencies. Each man was a law unto himself, dependent for protection on himself alone. The fierce individualism which resulted has persisted among those who live in the Central and Western states. And such an individualism produces resentment when a far-distant government interferes with the patterns of every-day living—particularly when interference is carried to the point of requiring military service for months or years in an army in which individualism is suppressed.

A third factor of no small importance is that a large part of our population is made up of immigrants or the children of immigrants, and that many of these immigrants who came to this country left their homelands expressly to escape the necessity of serving, against their wills, in the armies of kings, kaisers or emperors. They came to America as a land of freedom, in which such army service was not demanded. And their strong aversion to compulsory service was passed on to their American-born sons and daughters.

And still another factor is the attitude of the average American toward the Army itself. Americans in general hate and fear war; many of them feel that the very existence of a large army is a threat to national peace. They resent the Army as a militaristic agency; they fear that young men drafted into the Army will become war-minded. In brief, compulsory military training in the minds of many Americans is a policy which makes for militarism, and militarism leads to war.

And, of course, most Americans refuse to see any need for armies of millions of men. Since 1812, our country has never been invaded; for more than a century, our wars have been fought upon foreign soil. The broad Atlantic and the vast Pacific have been our defenses. And generations of peace or of easy victories in time of war have led the nation to question the need of large military establishments. The result has been that our national policy has been one of small armies made up of professional soldiers; the nation has preferred to wait until danger actually threatened before preparing for war. Of course, with war once declared, we have been willing to accept conscription— not eagerly, but reluctantly, as the best method of dealing with an emergency.

Whether the nation will hold to its opposition to compulsory service when peace has been restored at the end of World War II is for the future to decide.

THE CONSTITUTIONAL BASIS OF CONSCRIPTION [1]

ARTICLE I.

Section 8, paragraph 1. The Congress shall have power to . . . provide for the common defence and general welfare of the United States; . . .

Section 8, paragraph 11. To declare war, grant letters of marque and reprisal, and make rules concerning captures on land and water;

Section 8, paragraph 12. To raise and support armies, but no appropriation of money to that use shall be for a longer term than two years. . . .

Section 8, paragraph 14. To make rules for the government and regulation of the land and naval forces;

Section 8, paragraph 15. To provide for calling forth the militia to execute the laws of the Union, suppress insurrections and repel invasions;

Section 8, paragraph 16. To provide for organizing, arming, and disciplining the militia, and for governing such part of them as may be employed in the service of the United States, reserving to the states respectively, the appointment of the

[1] Quotations from the Constitution of the United States.

officers, and the authority of training the militia according to the discipline prescribed by Congress. . . .

Section 8, paragraph 18. To make all laws which shall be necessary and proper for carrying into execution the foregoing powers, and all other powers vested by this Constitution in the government of the United States, or in any department or officer thereof. . . .

Section 10, paragraph 3. No state shall, without the consent of Congress, . . . keep troops, or ships of war in time of peace . . . or engage in war, unless actually invaded, or in such imminent danger as will not admit of delay. . . .

Article II.

Section 2, paragraph 1. The President shall be commander in chief of the army and navy of the United States, and of the militia of the several states, when called into the actual service of the United States. . . .

Section 4. The United States shall guarantee to every state in this Union a republican form of government, and shall protect each of them against invasion; and on application of the legislature, or of the executive (when the legislature cannot be convened), against domestic violence.

Amendment II.

A well regulated militia being necessary to the security of a free state, the right of the people to keep and bear arms shall not be infringed.

THE DRAFT IN AMERICAN HISTORY, 1775-1860 [2]

Although the obligation of the citizen to give military service has been universally accepted at all times, the background of

[2] From *American Selective Service*. Pamphlet prepared by the Joint Army and Navy Selective Service Committee for use as a text by students in selective service extension courses. U. S. Gov't Ptg. Office. October, 1939. p. 2, 5-8.

American selective service lies in the history of Great Britain and of our own country. . . .

The drafting of soldiers in the United States did not begin in 1917, nor even in 1863; it is as old as white America. The first settlers brought with them the English militia system, the self-armed citizenry; and the grim necessities of pioneer existence strengthened the already recognized obligation of universal military service. The Continental Congress, among its earliest measures for the common defense, recommended "that all able-bodied, effective men, between 16 and 50 years of age, be formed into companies of militia. . . ." (July 18, 1775); the ancient obligation was thus reaffirmed at the very birth of the United States.

But while the frontier conditions had strengthened the established principle, and the Continental Congress confirmed it for the new nation, the conditions of American development had also accentuated the weaknesses of the ancient militia system. The thirteen Colonies were in effect separate and jealous nations, unwilling to relinquish power to the central Congress. Communities were widely separated, the men were but little influenced even by state authority, and it was inevitably difficult to get the militia very far from home, or to keep them in the field long enough to acquire discipline and training, much less to conduct a long campaign. The resolution of the Continental Congress, cited above, conceded that the militia could only be called out by the consent of the state legislature; it was intended for local defense, while a Regular Army, the "Continental Army," was created (mostly on paper) for the general war effort of the combined states.

In short, the raising of armed forces by the draft is the oldest military policy of the United States. But as exemplified in the old militia, the draft was ineffective, first because the drafted men were not available long enough for training, conditioning, and campaigning, and second because the militia was by tradition and practice a local defense force.

The evolution from the militia draft to 1917 selective service was long and difficult. The newborn United States received from the mother country a deep distrust of standing armies and a habit of relying on an unregulated militia. To these inherited handicaps in its conduct of war, the peculiar origin of the nation added state sovereignty as another obstacle to the national authority. The difficulties which resulted, the expedients which were employed, and the gradual development of a sound policy, will be reviewed briefly in succeeding paragraphs.

As had been said, Congress very early authorized a regular force for the general operations of the United States, and recommended that the states organize their militia for home defense. But sufficient men could not be induced to enlist in the Regular force. Even with offers of large cash bounties, voluntary enlistment was unsatisfactory. Washington therefore had to call constantly on the states for militia to assist in his operations. The militia by its very nature was completely unsatisfactory. The American army was in constant danger of final disaster. For example, Washington reported from Morristown, New Jersey, on March 14, 1777, that he had but 1000 Regulars, and 2000 militia whose engagement expired that same month, to face over 20,000 British in and around New York. Because the central government lacked power to raise an effective army, the war dragged out for seven years, during which the Americans employed a total of almost 400,000 men while the greatest strength of the enemy in any one year (1791) was but 42,000. . . .

The Constitution gave real powers to the central government, and thereby tremendously increased the war-making effectiveness of the nation. On this point the Supreme Court said in 1917:

When the Constitution came to be formed, it may not be disputed that one of the recognized necessities for its adoption was the want of power in Congress to raise an army and the dependence upon the states for their quotas. In supplying the (military) power, it was manifestly intended to give it all and leave none to the states, since besides the delegation to Congress of authority to raise armies the Constitution prohibited the states, without the consent of Congress, from keeping troops in time of peace or engaging in war.

The Supreme Court has thus most positively stated the power received by the federal government, and affirmed the deliberate intent to grant that power. But there were practical difficulties in translating theory into action. The federal government was at first an experiment, and was viewed with much distrust. The old English traditions were strong. Public opinion was entirely in favor of leaving national defense to the militia, the farmers with rifles, who were the heroes of the Revolution. It took generations to overcome these prejudices.

Washington, Knox, and Steuben believed in the militia. Indeed, they could hardly look toward anything else. But during the Revolution they had seen far too much of the old-style militia, and felt most strongly that it must be converted into "well-regulated militia," a vastly different thing. Washington proposed to the First Congress a true selective service. To avoid calling forth indiscriminate levies, of all ages and no training or discipline, he proposed to classify the men by age and physical fitness; to segregate the fit men between 18 and 25 years of age into separate tactical units; and to give them special training by selected instructors. He thus hoped to develop an effective citizen army.

Despite repeated recommendations by Presidents Washington, Jefferson, and Madison, these proposals never became law. Instead, the Militia Law of 1792 was enacted. This law did provide for universal military service, but the militia it organized was, if anything, worse than that of the Revolution. It arranged for the same old untrained and unregulated mobs, of every age and physical condition, and grandiosely combined them into innumerable regiments, brigades, and divisions. In 1808 there were 1033 infantry regiments in the country. Arms, equipment, and horses had to be furnished by the individual. Withal, no penalties were provided to give the law force. Training under this law consisted in most places of one annual "muster day," usually the occasion for a grand spree. It would have been difficult for Congress to have disregarded more completely the mature advice of our Revolutionary leaders and early Presidents.

Between Washington's conception of a "well-regulated militia" and its fulfillment lay over a century of mistakes. The first calling forth of "well-regulated militia" in the history of the nation was the Selective Service of 1917.

The lessons of the Revolution were repeated in the War of 1812. We employed all told 527,000 men, while the enemy never had over 16,500 in the field against us at any one time. The war dragged out futilely for three years.

A Regular Army of numbers adequate to win the war was authorized but could not be recruited. Even when bounties were offered, the volunteer system broke down. Conscription for the national army was then proposed, but the old prejudice in favor of the state militia was too strong, and it was decided to rely on it again. The states accordingly turned out their levies, undisciplined mobs under untrained officers, and all of the old weaknesses were demonstrated once more.

On at least three occasions they refused to cross the border, once abandoning to annihilation a force which had already crossed into Canada. The action at Bladensburg, in defense of the national capital, illustrates perfectly the working of the militia system; 4400 men were drafted a day or two before from their fields and shops, and obediently answered the summons; but they fled at the first shot. The obligation of military service which brought into battle merely untrained levies was obviously not enough; success could be achieved only by properly trained troops. Moreover, the authority which conducted the war, the national government, could not operate effectively with troops which were responsible to another authority, the state; nor could it hope for victory with troops which were exempt from entering foreign soil.

The Mexican War (1849) did not throw sufficient strain on national manpower and endurance to create proper laboratory conditions for studying recruitment policies. It offers one lesson.

In this war, two kinds of troops were employed: regulars enlisted for five years, and "volunteers" enlisted for only 12 months. As one result of the short enlistment period for "volunteers," General Scott had to send home 4000 men, over 40 per cent of his army, when he was in the middle of his advance to Mexico City, and at a time when Santa Anna was admitting that Mexico "no longer had an army." Scott then had to wait weeks for new regiments, while the enemy recovered. The mistake of not making enlistments for the "duration of the war" greatly prolonged hostilities.

EXPERIENCE WITH THE DRAFT, 1861-1865 [3]

The first troops raised by the North in 1861 were ten companies of District of Columbia militia, which could not be used outside the District, an area ten miles on each side. Next Lincoln called for 75,000 militia for three months, and their commander found that he was expected to win the war in that time. The South began with a one-year enlistment, which of course proved unsatisfactory but was a decisive advantage in the first battle. The Union troops in the Shenandoah region refused to remain beyond their three months, and the Confederate troops were free to move to Manassas where they proved to be the decisive reinforcement. Union troops in the Manassas area actually marched away to the sound of the cannon, because their time had expired.

Lincoln meantime had begun recruiting for "three years or the war," but within a year voluntary recruiting had virtually collapsed (July 1862). In desperation the government ordered that "a draft of 300,000 militia be immediately called into the service of the United States, to serve for nine months, unless sooner discharged." The state governors were called upon to raise their quotas of this force, and regulations for carrying

[3] From *American Selective Service*. Pamphlet prepared by the Joint Army and Navy Selective Service Committee for use by students in selective service extension courses. U. S. Gov't Ptg. Office. October, 1939. p. 9-11.

out the draft through the agency of the state governors were issued by the President. But calling militia for nine months killed whatever vitality remained in the efforts to recruit volunteers for three years or the war. The grim fact became clear, that unsound hour when the South was winning everywhere; when Jackson's Valley Campaign, McClellan's failure at Richmond, and the Second Battle of Manassas, all cumulatively darkened the Northern skies. Such troops as were raised under this militia call were too green for use during the summer and autumn crises; they were maintained at great expense throughout the inactive winter period; and they claimed discharge when, in the spring of 1863, they could have been used to advantage. The only profit from this militia call was that it prepared public opinion somewhat for the inevitable: the words "draft" and "conscription" had been spoken out loud. For if the North wished to win the war, there remained only one way to raise the necessary armies.

National conscription was accordingly introduced in the spring of 1863. The methods employed furnish a text on "How Not To Do It." They aroused public resentment so greatly that the authority of the federal government was gravely threatened in many of the states which had remained loyally in the Union. . . .

In the first place, the draft was introduced two years after war began. Instead of being a popular measure to insure orderly mobilization of the nation's manpower, it was by now only a means of coercing those who had declined to volunteer. It was not made the sole method of recruitment; on the contrary, voluntary recruiting continued full blast, and the draft was applied only in those districts which failed to fill their quota with volunteers. Hence public odium quickly attached not only to the drafted man, but to the district where the draft was necessary. . . .

Second, the machinery set up to conduct the draft was simultaneously assigned the duty of apprehending spies and deserters. The draft registration was conducted by the military, using force when necessary. . . .

Third, the federal government alone conducted the draft machinery. . . . It was made to seem that the federal government was using its army to drag men away without regard to fundamental democratic processes.

Fourth, the recruiting process was vastly expensive . . . . General Crowder reports that the cost of recruiting each man in the Civil War was $228, as against $8 in the World War . . . .

Fifth, the law fell heavily on the poor and allowed the rich to escape. After being drafted a man could either hire a substitute, or purchase exemption outright for $300 . . . .

Sixth, the Civil War draft induced corruption on a vast scale. "Substitute brokers" traded in the sale of substitutes. This commerce created "professional substitutes," who, after getting their money, deserted and sold themselves again and again in new localities . . . .

In short, the Civil War draft was enforced not by the will of the people but by the weapons of the army. . . It aroused bitter hatred and was resisted by riots amounting to serious insurrections. It can perhaps be excused as the measure of a desperate government; but it was about as bad as it could have been. . . .

LINCOLN ON THE DRAFT [4]

. . . In the London *Spectator,* for example, attention has been directed to the subject of the draft. An editorial article in that journal declares that Lincoln went through all the stages that England is now going through in the matter of raising troops, except that the voluntary system in America gave results which numerically and in proportion to the population were below those which the voluntary system has given England in the first few months of the war.

[4] From "English Conscription and Our Civil War Draft" *American Review of Reviews.* 51:357-8. March, 1915. Reprinted by permission.

Contrary to the general assumption that volunteering in Great Britain has not been as good as it was in the North before the draft was put in force, the *Spectator* declares that it has been very much better. It is assumed, however, that sooner or later the voluntary system will prove not to be giving as many men as are wanted and that recourse to compulsion will be necessary. . . .

The *Spectator* characterizes Lincoln as "a liberal and a democrat and an upholder of popular rights if ever there was one in the world. Yet, strange as it may seem to our Radical friends, he was from the very beginning a strong advocate of compulsory service, or, as he called it, conscription, as the fairest and best way of raising troops for a great national emergency."

This appeal to the people in defense of the draft which Lincoln wrote at that critical juncture is pronounced by *Spectator* "one of the greatest state papers ever produced in the English language." Lincoln's refusal to publish the document was based, not on any lack of confidence in his argument, but on the fact that after the draft was put in operation it proved to be less unpopular than had been expected, and it was feared that the strength of the language used by Lincoln might possibly have irritated certain men who were rapidly becoming reconciled to the measure. Among the striking passages in Lincoln's address which have been marked by the *Spectator* as peculiarly applicable to the present situation in Great Britain are the following, which the editor commends to his English readers:

At the beginning of the war, and ever since, a variety of motives, pressing, some in one direction and some in the other, would be presented to the mind of each man physically fit for a soldier, upon the combined effect of which motives he would, or would not, voluntarily enter the service. Among these motives would be patriotism, political bias, ambition, personal courage, love of adventure, want of employment, and convenience, or the opposite of some of these. We already have, and have had, in the service as appears, substantially all that can be obtained upon this voluntary weighing of motives. And yet we must somehow obtain more, or relinquish the original object of the contest, together with all the blood and treasure already expended in the effort to secure it.

To meet this necessity the law for the draft has been enacted. You who do not wish to be soldiers do not like this law. This is natural; nor does it imply want of patriotism. Nothing can be just and necessary as to make us like it if it is disagreeable to us. We are prone, too, to find false arguments with which to excuse ourselves for opposing such disagreeable things. In this case, those who desire the rebellion to succeed, and others who seek reward in a different way, are very active in accommodating us with this class of arguments. There can be no army without men. Men can be had only voluntarily or involuntarily. We have ceased to obtain them voluntarily, and to obtain them involuntarily is the draft—conscription. If you dispute the fact, and declare that men can still be had voluntarily in sufficient numbers, prove the assertion by yourselves volunteering in such numbers, and I shall gladly give up the draft. Or if not a sufficient number, but any one of you will volunteer, he for his single self will escape all the horrors of the draft, and will thereby do only what each one of at least a million of his manly brethren have already done. Their toil and blood have been given as much for you as for themselves. Shall it all be lost rather than that you, too, will bear your part?

I do not say that all who would avoid serving in the war are unpatriotic; but I do think every patriot should willingly take his chance under a law, made with great care, in order to secure entire fairness. . . . The principle of draft, which simply is involuntary or enforced service, is not new. It has been practised in all ages of the world. . . . Shall we shrink from the necessary means to maintain our free government, which our grandfathers employed to establish it and our own fathers have already employed once to maintain it? Are we degenerate? Has the manhood of our race run out?. . . . With these views, and on these principles, I feel bound to tell you it is my purpose to see the draft law faithfully executed.

CONSCRIPTION: AMERICAN VIEW—1917 [5]

America has arrived at democracy. It is face to face with equality. It must take it or leave it, and the choice must be made now.

For a hundred years we have talked democracy and professed it. At an earlier time we had it; for in the days of the Indian

[5] From an editorial titled "Conscription." *The Independent.* 90:191-2. April 28, 1917. Reprinted by permission.

wars all men were equal before God and the scalping knife. There were volunteers, but also there was obligation. Every man had to train. Every man had to provide himself with gun and ammunition, and he was under no misapprehension about his duty.

Then came independence, nationality and the professional army. The military obligation of every citizen continued in legal theory. Practically, it was ignored. Training day was forgotten, and even the militia was filled by voluntary enlistment.

The Mexican War made no real demand upon resources or people. The Civil War was won by the North after four years of ghastly, murderous blundering. The response to Lincoln's call for volunteers was quick and brave, by souls whose natures were quick and brave. But to our eternal shame a million men who loved America for what America could do for them found ready reasons why they should sell shoes or army blankets, or other useful stuff instead of serving at the front. The draft became necessary. But instead of being made equal and democratic and intelligent it was bungled and made a cause of bitterness. Any rich man could evade it by buying a substitute. The poor man could not.

The experience taught us nothing, and we went into the Spanish War the most incompetent, unthinking, irresponsible lot of warriors that ever preferred typhoid to bullets. Some day the true history of those years will be known by the people as it is now known by students, and the people will understand what would have happened to us if Great Britain had permitted German intentions to work their will.

Democracy means equality of obligation even more than it means equality of opportunity. It means equality in the supreme obligation, to give everything that one has, both property and life, when the necessity arises. A small professional army is necessary to maintain instruction, to study problems, to meet emergencies, to organize. But a professional army, relied on as the defense of a government, is a fit arm for monarchy only. A volunteer army is an aristocracy, in about the best sense of the word; but an aristocracy it is, and a volunteer army system is irreconcilable with democracy. Democracy must come to universal military obligation, or it must go out of business.

This country in particular needs conscription for military and for other than military reasons. We need it for patriotic and moral reasons. It would bring men together, the East with the West, the North with the South, the men of the seaboard, the prairies and the mountains. It would open the hearts of men to the realities of comradeship and brotherhood. It would improve the health of a population that has become too sedentary. Through discipline it would make men more efficient for business and industry, and as the experience of Australia has demonstrated, it would rid the community of hoodlumism and loafing.

Our prejudices against universal service have been fed by a proper hatred of the Prussian system, but between that and the universal requirement of French or Swiss or Australian democracy the difference is as wide as between light and darkness, or good and evil. Universal subjection to a kaiser and universal co-operation of free patriots are two different things.

We must have conscription now. We must have it because it is necessary. We are entering into a war that will call for all our strength and for all our common sense. We cannot play war this time. We must have selective conscription, and it must be so broadly conceived that it will enable the Government to put the right men in the right places, sending every man into precisely that service, military or noncombatant, where he, rather than some one else, is particularly needed. We must have such conscription because it is vital to our national unity, vital to our democracy, and vital to our manhood.

UNIVERSAL SERVICE IN WORLD WAR I [6]

Although upon entering the World War the United States adopted compulsory universal service, it would be a mistake to think that the country as a whole had perceived the errors of the past and was agreed upon the remedy. On the contrary, the public temper was far from certain. It was a courageous President, backed by wise advisers, who induced Congress to begin the national effort on a sound basis.

The Selective Service Law, signed by the President on May 18, 1917, was, in its own words, "based upon the liability to military service of all male citizens." It authorized "selective draft" for the Army from citizens between their twenty-first and thirty-first birthdays; authorized concurrent voluntary recruiting, at Presidential discretion; and prescribed service for the period of emergency. It forbade bounties, substitutes, and purchased exemption; exempted outright only ministers, divinity students, and a few groups of high public officials; exempted conscientious objectors from combatant service only; and authorized exemptions at Presidential discretion for essential occupations and dependency. It established the state as the unit for quota allotments; based allotments on total population; authorized local boards and district boards. . . . Penal provisions gave the law teeth. . . .

All of these laws vested in the President plenary powers for the regulation of administrative details to give them effect.

The Selective Service Law of May 18, 1917, was upheld by the Supreme Court in the most unequivocal terms. . . .

On the date set, June 5, almost 10,000,000 men registered at their regular precinct polling places. . . . There were three subsequent registrations. In June and August 1918, about 900,000 men who had recently become 21 years old were registered at their local board offices. In September 1918, over

[6] From *American Selective Service*. Prepared by the Joint Army and Navy Selective Service Committee for students of selective service extension courses. U. S. Gov't Ptg. Office. October, 1939. p. 12-17.

13,000,000 men between the ages of 18 and 45 were registered at the polling places, under supervision and control of the local boards. The total World War registration was over 24,000,000.

The first draft of 1917 furnished 687,000 men to the Army. Under emergency conditions, classification was simple, expeditious, and uncritical. . . .

The "Work or Fight" order was issued on May 17, 1918, after some months of consideration. Briefly, it provided that any registrant who was idle or engaged in a nonproductive occupation became liable to induction immediately, regardless of his class or order number. Nonproductive occupations included, for example, gamblers, bartenders, bell boys, elevator boys, ushers, waiters, sales clerks, professional athletes. The order was inspired partly by a sense of the unfairness of drafting useful workers while other men loafed, and partly by the intent to push into essential industry a flow of replacements for men taken into military service. . . .

Selective service was instituted at the proper time—the beginning—and thus avoided the effect of belated coercion after other methods had failed. The obligation of service was held to be personal and nontransferable; devices favorable to the rich, such as purchased substitution and purchased exemption, were forbidden.

Responsibility was dispersed to units of population so small that officials were accessible to the public. The officials were not military men but civilians, well known in their communities. A man's liability and availability for service were decided by his own neighbors. If favoritism crept in, it did so in full view of the community and no blame attached to the armed services. By careful education, the understanding and confidence of the public were obtained, so that the draft received popular support, and odium attached to those who tried to evade it.

Thousands of drafted men thoroughly disliked military service; resentment and disgust made the Army unpopular for several years after the war. But the sentiments only emphasize the absence of such reactions against the draft itself.

The dominating features of selective service were its strictly civilian nature and its intimate local administration. The armies were raised by the nation itself, and public realization of this fact was the strongest element in the success of the system.

UNPREPAREDNESS IN WORLD WAR I [7]

The writer of this letter at 22 years of age was in the first draft in September 1917. He writes as follows:

April 1917 United States declared war on Germany. A blaze of black headlines captioned every newspaper in the land. At first it failed to arouse much interest. It seemed just another event in the world news. The United States was terribly unprepared for war. At first officers had to be trained. That took many months. In September of the same year the draft got under way, and the able-bodied were drafted into the service. I was in the first call. For the first time in my life I felt a comforting satisfaction from the fact that I had had two years of compulsory military training in college.

Upon arriving in Camp Lewis we were assigned first to the depot brigade. It was in this brigade that we were to receive our elemental training. For three months we were put through the paces of training and discipline. Then our company, 250 strong, was called for transfer into active service abroad. Just before boarding the troop train a rush order came from headquarters requesting the company commander, clerk, supply sergeant, mess sergeant, and first-line sergeant (myself) to return to our barracks to train another hundred raw recruits who had just arrived in camp. It was not our privilege to object to this order, although we were disappointed that we could not go on with our men.

We were only with these hundred new recruits about a week when another order came from headquarters ordering these new, green men to prepare for transfer—overseas and into the fight. When I read this order to these men it struck them like a thunderbolt. For a moment they stood motionless and speechless. They were stunned. They had not realized that we were at war. Now they knew it. Their faces were pale with fear—the fear of the helpless, the unprepared, the untrained. "Why Sarge," they uttered, "they can't do this to us when

[7] By Senator Edward R. Burke of Nebraska, presenting a letter from a Montana citizen to the Senate. *Congressional Record*. Vol. 86. August 13, 1940. p. 15661.

we have had so little training. We are not soldiers yet. We can't shoot. We know nothing of taking cover for our own protection. They may just as well take us out and line us up before a firing squad. It is downright murder."

The verbal barrage of these green men was all too true, but orders were orders and war was war. I tried to console these boys by telling them that they probably would receive several months of training in France before going into active service. But they were not to be consoled. Knowledge of their unpreparedness only added to their helplessness. But democracy had to be saved and we had to win this war. If seasoned, well-trained soldiers were not available, then the green raw recruits had to go to fill up the ranks that had been thinned by gunfire at the front.

I shall never forget one man of this group as he sat on his bunk just before marching to the train. He swore profusely. He cursed those in authority for allowing our country to be so unprepared. He accused them of being murderers for sending him into active service with no training. He wanted to know why they all had not had military training in peacetime so that if they must fight they would know how and stand some chance—an equal one—for their lives.

It was about 3 p.m. on the same afternoon that we received the order to "fall in" these men and march them to the train. Several of these hundred men were from nearby points and had telephoned their parents early in the day that they were leaving. Parents came to camp to see them off. I hope that I shall be spared to see an equally pitiful sight again as the one I saw as the troop train pulled out. Several mothers went into hysterics. They had realized their sons were not prepared. One mother sobbed bitterly and exclaimed, "We did not raise our boy to be a soldier and here he is going to war untrained and a perfect target for an enemy soldier. If he is killed, I shall never forgive myself for not sending him to a military school. We would easily have given him a year of military training. But we could not foresee this. May God bless and help him."

If our present members of Congress had seen such scenes as I have mentioned, I am sure that our country would not be in the unprepared predicament in which we find ourselves today. Our country would be prepared to meet any emergency.

I have a boy growing up. Though not old enough as yet for military training, I have vowed that he surely will be prepared if I am possibly able to see that he gets it. I love him too much not to give him a chance for his life if his country ever calls him. If my country needs him, I shall want him to respond but only on the condition that my neighbor's boy and all other boys also respond to the call, therefore universal service and compulsory military training is the only sane, safe, and humanitarian answer to our dilemma.

It is unfair to expect the boys who are now in our Army and Navy to do all of our defending for us. It is unfair to them not to have others trained so that if they need help that all can give it and give it quickly.

THE SUPREME COURT AND THE DRAFT [8]

The grant to Congress of power to raise and support armies, considered in conjunction with the grants of the powers to declare war, to make rules for the government and regulation of the land and naval forces, and to make laws necessary and proper for executing granted powers . . . includes the power to compel military service. . . . This conclusion, obvious upon the face of the Constitution, is confirmed by an historical examination of the subject.

The army power, combining the powers vested in the Congress and the states under the Confederation, embraces the complete military power of government, as is manifested not only by the grant made but by the express limitation . . . prohibiting the states, without the consent of Congress, from keeping troops in time of peace or engaging in war. . . .

The service which may be exacted of a citizen under the army power is not limited to the specific purposes for which Congress is expressly authorized, by the militia clause, to call the militia; the presence in the Constitution of such express regulations affords no basis for an inference that the army power, when exerted, is not complete and dominant to the extent of its exertion.

Compelled military service is neither repugnant to a free government nor in conflict with the constitutional guaranties of individual liberty. Indeed, it may not be doubted that the

---

[8] From "Selective Draft Law Cases." *United States Reports.* Vol. 245. Cases Adjudged in the Supreme Court at October Term, 1917. p. 366. As reprinted in the pamphlet *American Selective Service.* U. S. Gov't Ptg. Office. 1939.

very conception of a just government and its duty to the citizen includes the duty of the citizen to render military service in case of need and the right of the government to compel it.

The power of Congress to compel military service . . . is even more manifest under the Fourteenth Amendment, which, as frequently has been pointed out, broadened the national scope of the government by causing citizenship of the United States to be paramount and dominant instead of being subordinate and derivative, thus operating generally upon the powers conferred by the Constitution.

ARMING IN AN EMERGENCY

DISCUSSION

Until the outbreak of World War II, the military policy of the United States has been to maintain the smallest possible professional army in times of peace, and to wait until disaster threatened the nation before attempting to build up the national defense.

As pointed out in earlier pages in this compilation, no effort was made to build an adequate army in the War of 1812 until British troops actually threatened Washington. Then both volunteering and conscription were used; the resulting untrained military force was hard put to defeat British armies one tenth its numbers. In the Mexican War, the use of a volunteer army enlisted for a 12 months' period prolonged hostilities for several additional months. During the Civil War, short-term enlistments of volunteers and an inefficient system of conscription combined to weaken the Union effort and threaten the safety of the nation.

In all of these early wars, and in the Spanish-American War as well, military training was practically non-existent. Raw farm youths, barely able to sight their muskets or rifles, were sent into the front lines, sometimes to face well-trained and seasoned troops. That our nation succeeded at all in its military efforts is a commentary upon the type of warfare which characterized the 19th century.

When the United States entered the war in 1917, the requirements of successful warfare were vastly different. Instruments of destruction were more complex. Soldiers had to learn the use of gas masks, hand grenades, machine guns; they had to know how to take cover in an artillery barrage, how to take an enemy machine gun nest, how to advance across shell-pitted,

barbed-wire protected terrain before they could be of value as
soldiers. So a long period of training was essential before
draftees were sent to the front. As usual, the nation waited
until we were actually at war before taking steps to build up
an army. After the declaration of war, three of four months
were required for the enactment of a conscription law, registration of men of military age, and induction of the first contingents
of trainees. After the drafted men had actually been brought
into the army, they had to be given training for six or eight
months before they were ready to be sent overseas—so that
it was fully a year after our declaration of war before any
appreciable number of American soldiers were available for
fighting.

Today, the nature of warfare has changed still further, and
the need for specialized training has increased even beyond the
needs of World War I. This time, armies are mechanized;
men fight with airplanes, tanks, mobile artillery. But this time,
the United States has abandoned its policy of waiting until
war has been declared before starting its preparations for war.
We have begun to prepare while we are still at peace; machinery
has been set up for a system of selective service; a million men
have been called to the colors for training; should the United
States be forced to enter the war, we will have a force of a
million and a half trained men to carry the brunt of battle while
others are being prepared. For the first time in our history
as a nation, we have accepted the policy of training for war
before war is declared; and with that policy, we have accepted
the principle of peacetime conscription of men for military service.

ORIGIN OF THE 1940 DRAFT LAW [1]

Last week an unprecedented movement was under way in
the U.S.: military conscription. In only two wars—the Civil
War and the World War—has the U.S. conscripted men for

[1] From "Service for All?" *Time*. 35:17. June 17, 1940. Reprinted by permission.

its armed services. But this movement was unprecedented. It was for peacetime conscription, conscription as a preparedness measure. The changed technique of modern war and the changing temper of the U.S. people raised the issue.

The first steps were not taken by the government, but certainly the War and Navy Departments in Washington knew what was going on, heartily approved. So did Franklin Roosevelt. One morning last week he read in an editorial in *The New York Times*: "The time has come when, in the interest of self-protection, the American people should at once adopt a national system of universal, compulsory military training. We say this . . . because the logic of events drives us remorselessly to this conclusion." Mr. Roosevelt said he liked the paragraph.

Initiators of the plan for universal training were the *Time's* Colonel Julius Ochs Adler and Manhattan lawyer Grenville Clark, whose Military Training Camps Association set out to raise $250,000 to promote acceptance of a peacetime draft. Last week genial Colonel Adler, who served overseas with the 77th Division in 1918, told a group of Princeton alumni and students about a bill which was being drawn up for Congressional action. Most interesting detail: not only young men would be drafted, but about 15 per cent of the draftees would be men from 32 to 38, and five per cent, men of 38 to 45 (on the proved theory that groups combining different ages and various levels of intelligence do the best soldiering).

Meanwhile New Jersey's State Director of Relief ordered his subordinates to strip from the rolls all able-bodied, single men who are eligible for military service. His ungentle hint: the Army provides employment. Illinois's old, gentle Congressman Adolph Sabath, who has long opposed school military training retreated so far as to favor conscription for collegians. A Gallup Poll published last week showed voters divided 50-50 on peacetime conscription; last October, they were 61 per cent against it. Massachusetts' 38-year-old Senator Henry Cabot

Lodge (an Army Reserve Captain) proposed to require six months' training for all able young men as they turn 18. The Army's Chief of Staff George Marshall advocated some limited form of peacetime conscription.

The Army in a report last year announced that volunteer enlistment will not work for wartime service. But the reason for peacetime conscription is that volunteer recruiting is inadequate. Recruiting districts throughout the U.S. are behind in their quotas, will have to drive hard to up the Army from 242,000 to 280,000 by next September 1. How big an Army may be needed to face down the threats of Blitzkrieg no one last week calculated publicly. Some idea of possible requirements could be got from the fact that, if the U.S. ever has 50,000 warplanes in actual service, it will have to have around 75,000 pilots and 750,000 men on the ground (at the rule of thumb of ten men on the ground to keep one man in the air) for its air force alone.

THE DRAFT IN THE PRESENT EMERGENCY [2]

One short year ago the United States was beginning large scale preparations for its own defense. A year ago the Gallup poll showed that approximately one-half of the people of the United States believed that we should enact a Selective Training and Service Act. Nine months ago, after a period of discussion and study, Congress passed and the President signed the Selective Training and Service Act of 1940. A month later on October 16, 1940, more than 16 million young men presented themselves for registration. Two weeks after registration the national lottery was held here in the nation's capital to determine the order in which the nation's manpower would be selected for service. The process of classification and selection was begun

[2] By Brigadier General Lewis B. Hershey, director of Selective Service. From "The Present and Future of Selective Service," a radio address over the Blue network of the National Broadcasting Company, June 23, 1941. Reprinted by permission.

immediately. And just two months and two days after the Selective Service Law was enacted, the first contingent of citizen soldiers marched away to camp for a year of military training in the service of their country. . . .

The exact number of individuals in the land and naval forces who were there because of selective service cannot be accurately calculated. In fact it never will be known because in addition to those who have been selected for induction there are many others who have enlisted for three, four or six years in the Army, Navy and Marine Corps due to the fact that the Selective Service Law places the liability for military service upon all who are between twenty-one and thirty-six. We do know, however, that by July 1 of this year, more than 600 thousand young men will have been inducted into the Army of the United States through the selective service process. They have been inducted in a manner which is, I am sure, most satisfactory to the Army in general. I have heard many very flattering remarks about the quality and the type of the individuals who have come to our Army through selective service.

The general physical condition of America's young men, as revealed and deliberately publicized by selective service, has deeply shocked our entire nation. It is indeed a cause for disturbance—for study and for action—when we must reject almost one-half of those who appear for examination. It is true that many of the defects are not of a nature which prevents a man from carrying on many of his normal activities. It is likewise true that many of the disabilities are such that they can be corrected if adequate measures are taken. It is also true that a reasonably high standard is maintained in our examinations. However, it is a standard which is little, if any, higher than the standard which should be maintained by a healthy citizen.

If the selective service had done nothing more than to emphasize the necessity for remedial and immediate action in connection with the physical disabilities of our citizens, it has thus justified its existence and is worth many times its cost to the nation. The decision as to whether or not an individual is fit for military service is decided on the basis of the standards of the service to which he is sent. . .

It seems that there should be established, among all our people, a feeling that each individual should put forth every possible effort to make himself physically fit to render service to his country.

Approximately 70 per cent of those who have been classified have been deferred because they have dependents. This is a most difficult field. In the first place, it is a field in which no two cases are ever alike. There is every possible type of variation in the problem of deferring or not deferring the individual, because others are dependent upon him for support. . . .

The basic function of selective service is to procure men for the land and naval forces of the United States. It is also the duty of selective service to procure these men without disturbing unnecessarily the production of arms and munitions, the growing of food, and the doing of many other things, that are essential to the national health, safety and interest. For this reason the selective service system has provided for the deferment of those who are necessary in the many activities connected with defense, and the maintenance of our national life.

The purpose of selective service is to make a man available for service in the place where he can do the greatest good for the nation. In the application of these general rules and regulations, the initial decision has been placed in the hands of those who live near the individuals in question. Every effort has been made to insure personalized, individualized administration of the selective service system.

There is and undoubtedly will continue to be a growing demand for individuals to work in industry and to grow food on the farm. Not only must the men who are engaged in these activities be deferred, but it is most necessary that others who are now engaged in training and preparation for their place on the production line, or on the farm, should also be deferred so that the supply of skilled workers, whether it be in agriculture or in industry, will be ample. . . .

We are in the process of an educational program . . . The American people have not yet come to believe that an individual in times of stress can serve his country as well at some other task, as he can in the land or naval forces. This is the result of long custom—it is the result of days when warfare was quite different in its nature than it is today. This fundamental and basic fact presents a problem of education to the selective service system.

Not only is it necessary to bring to the attention of 20,000 members of our local boards the critical need for skilled labor in the fabrication of arms and munitions, and in the production of food, but it is equally important to bring this fact to the attention of 130 million people. . . . It is our hope and belief that in time our people will understand the necessity for each man to do that task for which he is best fitted, provided that task aids in defending America. . . .

The method of application of selective service to all classes of society has been an excellent force for the solidification and unification of America. It is encouraging to those whose share of worldly goods is small to see their more prosperous fellow citizens accepting their obligations of military service and giving their time and their energy in the same organizations. It is an example of real democracy.

Selective service has given an opportunity to have in the same units a cross section of our American citizens. From this association they will gain a mutual respect which will remain a solidifying influence in our life—in the years that are before us.

Selective service has reemphasized the relationship of the citizen to his duties and to his obligations. For too long a time the emphasis has been placed upon our rights and our privileges. Selective service is an application of practical democracy. It is a decentralized process whereby the neighbors of the

individual to be chosen for service apply to him general rules
and general principles on a personalized and individualized basis.

Of course, in a system of this kind, there will be those
who look at others and believe that they themselves have been
less fortunate, because of an apparent lack of uniformity. But
granting that all charges of lack of uniformity are true, yet
the fundamental principle of the community having the right
to say, within certain limits, what citizen shall serve, is the
very essence of democracy. It is the very essence of community
responsibility.

In spite of many faults and in spite of many shortcomings
that it may have, selective service has more elasticity—it is
quicker to keep in tune with the demands of the local community
—than any other system that can be devised for this particular
purpose.

Lastly, selective service has aided materially in the formation
of a national army—an army that is not the property of the few,
but an army that belongs to all—an army that is made up of
sons of the rich, sons of the poor, sons of all classes and races,
united on a common ground for a common purpose,—the defense
of America.

THE STATE OF NATIONAL DEFENSE TODAY [3]

Black Jack Pershing in France with the A.E.F. 24 years
ago would have been pleased to have many of the resources
which are today available to Chief of Staff George Catlett
Marshall. Even General William Crozier, boss of the Army's
Ordnance in 1917, would have jumped at the chance of obtain-
ing as much or as good equipment as the U. S. Army's Ordnance
chief, General Charles M. Wesson, is able to provide today.

For in its basic national readiness for war, in the energy
and quality and amount of its pre-war planning and production,
the U. S. of last week was incomparably ahead of the U. S. of

[3] From "National Defense: The U. S. Effort, Preparedness 1941." *Time*.
37:21-3. May 19, 1941. Reprinted by permission.

pre-war 1917. It was even ahead of the U. S. of mid-war 1918. By the dollar measure alone the U. S. in that war spent a total of $22,000,000,000; last week, the U. S. had already spent or committed itself to spend $51,800,000,000.

The U. S. during World War I manufactured 64 tanks; last week it was producing 13 per day. It produced 1642 light and heavy artillery pieces during World War I; its planned (but by no means attained) production of a single type of anti-tank gun for World War II is almost four times that total. The U. S. last week had an Army of 1,300,000 poorly equipped, as yet half-trained men; not until nine months after World War I was declared did the U. S. of 1917 have that many poorly equipped, skimpily trained men.

But all these pleasant comparisons are no guide to the adequacy of present U. S. preparedness. The number and quality of tools adequate to win World War I are utterly inadequate to make even a creditable showing this time.

And in some respects the U. S. is no better off than in the last war. Washington last week was phenomenally like the Washington of January 1918. Then, as last week, there was a central agency (the early War Industries Board in 1918; the Office of Production Management last week) without a head empowered to decide, to act, to compel obedience. Then, as last week, there was a President passionately dedicated to the purposes of production, yet unready and unwilling to delegate final power to get that production done. . . .

Then, as last week, such men overlooked a large fact that with all the bobbling and mistakes, the nation was learning how to produce for war, in spite of everything was building the wherewithal to produce. And then, as last week, there was a cumulative set of circumstances which required the event which finally came (in March 1918): the naming of one able administrator with power to direct the whole effort. In 1918, that man was Bernard Mannes Baruch. Up to last week, that requirement was still to be met.

The fact that the U. S. has always muddled its preparations for war does not condone another such muddle. But if all these facts loom large and dark, their ultimate sum is smaller than the ultimate sum of U. S. vigor and resource. . . .

"In one breath I say we are not producing much, but in the next breath I tell you that an outstanding job of production preparation is being done." So said last week Alfred Robinson Glancey, chief of the OPM section in charge of getting ordnance, the stuff to fight with: guns, shells, tanks, etc.

Navy, Army and OPM ordnance officials no longer think solely in terms of so many thousand guns, millions of shells to be produced. The limit of U. S. effort is their limit. Nearest they could come to a statement of their goal last week was: full equipment for a U. S. Army of 2,000,000; partial equipment for 800,000 more; facilities for the rapid equipment of a 4,000,000-man Army, when and if it is called; armament for the two-ocean U. S. Navy; supplies for Great Britain; supplies for the rest of the democratic world. . . .

"At least a year will pass before we can have an Army and an air force adequate to meet the air and ground forces which could be brought against us. . . . We have . . . a naval instrument prepared and ready. . . ." So said Secretary of War Stimson last week. Army and Navy officers add some important qualifications to this estimate, but in general they agree with Mr. Stimson.

The Marines are expanding from a force of 35,000 to 80,000 men. They are well fixed for seasoned, ranking officers, will soon be short of qualified junior officers. Rated first though they are for fighting now, they need more automatic and semi-automatic weapons, pack artillery, transport vessels. Said a ranking Marine last week: "We are going to have an amphibious war, and damn soon. I wish we had another year to train our people. I don't think we'll get it. . . ."

The Army's prodigious expansion since last fall speaks for itself: 1,300,000 men put into uniform, 45 new cantonments completed or nearly so, a new Armored Force (two divisions) now doubling, and soon to triple, many and many another example of conquered difficulties, great accomplishment. Against the physical, visible facts of that record, the sum total of delays and mistakes seems picayune. Army men need not blame themselves when they accept Secretary Stimson's estimate that they are at least a year from readiness for modern war.

The U. S. and its Army will be doing very well if that estimate is made good. If General Wesson's fears for delayed ordnance productions are fulfilled, it will take more than a year to equip the Army. At super-human best, peak production on most of the schedules already drawn will not be reached before 1942. . . .

The Army has a vast problem in training men and officers as well as producing machines. Not till 1941 will most members of the draft Army have a year's training as soldiers. With shortages of equipment and of trained field officers the training of the men will probably be none too far advanced by then.

Among field officers a thorough weeding will have to be carried out. A similar process has already begun in the high command. . . .

Today the Army in the field is a great school force, whose officer-teachers themselves have to be taught. Given equipment, given time, given competent command, the job ahead can be done, but so far it has only been begun.

THE SPECIALIST BOTTLE-NECK [4]

The War Department has not obtained as many specialists from the ranks of selectees as it had expected. There is a shortage of skilled men in sixty-seven categories, including truck drivers, cooks and radio operators.

The shortages range from a fraction of one per cent to more than 24 per cent.

[4] From "Lack of Specialists Disappointing to Army." *New York Times*. July 6, 1941. p. 22. Reprinted by permission.

Leading shortages are truck drivers, 6.5 per cent; automobile mechanics, 14.6; cooks, 24.8, and commercial radio operators, 15.3.

The Department expects that in a majority of cases men can be trained in the Army to fill the gaps.

THE ARMY IN TRANSITION [5]

The adoption of selective service and the hasty expansion of the armed forces provide the most stringent test of the army's organizing capacity since 1918. At that time serious flaws were revealed, not only in the administrative work of the War Department but in the ability of many army officers and the whole regimen of discipline and command as applied to citizen soldiers. In the intervening years, critics of the system have made many suggestions for change. Today, after a static period following the last war, army organization and methods are gradually being modernized in many respects.

One important development has been a recent reorganization placing all of the field forces under a chain of command specifically designed to facilitate troop training. Prior to July 1940 there were no effective tactical—i.e., fighting force—commands in the continental United States larger than the division, except for the General Headquarters Air Force. Supervision of training ordinarily rested with the Corps Area Commander, who was also burdened with the many other functions of supply and administration. Now, however, the responsibility for training in the field is lodged in a newly organized General Headquarters, while the War Department General Staff serves as a planning and policy-making body. Beneath the GHQ stands the basic structure of the army, adapted to current training necessities. . . . The new system leaves combat troops free for the greatest possible measure of intensive training.

[5] By David H. Popper. From "The United States Army in Transition." *Foreign Policy Reports.* 16:220-7. December 1, 1940. Reprinted by permission of the Foreign Policy Association.

The expansion of the army, moreover, has resulted in an increase in the number of active general officers to 230, thus providing an infusion of new blood in the higher command as well as the possibility of more rapid promotion in all ranks. Opportunity is therefore afforded to reward outstanding leadership in training. Military instruction methods are gradually being altered to prepare the soldier for battle efficiency with a minimum of wasted time and effort. The preoccupation with close order drill, for ceremonial purposes and the inculcation of discipline, has been reduced by adoption of simpler and more flexible formations. Guardhouse confinement is to be minimized in favor of forms of disciplinary actions which do not involve absence from training. Some of the rigidity of military etiquette is in course of modification. Maneuvers and exercises are being made more realistic, now that sufficient funds have been provided. And much has been done to lessen the time spent on fatigue, administrative service, and camp construction by combat troops. The army is making a special effort to preserve a high morale among those recently called to serve.

Germany's successful offensives in Western Europe have profoundly influenced military thought and organization in this country, but they have not for the most part invalidated the basic doctrines and principles on which American practice rests. . . .

In no component save the air corps were the consequences of the *Blitzkrieg* more immediately apparent than among the army's mechanized units. Prior to the smashing success of the German armored divisions, the War Department had been experimenting with mechanized formations, but only on a tentative scale. As late as February 1940, the protective mobilization plan requirements for the infantry called for only 734 light and 194 medium tanks, while the immediate cavalry program stipulated the addition of but two combat car squadrons and a scout car troop. A force approximating a mechanized division was made up for test by adding other units to the mechanized

cavalry brigade, notably a motorized infantry regiment to serve
as a holding force for captured territory. A group of about
300 infantry tanks was also concentrated for experimental exercises. Maximum progress, however, had been hampered for
years by the division of responsibility for mechanized forces
between the infantry and the cavalry.

This defect was remedied, and a marked impetus was
given to the development of mechanization, by the incorpora-
tion in July 1940 of infantry and cavalry tanks in an armored
corps of two divisions, under the direction of an armored field
force commander. Each division is to contain about 9500
officers and men. It will include field artillery and motorized
infantry, and will consist of approximately 700 armored vehicles,
300 guns and howitzers of various calibers, and over 6500
automatic and semi-automatic weapons. . . . Two more armored
divisions are to be formed in June 1941, with an ultimate goal
of ten; and a force of heavy tanks of perhaps 40 to 70 tons
is in prospect to serve as "land battleships" accompanying the
infantry in a break-through of the enemy line.

At present the matériel available is not yet sufficient even
for the existing units. When it was formed in July 1940
the armored force possessed approximately 400 tanks of all ages
and types. Recently, however, light tanks have been delivered
at a rate of 100 per month. The trend is toward heavier units;
the weight of the so-called light tank has risen from 10 to 13
tons in latest models. Medium tanks, redesigned as a result of
German operations, are receiving heavier armor and armament,
and will be delivered beginning in May 1941. They will
weigh approximately 25 tons, as compared with 17.5 to
19 tons for older models. New developments and tactics will
be studied and approved by the Armored Force Board, and
instruction will be carried on by the Armored Force School,
as in the case of the combat arms.

The psychological as well as the military consequences of
air power in the European war have fired the imagination and

aroused the fears of the American people, and have given rise to a phenomenal drive for expansion of the United States military and naval air forces. With 14,300 planes on order in this country for Britain, the purchase of 12,000 more planned, and manufacturers under contract for 26,000 for our own defense needs, it seems strange to recall that under a construction program adopted in 1939 the army set as its goal a force of 5500 airplanes, 2200 of which were to be kept in reserve. Pursuant to this earlier objective, the personnel of the air corps was to be increased from 21,500 to almost 45,000 enlisted men during the fiscal year 1940.

But in May 1940 the War Department, apparently caught unprepared by the overwhelming demand for scores of thousands of planes, began rapidly to plan for larger forces. For months the air corps' objectives remained indeterminate. By October 1940, however, it was clear that approximately 18,000 planes had been ordered or received. Of these, 12,800 of all classes and types, including basic and advanced training planes, are to be delivered and manned before the end of 1942. The remainder are to serve as an equipment reserve. . . .

While critics may dissent from individual features of the army's great augmentation programs, it can scarcely be denied that they represent a tremendous stride in the direction of "total defense" of the country. On the whole, they reveal that the General Staff is fully aware of modern military trends and is applying them with all practicable speed. Announced objectives are in many cases still tentative, permitting a high degree of flexibility to meet changing conditions. If there has been evidence of confusion, it has not, given the unprecedented circumstances, been excessive.

The gap which separates proposal and performance, however, may provide grounds for concern. The army as it exists today is but a nucleus for the great force of the future. In two respects—matériel and personnel—it is and must remain deficient for many months to come. For this, responsibility must be divided between Congress, the Bureau of the Budget, and the nation on the one hand, and the War Department on the other. Until recently, Congress and the Budget Bureau have pruned down the army's requests for funds—to such an extent, indeed, that in the sixteen years 1925-40 only $854,556,000 was devoted to augmentation, modernization and replacement of arms and equipment. Of this sum, $509,900,000 went to the air corps and only $344,656,000 to the ground elements of the army—an average of only $21,500,000 per year for the latter. On the other hand, the War Department has been censured for lack of vision and imagination in planning for the future. It has been accused of delaying the adoption of new weapons; ordering constant changes in design and unduly complicated specifications instead of rushing production; and retarding progress by excessively bureaucratic procedure.

In any event, the shortage of new matériel is pressing and must remain so for a considerable period. It is difficult to measure the precise extent of this shortage because the reorganization of tactical units and the addition of new units have resulted in an ascending spiral of requirements for equipment. The latest official summary of matériel on hand and on order —which by no means includes all future needs—reveals the status as of August 1, 1940. . . .

Because of the time necessary to place many of these items in production, deliveries will not be great until the summer of 1941, but should flow in increasing volume thereafter until completion of existing programs for "an army fit to meet any challenge" about March 1942. Meanwhile, there are glaring deficiencies in the equipment of many units, some of which have already been mentioned. The semi-automatic rifle adopted as standard for the infantryman—a weapon which greatly increases infantry fire-power—is supplied to only a fraction of the troops. The newer models of tanks, artillery, and anti-tank and anti-aircraft weapons are still almost completely lacking. Of a total of 186,000 motor vehicles needed for a field force of 1,400,000, only a minor portion have so far been delivered. As for airplanes, General Marshall revealed in September that the army had approximately 1500 planes that might be used in modern warfare, although only 500 were of the most modern types containing self-sealing fuel tanks and armored fuselages. At that time one prominent observer estimated that the regular army divisions were 75 to 90 per cent equipped with modern arms, and the National Guard 50 per cent equipped. As the number of troops in service increases, these figures temporarily decline.

Serious though they are, these deficiences may be less significant in the long run than flaws in organization and personnel. The seventeen military bureaus of the War Department, not to speak of the five sections of the General Staff, are said to present many examples of overlapping functions and lack of coordination. Officers are commissioned not in the line of the army but in one of the arms or services—for example, the infantry, field artillery or cavalry—and each of these is headed at Washington by a chief representing men who use the same weapons wherever they may be, when representation might more desirably group individuals from the various arms engaged in a specific task, such as coast defense. Despite the existence of a number of joint boards, coordination of army and navy activities seems insufficient, especially in such matters as landing exercises and division of functions in over-water aviation.

The abilities of army officers, moreover, will be subjected to the severest tests in the years ahead. There are large numbers of highly qualified officers in the service, but there are also some whose professional ability is open to doubt, or who may not be willing or competent to train their men in accordance with the new developments sanctioned by the War Department. This situation is partly due to the failure, through political interference, of attempts to weed out inefficient leaders, and partly to the absence of any system of selection for promotion by merit below the general officer grades since all commissioned personnel is normally advanced to the rank of colonel on a straight seniority basis. Many regular army officers have had too little experience in handling large bodies of troops, and the number of reserve and guard officers—generally much less well trained —will be about five times the number of regulars in 1941.

Enlisted men, too, suffer from lack of training and appreciation of the nature of modern war, as well as a varying degree of physical softness. Maneuvers held by the four field armies in the summer of 1940 revealed the existence of these deficiencies and convinced officers that it might take six months to make qualified combat troops of some regular army divisions, and one year for the National Guard.

The flood of recruits obtained by voluntary enlistment and conscription will necessarily prolong this process. Trained men have been formed into cadres which have been filled by assignment of raw troops for instruction. Instead of diluting almost all regular units in this manner, the War Department might have done better to put two or more divisions of seasoned soldiers in full readiness at once for any contingency during the critical period immediately ahead. As it is, one commentator believes it "obvious that for the next eighteen months we shall not have an army so much as an aggregation of half-trained units —both in the air and on the ground."

Thus the army has chosen to plan not for the immediate future but for more distant eventualities. It seems a reasonable deduction that the General Staff is not greatly alarmed by the prospects of an invasion of the Western Hemisphere in 1941. Many unofficial observers would concur in this judgment. Given the difficulties of transporting and supplying an Old World force in the New, they would say that the United States military needs for hemisphere defense could be met by a regular army of 400,000 to 600,000 completely equipped mobile troops ready for quick transportation to any threatened point in the Americas.

Preparations for training three to four million men may, however, be justified by other considerations beside the possible value of compulsory military service as an instrument of national education in a period of crisis. A mass army may conceivably be necessary whether the United States stands its ground in the Western Hemisphere against a hostile world outside, or whether it chooses to aid Great Britain by force of arms. In defending the hemisphere large forces may have to be used under two conditions. In the first place, there is a possibility of a concentrated German-Italian-Japanese attack after Axis triumphs in Europe and Asia and many months of feverish preparation unhampered by resistance from the conquered nations. Second, great numbers of troops would be required for occupation of large areas of Latin American territory. The prospect of the first eventuality is remote but undeniable; and there seems to be very little likelihood of the second. In either case, this country should have sufficient time for the training and equipment of hundreds of thousands of newly inducted men.

It is less certain that the option of extending military aid to Britain will remain open indefinitely. If British resistance continues, the actions of its enemies or the measure of Britain's need may call for the dispatch of small, mobile units to occupy outlying points like Dakar or even Singapore, before existing American units are fully trained. Ultimately, assuming that Britain and the Axis are locked in a stalemate conflict for years to come, large American forces might participate in a British offensive on the European continent. . . .

EQUIP THOSE WE HAVE [6]

I stand here on the floor today in the capacity of an individual member of the Military Affairs Committee of this House to implore my colleagues to weigh carefully and consider calmly any measure that proposes to saddle compulsory military training upon the people of this nation. Before we embark upon any such course, which by its very nature is inimical to democracy let us ask ourselves a few pertinent questions. The first and

[6] By Congressman Arthur Anderson of Missouri. *Congressional Record*, Vol. 86. September 3, 1940. p. 17334-5.

greatest question is, What are we preparing to undertake? Is it defense or is it preparation to join in the folly of war? What more could we do than conscript our youth, if we were actually at war or imminently in danger thereof?

The second great question to consider is, Have we learned anything at all of military value from the war in Europe? It strikes me that the American people have learned a great deal from that terrible war that our military and naval experts cannot or will not see because their eyes are dimmed by tradition and their minds are adverse to progress.

If the men who dominate and control the policy of our military machine have given any thought to the military, and not the political, significance of the war in Europe they would not be crying for conscription; for men and more men. They would, rather, be bending their every effort to properly equip and train the troops we now possess or have authorized. Anyone who will take the time to examine the records can see that the so-called progress in the manufacture of essential arms such as planes, tanks, large guns, and so forth, is not adequate nor is it proceeding with proper speed. Witness the maneuvers now being held, with trucks taking the place of tanks, and gunners practicing, schoolyard fashion, with cardboard and wooden guns. The men thus engaged are not conscripts nor raw recruits. They are trained soldiers of the Army and National Guard. The theorists at the War Department may feel satisfied with a truck with a sign on it, Tank, but before they come here and ask to conscript millions of young men, let them devote their energy to the task of equipping the forces we now have. Until that job has been done, the appearance of these men to plead for conscription strikes me as a deliberate attempt to direct the attention of the American people away from the fact that these gentlemen, up till now, have failed to provide our existing Army, including the National Guard, with the essential weapons of modern war. Do they propose to train the conscripts under the tutelage of an officer who has received his own training in a cardboard tank or with a wooden gun?

It seems clear that the dominant forces in our military setup are still ignorant of the fact that the wars in Europe and in Asia have more than proved that manpower alone means very little to military success and that equipment, machines, real tanks, real airplanes, real guns, are what spell the difference between defeat and victory.

Let us not forget that France had a trained army of nearly 5,000,000 men. These men were not conscripts, but trained, hardened troops, said to be the finest in the world. Yet this supposedly greatest of armies, was utterly routed and destroyed by an enemy admittedly far less trained but one that possessed every modern weapon capable of production.

Did our military experts learn anything from the destruction of the French Army? Do they still believe that men and more men are what make an army? Can it be that they have failed to study the plight of China where manpower exists in its greatest abundance? Are they learning anything? Are they even trying to learn anything from the Battle of Britain? The boys and girls in the street who read the papers and listen to the radio know that the success of the British in defending their island will depend on how long they can keep about 5000 airplanes in the air and how long they can keep a few thousand anti-aircraft guns firing. If these planes are downed or the guns silenced by the enemy an invasion of England would be comparatively easy. All the millions of men in the British Empire will be of little avail unless their air force and anti-aircraft guns can offer resistance to the enemy. Machines and equipment mean life or death in modern war. Men alone mean nothing.

Here in the United States we have authorized a Regular Army of 375,000 men. The National Guard number about 250,000 trained men. This number is augmented by Organized Reserves and by partially trained men who have had C.M.T.C. experience. Together that is a fair-sized army. Properly trained and equipped with the tanks, planes, guns, and so forth, that American ingenuity is capable of giving them, they represent a force well-nigh invincible—if you are speaking of defending the United States.

If the Army we now possess, including the National Guard, was equipped with the necessary planes, with the necessary guns, anti-aircraft and otherwise, with the all-essential tanks, and with the other machines of modern war, and if that Army was trained fully in the use of such equipment, which it is not at present, then there could possibly be a sounder basis for considering conscripting additional men for military training. Until that point is reached and until a voluntary system of enlistment in both the Regular Army and National Guard has been given a fair chance, agitation for conscription can serve only to disrupt the proper training of a modern war machine, to weaken industry and agriculture by sapping it of the vigor of youth, and to dampen the faith of the people in the democratic form of government.

During my service in this House I have worked conscientiously for a modern and sufficient Army to defend this nation and the principles for which it stands. I have pleaded for aviation and mechanization. I have supported every defense measure that has come before this House. I have studied every report I could get of the war in Europe for the purpose of being enlightened on the needs of our armed forces in the world of today. Everything that I have done and do now is with the firm conviction that this country will not participate in the European conflict. I have studied the problem from the standpoint of defense only. Having thus defined my course, I cannot conscientiously support conscription at this time.

With our present Army sadly lacking in proper equipment and in the training for use thereof, I cannot perceive a legitimate basis for conscription. I am ready to support any measure for the defense of my country. I am not ready to call millions of young men out of the factories and fields to be trained, if you can call it that, by men who have not had training themselves or very little training, in the methods and equipment that is all-essential in present-day war.

Until such time as we are prepared to train men in the use of modern equipment which is now sadly lacking even in the Regular Army, we are wasting time in talking conscription and we are jeopardizing the defense of this country.

Those who profess to have such great and boundless concern for the future of our nation would do far better just now to exert their influence in the proper places to see that the Army we now have is equipped with the best planes, the best guns, the best tanks, and the best ammunition that America is capable of producing. Why sabotage the whole defense program by calling in millions of men when we are not yet prepared to school them in modern warfare?

ARMY DEFICIENCIES AFTER THE FIRST YEAR [7]

The United States Army today—after a year of expansion and preparation— is still months away from adequate combat efficiency.

In the opinion of most high-ranking officers not a single division is yet ready for war, although all our organized divisions are already superior in training to the divisions we sent to France in 1917.

Only in the physical condition of our soldiers, already hardened to field service and capable of extended effort, considerable endurance and twenty-five mile marches, can the condition of the Army be considered satisfactory. There are grave deficiencies in equipment, in training and tactics and leadership and to a lesser extent in discipline and morale.

Most serious by far of all the criticisms leveled against the Army is that which relates to its basic tactical concepts and to

[7] By Hanson W. Baldwin, *New York Times* military and naval expert. From "Army is Far Short of War Efficiency After Year Effort." *New York Times.* June 29, 1941. p. 1. Reprinted by permission.

its leadership. Military lack of vision is freely criticized within the Army itself and some officers say that the only hope of progress is to sweep the Army clean of the "Colonel Blimps" and military reactionaries who, in the past, have blocked and who still are blocking tactical progress. Incompetent officers of all grades, but especially general officers and colonels, must be weeded out, it is held, if we are to have a battle-worthy army.

There seems no question, in the opinion of many Army officers, that our conception of modern tactics—as exemplified by recent maneuvers in Tennessee and elsewhere—is even started to develop, in field exercises, real cooperation between ground and air; we still extol the foot soldier—who, some officers believe, is "as dead as the dodo"—as the "queen of battles"; we are still training with bayonets and grenades and essentially in the war of position rather than the war of maneuver.

Many officers, military iconoclasts though they may be, have put it bluntly and probably correctly:

"We are still training for a 1917 war."

The strengths and weaknesses of the Army today and its position after a year of preparation are perhaps best illustrated by a review of the different items, tangible and intangible, that go to make up an army.

Shortages of modern equipment are still very serious. In equipment not a single division equals the majority of the German divisions. Certain divisions and special units are much better equipped than others.

Thus, the two marine divisions and the First and Second Divisions of the Regular Army, which have had priority, are rather completely equipped. Missing in these divisions are the 105-mm. howitzers, which are to replace the 75-mm. guns. The Army still has considerably less than 100 of these new weapons.

The Forty-fourth Division and three other National Guard divisions which entered Federal service last September before any of the other Guard units, are also fairly well equipped, though there are still shortages in motor transport, .50 caliber machine guns, 37-mm. anti-tank guns, radios and many miscellaneous items, as well as in the 105-mm. weapons.

Divisions which have not had such high equipment priority, like New York's Twenty-seventh Division, or the Regular Army Fifth Division, are still short many items of essential equipment, such as trucks, .50 caliber machine guns, mortars and even Colt automatics. There are plenty of rifles. Ammunition shortages are still acute, not only in anti-aircraft and larger-caliber shells, but even in cartridges for small arms.

None of our four armored divisions has as yet received a single new medium tank, although the Second Armored Division has more than thirty medium tanks of out-moded design. Its quota of medium tanks is 110. New light tanks are available in quantity, but not in the numbers required by the tables of organization. Half-track personnel carriers and prime movers and other items of mechanized equipment are just beginning to be delivered in rather limited quantities. There are no self-propelled gun mounts.

The anti-aircraft situation is still very unsatisfactory, with none of the new 90-mm. A.A. guns yet in the hands of tactical units and with some "bugs" still to be ironed out in this gun.

In the air—particularly in the type planes required for support of and cooperation with land forces—the Army is weaker than in any other field. There is not today a single army dive-bomber available. There are only a few modern attack planes or light bombers especially designed for attacking ground forces.

There are considerable numbers of observation types, though some of them are obsolescent. Many of our new plane types, though basically sound, have developed faults, some of them serious, which require rectification—some at the factories.

This continued shortage of equipment may be surprising to the American public, but it is due in large measure to past public apathy to Army needs. Equipment for a modern army cannot be produced overnight. When the program started a year ago the Army did not expect to be even fairly well equipped until the spring of 1942. This schedule has since been further delayed by the extensive nature of the material aid sent to Britain. A considerable part of our continued equipment shortages, particularly our serious ammunition shortage, can be explained in part by the shipments abroad.

The quality of our new weapons in comparison with German weapons is in some ways encouraging, in others profoundly discouraging.

Our planes are, in general, as good or better than those of the Nazis, although many "bugs" in many types still remain. Our tanks are faster, about as well armed, but with less armor.

The new light tank is probably the best of its type in the world. The new thirty-ton medium, which will not be produced in quantity for another two or three months, has a high silhouette, too little power for those who would like to see greater mobility, and its main weapon—a 75-mm. gun—has limited traverse, particularly to the left. It has other "bugs" which will require rectification.

It is seven to eight tons lighter than one of the best German tanks. Nevertheless, it is essentially a fine combat tank, and a good example of American industrial genius at its best—from blueprint dream to steel monster in a year.

We have no heavy tanks, although a 60-ton model, armed with a high-velocity gun which will penetrate any tank armor now known will be ready for test soon.

Our rifles and machine guns are good, although need exists for a new type of short-barreled "Tommy" gun and for a new light machine gun.

Our field artillery is basically good, though great need exists for a self-propelled mount—a gun on tracks, such as the Germans have used effectively. Aberdeen Proving Ground is experimenting with such mounts, but none are yet in production.

Anti-tank guns are mainly of the 27-mm. type, a considerably improved model of the German standard weapon, plus the

75-mm. field piece, modified for anti-tank use. At present prevailing opinion holds that it is technically unsound to build calibers between these two, although the British are building a 57-mm. anti-tank gun and some officers in our Army want such an intermediate caliber.

More and better anti-aircraft guns of two types, one of heavy caliber to fire projectiles far into the heavens against high-flying bombers, the other a small or intermediate caliber to guard ground troops against dive-bombing, are urgently needed and are being developed. The Germans and the British are far ahead of us in the variety and, in some respects, in the quality of their anti-aircraft equipment.

The most urgent needs for quick improvement of planned or existing weapons are in anti-aircraft equipment and in mechanized vehicles. Tanks with greater armor protection and self-propelled mounts for field artillery and anti-tank and anti-aircraft guns should be quickly developed.

There is also a need—though, of course, a far less important one—for a durable battle uniform, roughly similar to that of the British. Only the Armored Force, which wears a zipper-type coverall, with big pockets, has solved this problem. At the maneuvers of the Second Army in Tennessee the soldiers quickly became a rag-tag and bobtail army.

After three weeks in the field, sleeping on the ground and fighting through thickets, the cotton khaki uniforms were stained, torn, frayed or ripped. Many of the men, by orders, wore blue denims; this discolors less easily and is perhaps more rugged than the cotton khaki, but nevertheless is not durable enough for field service and is at best sloppy looking.

Greatest need of all is technical and tactical vision, not only in the services that develop the arms and equipment, but in the units—infantry, field artillery, etc.—which make use of them. Many of the weapons which the Germans have used successfully in this war were envisioned here; some of them were tried out in embryo form here, but their development was abandoned. We must think—and act—ahead of the Germans.

THE EQUIPMENT SHORTAGE [8]

There seems to be a tremendous, organized propaganda movement, behind the appropriation. Moving-picture news reels and
newspaper photographers have shown the National Guard and
the Organized Reserve, in training, in various parts of the
country under the most astonishing conditions. The men have
been shown drilling with broomsticks, and sometimes with iron
pipe, in place of guns. There are shots of them using pieces
of large iron pipe to imitate trench mortars, and beer cans for
shells. Some of the pictures show Army trucks with signs on
the side of them, labeling them "tank." And altogether, it's a
very alarming and shocking impression that is given to you, the
general public, the idea that we are almost criminally short of
essential equipment for the Army.

Now, I know I'm inviting a lot of trouble for telling you
what I'm going to tell you now. I'm going to be accused of
being a "fifth columnist." Some people are going to be very
critical, and they're going to accuse me of trying to discourage
the national defense program—which I'm not doing at all—
it's not my business to be propagandizing you, one way or
the other, but in view of these news-reel scenes, and the news
pictures, and a lot of things along the same general line that
have been written in columns and spoken over the air—there are
certain cold facts which I think you ought to know, and I can't
help feeling that I would be letting you down if I didn't pass
them along to you.

After all, everyone agrees, I think, that we ought to do
everything that is necessary, and we ought to spend whatever
money is necessary, to build up a national defense that is absolutely adequate and completely modern, for any possible emergency. What's more, I think almost everybody will agree
that we ought to lean over backward in deciding how much

[8] By Fulton Lewis, Jr., radio commentator. Quoted on floor of the Senate
by Senator Gerald P. Nye. *Congressional Record.* Vol. 86. August 23, 1940.
p. 16513.

we need, and if there's any controversy at all, take the higher figure, just to be on the safe side.

But at the same time, it's your money that's being spent, and it certainly is not fair for you to be propagandized into thinking that one situation exists, when the facts are something else.

So here is the story, and these facts I'm going to give you are official figures from the War Department—they are not any imaginative dream—part of them come from General Marshall, the Chief of Staff of the Army, in person, and the rest come from the Official Information Section of the War Department.

About the National Guard men, and the Organized Reserve men using broomsticks and pieces of pipe for guns, the actual figures are these:

When all of the National Guard and the Organized Reserves are finally called out, and go into the Army on active duty, we will have about 600,000 men in the Army—including the regular force that already is there. Six hundred thousand men.

So far as rifles go, the Army now has on hand 2,000,000 Enfield rifles, which they say are excellent for training, and 800,000 Springfield rifles, which are considered to be the best in the world. Using just the Springfields, that means there would be one and a third rifles for every enlisted man in the Army; if you want to include Enfields, too, it means 4 2/3 guns for every man in the Army, but actually, according to the Army, there is only about one man in every four in an army who carries a gun; the others are in cavalry, artillery, various other branches.

On that basis, only 150,000 of these 600,000 men would carry guns, and if you'll use a little arithmetic, you'll find that figures out to just exactly this: while the pictures show these men being trained with broomsticks, and iron pipes, the fact is that the Army has enough actual rifles on hand, in perfect condition, to supply every man who is supposed to carry a gun—not with one gun, but with 19 guns.

As for using sewer pipe to imitate trench mortars, the facts are as follows: The War Department has on hand, at the present time, about 3000 3-inch trench mortars. They told me today that that is enough to supply an army—not of 600,000 men—but an army of 3,000,000 men.

As for machine guns—in which there also have been some fancy publicity pictures taken—the Army has 75,000 machine guns on hand, in perfect condition, ready for service—and that does not include the machine guns that are installed in airplanes—75,000 of them. The War Department says that is enough to supply an army of 3,000,000 men.

In fact, General Marshall said today that the Army has on hand sufficient basic weapons to completely supply a full army of 3,000,000 men; that means rifles, pistols, machine guns, 75 millimeter cannons (the famous French 75's—we have 3400 of those French 75's), and the 3-inch trench mortars.

He said there are a few lines in which we are short. There is a brand new type of trench mortar—in two different sizes—60 and 81 millimeter. We have just started production on them, so naturally there is a shortage of them.

The same thing is true of the 37-millimeter anti-tank guns, which are developed from the lessons of the present war; and also a new type of anti-aircraft gun; and also tanks. There is a shortage in all those things, and to get back to the matter of rifles, there also is a shortage of the new Garand rifle, which has certain improvements over the Springfield and Enfield. For one thing, it is semi-automatic, and so it fires more rapidly than the Springfield does; for another thing it has a sort of shock absorber built into it, to take up the recoil each time the gun is fired, which cuts down the shock on the shoulder of the man who is using it. But even so, we have 50,000 of those in use in the Army at the present time, and they're being turned out at the rate of hundreds every day. One officer said about a thousand a day.

ONE YEAR OF DEFENSE [9]

At the start of the defense effort . . . the Regular Army consisted of 230,000 enlisted men and 13,500 officers, a total of 243,500, besides 225,000 National Guardsmen. By contrast, the General Staff submitted a plan for organizing, equipping, and training four armies and nine army corps, or a total of 1,418,000.

The first moves toward attaining that goal were to step up recruiting for the Regulars, to federalize the National Guard, and to launch a vast program for building 46,000 barracks and other structures to house the new defense Army. Then, after months of debate, Congress passed the Selective Service Act, providing for one year's training of up to 900,000 draftees in 21-to-36 age categories annually.

Despite the fact that preliminaries consumed six months valuable time, the Army rapidly caught up, and by last week its strength had been increased to 1,302,500, including 473,000 Regulars, 270,000 Guardsmen, 480,000 Selectees, and 79,500 Regular, Reserve, and National Guard officers. Hence, with draftees now being inducted rapidly, the Army is expected easily to meet its first objective, of 1,418,000 men by the end of June. And, meanwhile, the War Department is studying tentative plans for a still larger force should Congress decide that the world situation makes this necessary.

But the strength of the Army cannot be measured by numbers alone. The true yardstick is the fighting division, and the War Department has already made good progress in organizing combat units. A year ago, there were six divisions—five infantry and one cavalry. Today, this total has been stepped up to 30, including 27 infantry, one cavalry, and two armored divisions similar to the German panzer units. Moreover,

[9] From "First Year of Defense Effort Spotlights Vitality of Nation." *Newsweek*. 17:35. May 19, 1941. Reprinted by permission.

another cavalry and two more armored divisions are being organized, and still another pair of panzer units are planned.

ARMY STENGTH ESTIMATED [10]

The strength of the Army of the United States as of July, 1941, is estimated at 1,448,500 officers and enlisted men. The breakdown is as follows:

Officers

Regular Army	14,700
National Guard	21,800
Reserve Officers	55,000
Total	91,500

Enlisted Men

Regular Army, 3 year enlistments	476,000
Regular Army, Reserve and one year enlistments	18,000
National Guard in Federal Service	266,000
Selective Service Trainees	597,000
Total	1,357,000

Total Combined Strength

Regular Army	508,700
National Guard	287,800
Reserve Officers	55,000
Selective Service Trainees	597,000
Total	1,448,500

[10] From "Army Strength Estimated." *Educational Bulletin No. 8.* July 7, 1941. War Department. Bureau of Public Relations, Radio Branch.

PREPAREDNESS AND THE FUTURE

DISCUSSION

Regardless of the outcome of World War II, there seems little possibility of a major reduction in the size of the American military establishment for years to come. Should Britain be defeated by Germany, we will need a stronger army and a larger navy than ever before to protect our own territories and those of Latin America. Should the war end in a stalemate, with the belligerent powers in a state of armed truce, a powerful military establishment must be maintained against the time when hostilities break out again. And even should Germany be defeated, the plans of Britain and the United States to "police the world" will demand large numbers of Americans under arms.

Even if the world should settle down to a peace based on military and economic exhaustion, it is unlikely that the United States would return to the state of unpreparedness which has characterized our military forces during the past fifteen or twenty years. Our leaders have become aware of the dangers of such lack of preparedness, and of the costs of last-minute preparation to meet emergencies. Only in the unlikely event of a completely disarmed world does it seem possible that we will fail to keep ourselves fully prepared and in readiness for the next possible war.

THE NEED FOR A PERMANENT MILITARY PLAN [1]

Regardless of the outcome of the present world conflict, I am convinced this country will not follow a disarmament policy for the next 25 or possibly 50 years. On the contrary, we are going to maintain a much larger Navy and standing Army than

[1] By Congressman Butler B. Hare, of South Carolina. *Congressional Record.* Vol. 87. August 14, 1941. p. A4231.

at any time in our history, and the question now confronting us is how we can best achieve these objectives. We have already made provision for a two-ocean navy, and it is high time we begin considering a program for strengthening the Army. . . .

Instead of trying to plan a long-time policy for our land forces when the existing emergency arose, we proceeded with a temporary expedient. Possibly this was the best that could be devised within a short time. The prevailing thought a year ago was that we should proceed to provide for a very large army, and we were told the best way to do it was to train some for 12 months and place them in reserve and then train others. However, we are now told that it may not be necessary to train an enormous number of men but it will be best to train them longer and make them more efficient.

A PERMANENT ARMY PROGRAM [2]

The outstanding feature of the Army's expansion program is its apparent rejection of the idea that it is building for an emergency. Instead, all efforts are aimed toward permanently increasing the nation's military plant. In most cases, land for training centers is being bought outright instead of leased, and every care is being taken to avoid makeshifts in troop housing facilities. This reflects the feeling of many Army officers that our training program must continue for some years to come, possibly changing over to some universal military training plan.

The future of any such program, however, depends upon events in Europe and Asia. Should the Axis win the war, it seems certain that we would deem it necessary to maintain a large standing army to protect the Western Hemisphere against any European penetration. But even if Britain should be victorious—an eventuality that it is generally conceded would take some years—it appears unlikely that we would permit our military strength to dwindle anywhere near the post-World War low point for many years.

[2] From "Army Expands Military Plant with Eye to Permanent Setup." *Newsweek.* 16:36-8, November 18, 1940. Reprinted by permission.

While continuance of the training program may mean many changes in our way of life (for instance, many more men would spend their vacations in refresher camps as the Reserve components increase) as long as there is a chance of war, such training is invaluable to the individual as well as to the military. This is particularly true in the light of World War Army statistics which show that a well-trained soldier is only half as likely to become a casualty as a poorly trained one. . . .

ARMAMENTS IN THE FUTURE [3]

Win, lose or draw, the United States, after the war, will have to go armed to the teeth if it wishes peace—or wishes even to survive.

One of the announced peace aims of President Roosevelt and Prime Minister Churchill is to "lighten . . . the crushing burden of armaments" for "peace-loving peoples." "After the final destruction of the Nazi tyranny," said their statement, they "hope to see established a peace which will afford to all nations the means of dwelling in safety," free from fear and want.

But how?

American taxpayers will find it necessary to support a gigantic defense program after the war whether or not the Nazis are wiped out. The reason is this:

Unless Hitler and Hitlerism are destroyed completely, as a matter of course we shall have to defend the United States and the Western Hemisphere against a Europe, Asia and Africa dominated by Germany and Japan—a group of aggressive militarists gone berserk. If, on the other hand, Hitler and his ilk are smashed, "the peace-loving peoples," to live "free from fear," must remain sufficiently armed to squelch another comeback staged by another potential Hitler. And the people of the United States will have to provide most of the armament.

[3] By William Philip Simms, Scripps-Howard foreign editor. From "U.S. Faces Years of Arming Regardless of War's Result." *New York World-Telegram*, August 25, 1941. p. 1, 8. Reprinted by permission.

Splendid as it is, the Atlantic pronouncement is no automatic peace contrivance. It will no more stop international outlawry after this war than did President Wilson's more-thorough program after the last war. The Wilsonian League of Nations, with its Covenant, probably was the greatest single concept for law and order since the Ten Commandments—but it failed utterly to keep the peace because force, or threat of force, was needed to make gangster nations behave, and no such force was forthcoming.

That the world will accept the new Roosevelt-Churchill order any more readily than it accepted the new order of Woodrow Wilson and his collaborators is out of the question. A defeated Germany, Italy and Japan will be just as bitter against the victors and will seek revenge just as surely as did Germany after Versailles. The "four freedoms" of President Roosevelt are a magnificent ideal, but we are living in a fool's paradise if we think the whole world will agree with us. There are whole nations which will no more accept the proposed Anglo-American peace than the British-speaking world would accept the dictated peace of Hitler and Japan.

For that matter, one of our own allies—Soviet Russia— would not accept such an order. Stalin despises and denounces the democracies every whit as scathingly as Adolf Hitler does. Religious freedom long has been extinct in the Communist Fatherland, and one of Moscow's chief activities has been to interfere in the internal affairs of other nations.

In any event, it can be considered certain that Germany, Japan, Italy and their satellites will not remain unarmed after this war, or accept a position of national impotence of their own free will. They will be good only so long as a superior force makes them be good. Once the pressure is lifted they will assert themselves again. Just as Hitler scrapped the disarmament clauses of what he called "the diktat of Versailles," and marched into the Rhineland in 1936, the vanquished of this war will shoot their way out again if they can.

The Geneva League of Nations—with France and Britain as its instruments—could easily have thrown the Nazis out of the Rhineland and crushed Hitler into oblivion. But it balked at using force and the chance was lost forever. Sooner or later the United States, Britain and their associates will face a similar situation. The time will come inevitably, not once but repeatedly, when they will have to wage—or be prepared to wage—a preventive war, or see the rise of another Hitler preaching another "new order."

The justice of the Atlantic peace is no guarantee of peace. President Manuel Quezon of the Philippine Commonwealth used to say the Filipinos would rather go to hell in their own way than go to heaven under foreign direction. That is a thoroughly human sentiment and well-nigh universal.

The Roosevelt-Churchill peace, therefore, must be enforced if it is to endure—however good a peace it may be. The big question is what nation, or group of nations, will do the enforcing? Roosevelt and Churchill apparently envisage a new association or league of nations, and in that objective many of the world's best minds are with them. But the necessary armies, navies and air armadas would have to be provided by member nations. This means the world will have to be policed, with gangster nations kept in line by the United States and Great Britain—chiefly by the United States.

Conscription almost certainly will become a fixture in America, just as it has been so long in Europe. Our two-ocean navy will be permanent. And the painful dent made in the taxpayer's pocketbook by the annual defense budget likely will remain with us for a long time.

LESSONS IN UNPREPAREDNESS [4]

False doctrines of security and martial prowess have lost half the nations of Europe their independence within the past year.

---

[4] By Willard K. Smith. Editor, *News and Opinion*; member of American peace mission after first World War. From "The Legend of American Invincibility." *The American Mercury*. 51:295-7, 301-2. November, 1940. Reprinted by permission.

The Polish mud and the rough Norwegian terrain would stop the German machines; the Dutch dikes would save Holland; the impenetrable Maginot Line would safeguard France; and so on. Americans have been similarly beguiled by the myth of invincibility fostered by oversimplified history textbooks and patriotic self-congratulation. From the Fort Pitt frontier captain who in 1776 proclaimed, "Pennsylvany kin fight the world," to the able Congressman who in 1939 declared, "No European power dares send a hostile airplane carrier within a thousand miles of our coast," our people and our historians have fraudulently proclaimed our military genius. But the times are too crucial for complacent delusions. If we want to survive in a predatory world, it is high time we faced the bitter fact that our government, our volunteer soldiers and our resources have never given us anything but the most inefficient service in warfare. The program of genuine national defense on which the country is now working will be more realistic if we confront unflinchingly the facts of our past military record. . . .

The American Revolution is held by speechmaking patriots to be the classic example of a small colony's successfully resisting a great power. In that war we fought an enemy whose councils were divided; an enemy engaged at the same time with other nations. The Colonies had powerful friends in Parliament; they had the financial and military assistance of France—a first class military power. They were fighting on home ground against an enemy that had to transport troops, supplies and munitions 3000 miles in sailing ships. Incredible incompetence of the British army in the field, intolerable mismanagement by the Ministries in England, French aid and English sympathy saved us—not our own military superiority.

The records of the War Department show over 395,000 enlistments of American soldiers during the Revolution, against a total British force from first to last of some 150,000 men. Of course, many of ours were re-enlistments; nevertheless in 1775 our troops outnumbered the English two to one. When

Washington took command of the army in that year his troops fit for duty, according to Upton, numbered 14,500 men, against 6500 British effectives. Later, in 1775, we had 38,000 men under pay. In 1776 we called out 90,000 men to oppose only 27,700 British troops. The Revolutionary army constantly fluctuated in size and efficiency. In May 1778 we had only 15,000 effectives; then France came to our aid, and eventually our forces in 1778 totalled 51,000 men under arms, against considerably smaller number of British. 1779 and 1780 were years of major American defeats except for Stony Point and King's Mountain. At the beginning of 1781, mutinies and Congressional mismanagement had reduced Washington's army to 5000 men. . . .

When finally we had achieved our independence, "with chaos in the country and anarchy around the corner, with hostile Indian tribes on three sides, Congress disbanded the Continental Army and reduced our entire soldiery to eighty men." The quotation is from Huidkoper. Our survival during the next fifteen years can be credited to Divine good will.

In 1812 we fought another war with England. . . . Our government had two months' warning that a British expedition had been sent against Washington. The English troops landed on the Chesapeake and proceeded with the utmost caution because they could not believe the Americans had not set a trap for them. Finally, at Bladensburg, Maryland, the British General Ross had his first sight of his foe. On a hilltop some hastily improvised breast-works were defended by "a crowd of men with arms in their hands but utterly without military training." The real fighting was left to Commodore Barney and 600 marines. "Had the least support been given them," states a report of the engagement, "the day might have been turned, but the militia covering their flank broke and run away at the first English charge." Only 1500 English troops were in this action. The American government had called some 235,839 troops into service during the year, yet against this expedition it had hurriedly to organize 5401 Washington men "utterly without military training." Such incidents were common.

The war against the Seminole Indians was proportionately the costliest, as it was the most inefficient and disgraceful, in American history. After a first war in 1817-1818, the second Seminole campaign began in 1835 and dragged out until 1842. A nation of 17,000,000 people required seven years, 60,000 men had $70,000,000 to subdue 1200 warriors. . . .

In 1918 we had in France over 2,100,000 troops, somewhat fewer than half of whom were in the line at various times. It has been stated that at no time did the total German forces opposing us reach half our strength, although we might have been outnumbered in some actions. Our allies lost in less than a month more dead than we did during our entire fighting period abroad.

In spite of our enormous facilities for manufacture, we were able to put none of our own guns on the firing line. The First Army, which was our only real fighting body, did not fire a single cannon or a single shell made in America, except four fourteen-inch naval guns. No American-made tank was used by the A.E.F. One year after war was declared we had but three squadrons of airplanes at the front. By the time of the Armistice, there were forty-three American squadrons operating with 740 planes, but only twelve of them were using American-made machines.

When Secretary Bryan spoke of a million men springing to arms overnight, he neglected, in his oratorical fervor, to mention that they would have no arms to spring to. We had to buy 3035 of France's famous 75-mm. field guns, 514 tanks, 1190 six-inch howitzers, 9592 machine guns, 40,000 automatic rifles, and 5,000,000 rounds of 75-mm. shells. England had to furnish our troops 324 heavy field guns, 864 heavy six-inch Newton mortars, and 2550 Stokes three-inch mortars. We even had to transport our troops in foreign ships.

At the time of the Armistice we had material and men almost sufficient to continue the war single-handed, but it had taken seventeen months to reach that point.   Our determination was manifest, and that was perhaps a vital factor in the peace. Manpower we have, but some ally has to hold our line for us until we get it equipped and moving.

The great influenza epidemic of 1918 wrought terrible havoc in the Army. . . .   Altogether in 1917-18 we lost twice as many dead from sickness as from bullets, gas and shell-fire.

Today there is much talk of involvement in the second World War.   Our war preparations up to last year were represented, unintentionally perhaps, as adequate and efficient.   The veil has recently been raised, however, and the whole sad spectacle of our military, naval and air weakness is now on view.   No one any longer denies or tries to explain away the obvious.   For once the effort to make America strong and militarily independent is being undertaken before and not after the war catastrophe is upon us.

That, in brief, is the reality behind the textbook myth.   It is essential that the reality be faced without blinking, in order that the necessary steps be taken to bring some real help to our great traditional ally, a kindly Providence.

THE COST OF UNPREPAREDNESS IN 1917 [5]

"The great lesson of our wars is that they must be carried to a conclusion by citizen soldiers and these soldiers must be trained.

To thrust untrained citizens into the field is nothing short of death by government order."

THE SECRETARY OF WAR, August, 1915.

Twenty-six out of thirty general officers holding command in the A.E.F., who were asked what proportion of our battle losses was due to lack of training, replied: "At least half."   The

[5] By Henry Wysham Lanier, author-publisher.   From "Lest We Forget." *World's Work*. 39:33-6. Reprinted by permission.

other four were more conservative—one major general put it at about a third.

We paid:

Some thousands of fine young American lives,

Some tens of thousands of American maimed,

Some thousands of millions of American dollars, for—the privilege of inertia, till the time when we had to send our sons, brothers, husbands, fathers into the World War, inadequately prepared. . . .

The issue is now before Congress to decide whether we shall have universal military training. So, when you have read this plain statement, from men who know, you will only have arrived at the important point, which is:

What are you going to do about it?

The general beside me at the preparedness dinner was fifty-six and one tried in vain to recall some business or professional friend of forty who had so vigorously and usably ready all of his physical and mental powers. . . .

"General," said I, finally—with the hesitation of an outsider fearing to ask an absurd question before a group of experts— "I wish you'd tell me something. An artist friend, who painted a lot of our men on the French front, says he asked at least twenty-five general officers what proportion of our battle losses was due to lack of training—and twenty of them replied, 'Fifty per cent.' Despite his opinion of the men who said it, neither of us could believe that. How about it?"

"I think it was an understatement," was the quiet reply.

"You really mean that half our casualties might have been avoided with proper training?"

"Yes. . . . The whole thing would fill a big volume. It would have to go into every operation of the war, from the beginning of training to the Armistice."

The thing startled the imagination. Fifty per cent. And the record of killed creeping up to 50,000, with nearly 250,000 more wounded and missing! Had the American aversion to military training really run up so weighty an account as that? . . .

I tried a lieutenant general, who commanded one of the three divisions which bore the brunt of our advance:

"Fifty per cent is well within the truth," he declared. "I'll tell you an incident that actually happened to me.

"My division was attached to a corps under the French army of General Dubonnet. We had a French division on the right of us, a French division on the left. This was in the spring of 1918—the Germans were attacking savagely: it was lively work.

"The French commander spoke to me one day, before all his staff, at a council: 'General, I wish you'd do something about your losses.' Then he showed me a tabulation he'd had made up, showing that my regiments, under exactly similar conditions, were losing from *two* to *four* times as many men as the French on either side of us. . . .

"I was taken aback for a moment: there were the figures; I hadn't a leg to stand on. Then I said to him.

" 'General, I admit it's frightful. But I'm not going to tell them to be careful—that might take away some of the spirit which is our chief asset.

" 'We haven't had time to train properly. We have come in a spirit of sacrifice—to make up for our lack of training by readiness to die.'

"They had not a word more to say."

Let us call a few more expert eye witnesses. Here's a major general in command of the Chemical Warfare Service, speaking of his own specialty. . . .

"The gas casualties among untrained troops were about twice as great as among trained troops."

One more interview, the most impressive of all. . . . This was with a man whom more than one insider calls "the brains of our army in France." Certainly his was the main directing intelligence that worked out the actual plans for one of our advancing armies.

He had no doubts of the magnitude of our losses due to insufficient training:

"I suggest that you compare the British, French, German, and our own losses. I can't be certain, but I think you'll find, for instance, that the German figures are a third less—yet they were on the offensive more than anybody. What did it—except more thorough training?

"Keep this in mind," continued my informant. "Of the nine divisions which were all we could manage to scrape together for the opening of the Meuse-Argonne show—six had never been in a fight; two had never been in a trench. . . .

"The price of lack of training was due not only to mistakes by the men but also by officers. Indeed, the latter were generally more disastrous, because the officer, from the division commander down, had the responsibility for large bodies of men. . . .

"One day a colonel came proudly in, during the Meuse-Argonne push, relating how his headquarters detachment alone had captured a certain town. He clearly thought himself entitled to a D.S.C. at least. And it was a brilliant feat of arms. But his general asked: 'Where are the rest of your men?' 'Well, I—I don't know exactly.' 'Then, for God's sake, don't confess it to anybody else! But get back there quick, find them, and get them in hand.' He'd simply lost them: battalions and companies were fighting on their own, running themselves, needlessly exposed to artillery fire, almost ineffective. He knew enough to make a good corporal or sergeant. But he hadn't learned his job.

"There's no end to the details that illustrate the thing. Take the tanks.

"We have heavy tanks to knock down obstacles and open the way across trench positions; the light ones go forward with the infantry, somewhat like an accompany artillery gun, to give covering fire and hold the enemy down. They're worse than useless if they don't keep in the closest touch.

"During the first two days of the Meuse-Argonne, we had tanks that drove ahead through all three lines; they'd be reported by airplanes as being in enemy towns. They simply had to come back, with the consequent loss of time, or they were captured. Three or four per cent were lost in this way. You see, those light tanks can make nine miles an hour: they'd go shooting ahead on their own hook with nobody to support them, passing strong machine-gun nests, which the infantry had to wipe out afterward, most expensively.

"Like every other arm, they were worse than useless when they got to acting independently instead of in concert with every other branch."

That's the essential point: bravery, *élan*, marksmanship, readiness to die—all these are invaluable. But without the welding into unity of action which training alone gives, you give the enemy vast odds. You pay in human lives for every saving in such training.

Yesterday is gone. Its errors are paid for. Today we are called upon to decide our policy for tomorrow.

"Future losses of American lives in action will bear a close but inverse ratio to the extent to which training of infantry in time of peace is given to the leaders of infantry units."

PLANS FOR MILITARY TRAINING

DISCUSSION

The word "preparedness" first took a prominent place in the American vocabulary about 1915, when Europe was in the throes of the first World War. As American participation grew nearer, preparedness became the order of the day. And following the declaration of war in April 1917, the energies of an entire people were thrown into the effort to create and train a powerful army and to supply it with materials of war.

But after the Armistice in 1918, the American people lost interest in war and preparedness. The inevitable reaction set in; men hated the thought of war or of militarism. The world would never again experience a major war, Americans believed, so there was no need to maintain an expensive military establishment. And Congress, sharing the popular feeling, abandoned all efforts toward preparedness for war. The Regular Army was reduced to a force of less than 150,000 officers and men, and military and naval appropriations were cut to the bone.

But military leaders were less optimistic than the people of the United States as a whole. They envisaged the possibility of another war, and continued with preparations for war. With Army appropriations greatly reduced, their preparations were limited largely to reorganization of the reserve forces and to laying plans—plans under which armies could be called into service and trained with a minimum of delay and wasted effort.

At the instance of these military leaders, Congress passed the National Defense Act of 1920, reorganizing the National Guard and creating a stable officer reserve force. In 1926, the government created a Joint Army and Navy Selective Service Committee, to study methods of conscription and work out methods of training soldiers called into service in time of emergency. And in 1939, the Army perfected its plans for M-Day, or for general mobilization of men and industry for national defense. Many of the recommendations of these Army leaders have been put into execution in connection with the Selective Service Act of 1940, under which America is building up its military defense.

In connection with the Army program, several organizations or training agencies are worthy of special mention.

The National Guard, prior to the World War, was largely under the control of the several states. Training was limited to evening drill once a week or sometimes once a month, plus a summer camp lasting from two to four weeks. The National Defense Act brought the National Guard under more direct Army supervision, and made the various units a part of the Army organization. The strength of the National Guard has been increased from less than 50,000 at the beginning of 1920, to more than 250,000 officers and men in 1941. National Guard regiments were called into active service by the President in the fall of 1940.

The Morrill Act, passed during the Civil War and creating land-grant colleges in the several states, provided for military training for students attending such colleges. Since 1920, more than 150,000 students have been given basic military training each year by Regular Army officers assigned to land grant and other colleges and universities, in the Reserve Officers Training Corps.

Basic training covers a period of two years, with theoretical instruction and drill periods totalling from three to four hours per week during the school year. From 8 to 10 per cent of the students who receive this basic training are given two additional years of R.O.T.C. training; those who complete this extra two years' training and in addition, a limited amount of summer training in camp, are commissioned as officers in the Organized Reserve. According to testimony of Colonel Stephen A. Park, president of the Reserve Officers' Association, the number of Reserve Officers produced by the R.O.T.C. method averages 6000 per year; the cost of training averages $1100 per student commissioned, as compared with a cost of $10,000 to $15,000 for training of each officer commissioned upon graduation from West Point. Since 1920 the R.O.T.C. has provided the bulk of our Reserve Officer personnel.

Somewhat similar to the summer training given student officers of the R.O.T.C. is the military experience provided young men in Citizens' Military Training Camps, conducted each summer until recently at a number of army camps throughout the country. The term of training was usually six weeks; young men enrolled in the Camps were given the rudiments of military training, sufficient to fit them for service as enlisted men or as non-commissioned officers in the event of war.

Chiefly to provide officers for armies which might be created to meet an emergency, the military program established in 1920 created an Organized Reserve. Officers holding Reserve commissions were recruited in the early '20s principally from the commissioned and non-commissioned officers of the World War army, who had returned to civil life after the Armistice; in recent years, however, Reserve Officers have come chiefly from the college R.O.T.C. units. Men holding Reserve commissions are required to report for summer training at fixed intervals; raises in rank are given Reserve Officers who have received advanced training. Approximately 120,000 officers were enrolled in the Organized Reserve in June 1940. The Army General Staff believes that the Reserve organization will supply the officer material needed in case of war, without the necessity of creating Officer Training Camps of the type required in 1917.

Related to our military establishment, but not a part of it, is the Civilian Conservation Corps, created in 1933 to provide work for unemployed young men. During the past eight years nearly 3,000,000 men between the ages of 17 and 23 have been enrolled in the CCC, spending from six months to a year in CCC camps throughout the country. While the CCC camps are under the

direction of Army officers—in most cases, officers called into service from the Organized Reserve—the CCC enrollees are not given
military training. They are, however, given various types of specialized training which might well prepare them for work required by the Army, and the CCC might easily become an
essential part of our military system.

THE BACKGROUND OF PREPAREDNESS [1]

Let us consider the background for a moment. In 1920 Congress passed the National Defense Act, which for the first
time in our history fixed a military policy for the country. This
was based on an army of the United States made up of three
components: the Regular Army, the National Guard, and the
Organized Reserves. Perhaps our greatest need in the early
months of the World War was for trained officers. The Organized Reserves under the Defense Act of 1920 have now a strength
of more than 100,000 Reserve Officers. General Marshall, our
Chief of Staff, has stated that is one of our greatest military
assets today and the point of greatest difference with the situation
in 1917 is that today we have practically no need for Officers
Training Camps, but rather for the sergeants, corporals, and the
buck privates to make up the enlisted personnel of a trained army
many times bigger than our pitifully small Regular Army.

The Defense Act of 1920 had also directed the War and
Navy Departments to make continuing studies concerning methods
of building such an army in an emergency, of procuring the
necessary manpower quickly, efficiently, and fairly. Since 1926
the Joint Army and Navy Selective Service Committee has been
continuously planning to meet the requirements we face today.
Their conclusions had been unanimous and had been concurred
in for years by the War Department General Staff. The only

---

[1] By Col. William H. Draper, Jr., General Staff, United States Army. From
"Selective Service in Operation." Address before the Eighth Metropolitan Conference on Employment and Guidance, New York City, November 16, 1940. Reprinted
by permission.

democratic and sure method of raising an army quickly was by compulsory selective service. There was one fundamental difference between the War Department's planning and the bill proposed by the Military Training Camps Association. The War Department had looked forward to wartime selective service and the Training Camps Association was advocating peacetime selective service.

THE WEAKNESSES OF R.O.T.C. TRAINING [2]

A remarkable 71-page report on military training at the University of California recently prepared and published by the peace committee of the Associated Students at that institution . . . is by all odds the clearest and most convincing argument against compulsory military drill yet produced. . . .

Since the War Department has been empowered by Congress to extend military training to the high schools and colleges of the country, I propose to give the rest of my speech to part of the summary of this report. It begins by pointing out that, contrary to widespread belief, there is no federal legislation requiring compulsory enrollment and that the university would not suffer financially or otherwise by making drill voluntary. . . . The following are some of the other important points made:

Compulsory R.O.T.C. has little or no physical educational benefits:

    a. The exercise it provides for the cadets is of the wrong sort.

    b. The uniforms are the wrong kind to wear for exercise and physical exertion.

    c. The physical training that is presented is not compatible with that required by the type of society in which we live.

    d. Military instructors are in no way qualified to teach physical education.

[2] By Oswald Garrison Villard, former editor of *The Nation*. From "Issues and Men." *The Nation*. 150:394. March 23, 1940. Reprinted by permission.

Compulsory R.O.T.C. is of little value for national defense:

a. The War Department does not urge or even suggest that enrollment in the R.O.T.C. be made compulsory.

b. Men taking merely the basic two-year course are not potential reserve officers, would not be commissioned in time of war, and are not part of our system of national defense.

c. The training given in the two-year basic course could be given in one week of intensive training.

d. Voluntary R.O.T.C. is a much less expensive method of turning out reserve officers than is compulsory R.O.T.C.

e. The R.O.T.C. course today is not teaching the students the necessary things that fighting a war denotes: it trains students in outmoded methods of warfare, with outmoded weapons of war, with outmoded tactics: there is no bayonet drill, no gas-mask drill.

Compulsory military training does not provide good citizenship training or create good citizens:

a. The type of citizenship taught is not compatible with the needs of contemporary society.

b. Military "citizenship training" is not compatible with the needs of other departments in the university, or with those of education in general.

c. The military instructors are in no way qualified to teach citizenship.

d. In the R.O.T.C. courses no time is devoted to even that minimum of citizenship that the military department claims it gives.

Compulsory military drill does not develop character:

a. Compulsory R.O.T.C. makes for parrot-like repetition and unthinking, unquestioning obedience.

b. Character can only be developed where the curriculum is full of opportunities for individual decisions.

The R.O.T.C. develops a mind which accepts war as "inevitable":

a. The students are presented with a parade-ground version of warfare that ends on the parade ground and at the military ball.

b. Necessary truths are being withheld from the students in the R.O.T.C. as to what warfare will really mean in their lives.

TOWARD AN INDUSTRIAL CCC [3]

The above "Event" was already in type when President Roosevelt announced the plan for a training program of vast proportions to meet the needs of national defense under the conditions of present-day highly mechanized warfare. Suggested at once was an expansion of the CCC and the NYA to prepare perhaps a million young men, not for military service in the traditional sense of the term, but for the highly skilled duties involved in the construction, operation and repair of aircraft, tanks and other implements of modern war.

That this is a real need is evidenced by the fact that a serious shortage of skilled labor in many of the mechanical trades has been repeatedly reported ever since the long-awaited upswing in business and industry became a fact. The marked success of the CCC in the few occupational fields with which it has hitherto been concerned has led competent students of the problem to believe that the organization of an industrial CCC is by far the most promising way in which to meet the new needs on the side of specialized skills.

In addition to an army of highly skilled technicians, it is clear that specialized corps of technologists will be needed—men (and probably women as well) who are in a broad sense engineers rather than artisans. This means, of course, rigorous basic training in pure and applied mathematics and in the physical sciences.

[3] From "The New Educational Problems of National Defense." *School and Society.* 51:725. June 8, 1940. Reprinted by permission.

THE CCC AND DEFENSE [4]

Surprise often is expressed that the CCC has not been integrated more closely with the Army, or at least given full military training. Actually, of course, several factors have stood in the way of such a move. The vast majority of enrollees are from poorer homes; if they were impressed into service en masse, it might be said that "the poor men's sons" were bearing the brunt of selective service. Moreover, the age limits for the CCC—now 17 to 23—and those for the selectees are not the same; when the CCC boys become of military age, they are subject to the draft like anyone else. Then, too, the CCC enrollees signed up with the express understanding that they would not have to bear arms while in the Corps; the language of the enabling act would have to be altered to permit their being drilled with military weapons.

But the chief reason nothing has been done in this direction is that, under the selective service program, the Army is getting all the men it can handle, and hence finds the CCC more useful as a reservoir of trained noncombatant personnel.

GOAL OF THE CCC IN WARTIME [5]

Specific training for non-combatant defense service has been added to other forms of education in all CCC camps. As its contribution to the national effort, the CCC proposes to furnish: 90,000 trained truck and dispatch-car drivers every six months; 7500 to 10,000 truck and automobile maintenance men every three months; 3000 skilled mechanics a year; 6000 cooks and bakers each six months; 100,000 first aid men equipped with the standard Red Cross course, every six months; 3500 skilled dispensary attendants and medical orderlies every six months; 1000 competent welders in like period; 1,000 airplane motor mechanics in the first year; not fewer than 75,000 reasonably competent

---

[4] From "Eight Years of CCC." *Newsweek*. 17:24. April 14, 1941. Reprinted by permission.
[5] From "Specific Training for Non-Combatant Defense Service." *Survey Mid-Monthly*. 76:362. December, 1940. Reprinted by permission.

road, bridge and telephone-line workers; 2000 men with knowledge of map making and map reading every six months; 10,000 men reasonably competent in basic photography every six months; and 20,000 men reasonably familiar with sending and receiving code and with elementary radio repair skill, every six months.

THE CONTRIBUTION OF THE CCC [6]

The defense of our nation implies and involves more than the training of human material to man the military establishment. Our larger task is to create a nation of human material and of physical wealth which is capable of furnishing the resources for defense. There is further the implication that that nation must provide such aspects of economic and social advantage as will cause its people to regard it as worth defending.

The Civilian Conservation Corps has for seven years played a leading part in the conservation of natural resources and in the preservation of the fine qualities of a large segment of our young manhood. The forestry, the soil conservation, and the park programs of the CCC have contributed mightily to the increase of our national wealth and to the health and enjoyment of our people. The 2,600,000 young men who have served in the Corps have derived important physical, mental, and spiritual benefits which contribute to the making of a stronger and sturdier people. . . .

However great has been the results of the work of the Civilian Conservation Corps in terms of increased national wealth, still greater is its actual and potential value as an organization dedicated to the training of young men. No greater contribution can be made to the defense of the nation than in strengthening and disciplining the mental, physical, and spiritual qualities of its young people, and in providing those young people with a stable economic basis for life and citizenship in

[6] By Howard W. Oxley, national director of CCC education. From "The CCC and the Defense of the Nation." *Education*. 61:74-7. October, 1940. Reprinted by permission.

our nation. The defense of a country is no stronger than the desire of its people to defend it. The desire is largely the measure of the belief of the citizens of a nation that that nation and its institutions are worth defending.

The 2,600,000 young men who have served in the Corps during the past seven years have had an unrivalled opportunity to realize the greatness of their nation and to prepare themselves to preserve and strengthen that nation. Travel and work amid nature have shown the young enrollee the natural resources of the country. A well-balanced, productive life in the camps has shown the value of work. Daily hard physical labor and a regular regime of camp life produce physical vigor, disciplined muscles, alertness of limb. Health information and medical care serve to keep the enrollee in good health and to develop the physical qualities of the enrollee beyond that of most young men of this age group, and parallels closely the physical development of pioneer youth who helped to conquer the wilderness. Furthermore the enrollee learns good work habits, occupational skills, discipline, tolerance, and self-reliance. All in all, the young men who serve in the camps carry away with them important benefits which will prove of enduring worth to them as future citizens and in solving whatever problems they may face as citizens.

In addition to the manifold though often indirect values which the enrollee derives from the inherent life of camp, he receives the direct impact of a planned training program aimed to improve his ability as a worker and his capacity as a citizen. Since as a citizen he may be called upon, if necessary, to defend his country by arms, it may be appropriate to examine the training, actual or potential, which the CCC can contribute to the improvement of the capacity of the enrollee to aid in the defense of his country. . . .

The training provided by the CCC may be divided roughly into two types in consideration of its direct relation to national defense. First are those service operations of possible direct use in the military establishment. These are, of course, non-combatant operations, since the Civilian Conservation Corps does not provide military training. These operations are in the fields of food service, clerical, supply, motor transport and repair, medical, communications, and general engineering. For example, the CCC has trained and has in service at any one time 1500 mess stewards, approximately 9000 cooks and bakers, 1500 company clerks, 1500 supply stewards, 1500 camp exchange stewards, approximately 15,000 truck and other equipment drivers, 1500 infirmary attendants, several thousand orderlies and others whose training could be utilized directly should they ever be called into the military establishment.

In the light of the plans for mechanization it may be observed that the CCC operates daily the largest fleet of peacetime motorized units in the world—a fleet of 40,000 units, maintained by 63 central repair shops. The CCC operates a fleet of several hundred ambulances. Yearly its enrollees construct and operate thousands of miles of telephone lines with hundreds of exchanges. It has the use of a nation-wide radio signal service and operates radio sets reaching hundreds of camps with CCC radio operators. Yearly, also, thousands of CCC enrollees build hundreds of miles of roads and trails, hundreds of bridges, and hundreds of buildings of various types. These operations are turning out competent men who are successfully securing private employment and, if necessity arose, could make use of their training for purposes of national defense.

The second type of training provided by the CCC is that offered on its work jobs and in its vocational classes which lead to training for industrial and food production. The following are the principal specific fields under this phase of training: acetylene welding, electric arc welding, heat welding and forging, blueprint reading, machine tool and lathe operation, brick and rock masonry, concrete work, rough frame carpentry, plumbing, home gardening, poultry production, dairying, and food processing.

Following is a brief summary of certain fields of training which have provided many thousands of CCC enrollees with a basis for contributing to the national defense:

Nature of Training	Approx. No. Who Have Received Training Since 1934
Auto Mechanics	88,500
Carpentry	82,500
Truck Driving	75,000
Photography	26,000
Cooking and Baking	23,000
Surveying	21,500
Radio	17,500
Blacksmithing	13,500
Welding	13,000
Electricity	12,000
Drafting	12,000
Company Clerk	8,500
Supply Steward	5,000
Mess Steward	5,000

The extension and intensification of training for national defense by the CCC is indicated by the provisions of the Byrnes' amendment, offered to Congress on June 11, 1940, which directs that non-combatant training in the following fields will be set up in the camps: "cooking, baking, first aid to the injured, operation and maintenance of motor vehicles, road and bridge construction and maintenance, photography, signal communication, and other matters incident to the successful conduct of military and naval activities. . . ."

This training is an ever-sound basis for useful and satisfactory citizenship which is the soundest basis for the defense of our nation regardless of the emergency which may threaten it and its institutions from within and without.

THE SELECTIVE SERVICE PLAN [7]

At the end of the World War emergency, the selective service laws were allowed to lapse and selective service as a vital part of our national life ceased to exist.

[7] By Lt. Col. Victor J. O'Kelliher, United States Army. From "Selective Service During and Since the World War," a radio address broadcast by the Mutual Broadcasting System. Reprinted by permission.

It became a closed chapter of American history, and I take some pride in adding that no chapter of our World War history reflected greater credit or glory on American democracy.

It was a demonstration of democracy in action.

Despite the bitter controversy that preceded the enactment of the selective service legislation in 1917, the World War draft, even in the first few weeks of its operation, allayed the fears of its opponents and confirmed the convictions of its sponsors. . . . In a few short months, the 1917 selective service draft won the respect and whole-hearted cooperation of the American people. . . .

The outstanding characteristics of selective service in 1917 were its strictly civilian administration and completely local responsibility. And that was the secret of its success. . . .

Because dependency was a major cause for exemption, it is usually a surprise to most people to learn that only about four percent of the men registered in 1917 selected for service were married. . . .

During the operation of the selective service draft of 1917 about 11 million men were registered between the ages of 21 and 30; about 3,000,000 men were actually inducted into service. One in about every three.

It was a tremendous job, but when it was all over, the American people were agreed that selective service was the most democratic, most efficient, economical, and fair method of procuring men for our land and naval forces. . . .

In July of 1919 the Selective Service Administration was dissolved.

The following year the Congress of the United States passed the National Defense Act of 1920. That law provided that it shall be the duty of the War Department General Staff to prepare plans in conjunction with the naval forces for the mobilization of the manhood of the nation.

It was not until 1926 that the Secretary of War and the Secretary of the Navy created the Joint Army and Navy Selective Service Committee.

The function of this committee was to be the preparation of plans for the emergency procurement of men for our land and naval forces. The committee was composed of representatives of the Secretary of War and the Secretary of the Navy.

From 1919 to 1926 a small group of us, who had been in the Selective Service Administration, kept our interest in selective service methods alive by an interchange of correspondence.

We were called for consultation with the committee by Col. Harry C. Kramer, well known as the "spark plug" of selective service. A course of study and research was planned and a series of annual conferences was inaugurated.

From that small beginning selective service study and research has grown, until today there are some 700 officers in the Army, Navy, and Marine Corps, in the Reserves, and in the National Guard, who are especially trained in selective service methods.

In 1937 . . . I was made a member of the committee, which at the present time comprises nine officers.

Today there is available to the American people, a complete plan to be administered by civilians for the procurement of men for our land and naval forces with a maximum of efficiency, economy, and equity, and a minimum of disturbance to the social, economic, industrial, and agricultural life of our country.

In 1917, selective service was created and put into execution in a hurry and under the terrific pressure of then-current events, but it was based on such sound principles that, despite many handicaps, it proved itself to be one of our most successful undertakings.

The experience of the 1917 selective service draft, and the 23 years of study and research that have gone into our present selective service plans, are a positive assurance of the success of the American selective service system.

THE CIVILIAN EFFORT [8]

Selective service is a fair and efficient method, but it cannot be expected to produce a single man in the first 60 days of mobilization. The law must be enacted; the machinery set up; registration, classification, and selection must consume many days before a single man reaches camp. Were a selective service law enacted before M-Day, there would still be a lapse of perhaps 30 days before it produced any men.

Yet any war plan is useless unless it rests on a workable mobilization plan; and mobilization schedules depend utterly upon getting the necessary men. In the first 60 days, the Protective Mobilization Plan and corresponding Navy Department plans call for 790,000 new men. They must be obtained by competing agencies of the Regular Army, National Guard, Navy, and Marine Corps. In the World War, these agencies enlisted 290,000 men in the first 60 days. . . .

It cannot be hoped that official recruiting parties such as are used in peace and were used in 1917 will ever secure men enough to carry out the mobilization schedules. Recruiting offices will of course continue, in greatly increased numbers, and will accept suitable applicants, but far more effective means are required.

While the solution of this problem has not been worked out in complete detail, a comprehensive plan has been outlined and steady progress is being made toward its completion. This plan is called "The Civilian Effort."

The Army and Navy are not expected to produce money and supplies; these things are furnished them, and their job is to use them in the war effort. The same principle applies to manpower. The selective service process is production of men by each community according to its just quota. The idea behind "The Civilian Effort" is the same; each community of

[8] From *American Selective Service*. Prepared by the Joint Army and Navy Selective Service Committee for students of selective service extension courses. October, 1939. p. 24-7. U. S. Gov't Ptg. Office, Washington, D.C.

the nation shall contribute its share of the necessary men, as it contributes its share of the money and munitions. The armed services will be responsible for making soldiers of them.

Like the selective service system, "The Civilian Effort" is decentralized to the governor of each state, whose peacetime planning agent is his Adjutant General. . . . When the emergency arises, each governor will be called upon to organize a state-wide recruiting drive.

The governor will suballot a quota to each county or urban unit. A civilian committee in each community will produce the recruits. The promotional work to accomplish this result in each community is similar to other "drives," the mechanics of which are well understood and frequently employed. . . .

The Selective Service Administration is a semi-permanent organization; "The Civilian Effort" is an affair of two months. Selective service, selecting men who have no choice but obedience, is fundamentally a judicial process; "The Civilian Effort," existing purely to induce voluntary enlistment, is a promotional activity. Selective service requires complete and careful organization from top to bottom in order that its records and paper work may be properly handled; "The Civilian Effort" requires only sufficient organization to coordinate local drives, and can easily defeat itself by too much organization.

It sounds well to say that in wartime the people must furnish the soldiers to the Army, that the Army has no responsibility for getting them. But we know from history that the people will *not* furnish them for any length of time by voluntary enlistments. The government must sooner or later use some form of draft, and the longer this measure is delayed, the more confusion is bred in the entire war effort, military and industrial. "The Civilian Effort" which has just been described cannot be puffed into an alternative to selective service. It is only a makeshift, adopted more in the hope than in the conviction that it will meet the situation for a couple of months until selective service can begin producing men at the training stations.

"The Civilian Effort" is a stopgap.   Selective service is the only sound measure yet devised for the United States.

M-DAY [9]

A colossal war plan has been drawn up to control at the outset virtually every phase of American life. Shipbuilders and sales clerks, machinists and bankers, stenographers, bellhops, farmers, actors—everyone is included on this tremendous blueprint for war.

The backbone of the scheme has been drawn up by the War Department on the basis of studies begun just after the First World War.   And the whole plan rests on federal statutes giving wartime powers to the President.   Most of these powers are already authorized under existing laws.   A few others, covering the control of prices, resources and industry, are included in legislation approved by the administration and the heads of the defense services, and held ready for passage in an emergency.

There will be no haphazard entrance into war, as in 1917, with profiteering rampant, prices and wages running wild, chaos in industry delaying supplies and wasting billions of dollars. The entire nation will be controlled by the President through such superagencies as the War Resources Board, a War Labor Administration with a bureau of women and minors, War Finance and Price Control Commissions, War Trade Administration, Selective Service Commission, and an Advisory Defense Council.

Draft supervision officers for each state are being trained already.   Strategic war materials are being stocked.   Ten thousand industrial plants have been prepared for war production by hundreds of Army, Navy, and Marine Corps graduates of the Army Industrial College.   Regulation of capital, wages, labor, living costs, and other details of our economic life has

[9] By Donald E. Keyhoe, Washington newspaper correspondent. From "If War Comes—Uncle Sam's Plans for You." The American Magazine. 128:16-17+. December, 1939. Reprinted by permission.

been arranged, so that the "home front" will share the burden of war, even to the remotest village.

No matter what your sex, your occupation, if you are over sixteen your place on the blueprint for war is already marked. If you care to know your role in that war, take a glance ahead. . . .

The date is "M plus 30"—Army language for "30 days after Mobilization." War bills have been rushed through Congress, and the Stock Exchange has been closed, to block wild speculation. The National Guard, the Army and Navy reserves have been mobilized. Community drives, with their bands, speeches, and kisses for volunteers, have given way to the machine system of the Selective Service Draft. . . .

In modern war, for a nation to function efficiently, every phase of its life must to some extent be controlled. On the blueprint for war nothing has been overlooked. Communications—radio, telephone, telegraph—will be under government direction for M-Day, or before. . . . By price control and, if necessary, commandeering, agriculture will be regulated, as well as transportation, shipping, and general industries. Under the War Resources Control Act, even a Hollywood studio could be required to secure a Presidential license. . . .

Tax-profit rates will probably be fixed somewhere between confiscation of all profits and the allowance of a slight profit. But in the lower brackets many will pay who have never before seen an income tax blank. For, in spite of efficient planning, modern war will cost billions.

Besides its far-reaching industrial phases, the blueprint for war covers a thousand details of military and naval preparation, many known only to staff officers and strategy chieftains at the Army and Navy war colleges.

Others, less secret, include the "spotting" of Farmer Brown's south meadow for an emergency air base, arrangements with bakers and restaurant men . . . for furnishing food to cadre groups or National Guard units on some future "M plus X" day.

Plans, subplans, tiny details, all keyed back to the superagencies in Washington, to the great war machine ready to spring to life.

A tremendous Plan, to equal, within the legal limits of a democracy, the regimented force of a totalitarian country. To do this by sometimes curtailing, but not destroying individual rights.

But the Plan looks beyond even this, to the Armistice, to the dangerous days of demobilization. For the problems will not end with the war. The supercontrols must continue for a while, to slow down the vast war machine not too abruptly, for fear of falling prices, grim scenes of unemployment. There are women in men's jobs who must be moved as the fighters return. Closed "non-essential" businesses must be reopened, commandeered plants returned, the supermachine itself slowed down from its tremendous momentum.

No plan on such a gigantic scale can be perfect. But perhaps the knowledge that this great Plan exists, that America is geared for war, may be sufficient. The war machine may never have to be built.

A YOUTH PLAN FOR YOUTH [10]

Young men between the ages of twenty-one and thirty-one are in the news today because Messrs. Burke and Wadsworth, and others, think it necessary to draft them in order to preserve "the integrity and institutions of the United States."

We, who are among the youth to be drafted, are opposed to the compulsory military training bill for the following reasons: (1) It is not necessary. We see Fascist bullies making gains in the world, but we believe there are ways of raising an adequate army to defend America besides this selective conscription. (2) Placing hundreds of thousands of us under Army rule in peace time is a threat to our basic freedom of thought and action.

[10] By David Burgess and Leonard Detweiler. From "Youth and the Draft." *The Nation.* 151:179. August 31, 1940. Reprinted by permission.

Why not conscript our thinking into one mold for "efficient defense" of democracy? (3) Conscription is a temporary expedient to meet a "crisis" and not an answer to the underlying problem of unemployment, which is a real threat to American democracy.

We recognize that the problem before America is the defense of its democratic way of life. We propose the following: (1) A national program of functional education in the democratic way of life. Operated in the local community by local leadership and resources (schools, colleges, church, forum, etc.), its aim should be to rediscover the "grass roots" of democracy in everyday living. Emphasis should be placed upon the responsibilities as well as the freedom in democracy. (2) A national survey of the situation and a national and local effort to find youth a place in the present American system—a searching, scientific approach to the problem of youth's unemployment. (3) The establishment of voluntary, non-military work camps to teach young Americans skills useful in peace or war. These camps should be nation-wide but should take advantage of local conditions in planning the specialized training to be offered. The wages paid should be near the union wage minimum. (4) Voluntary one-year enlistment in the army for wages of $30 a month.

If the energies and imagination of youth are freed in an expansion of the democratic way of life, then they will of themselves rally to America's defense and development.

SHOULD SERVICE BE COMPULSORY?

DISCUSSION

Assuming that large armies are needed, should military service be compulsory or voluntary? America, like other nations, has had unfortunate experiences with the volunteer system in times of emergency—and equally unfortunate experiences with compulsory service. Never in a major war has the volunteer system been adequate to supply the necessary numbers of men for military service; in the War of 1812, the Civil War, and the first World War the United States was forced to turn to conscription to fill its armies. But conscription itself has been far from satisfactory; enforced service has bred resentment since the days before our War of 1812, when British warships "impressed" American seamen for service in the British Navy. Even in 1917, when our war with Germany was a popular crusade, 337,640 men were listed as draft deserters who refused to register for the draft or, after registration, to accept army service; thousands of draft resisters were thrown into military prisons.

And compulsory military service in peacetime has never received the support of the American people. One of the major reasons for emigration to this country from the nations of Europe was the desire to escape from the obligation of military training, imposed by rulers in Europe. On the other hand, few men would voluntarily give up a year of their lives to receive military training. Even in the depths of the depression, with millions of men unemployed, the Army and Navy had difficulty in securing the number of enlistments each year required to keep their forces up to authorized strength.

Arguments for and against conscription as opposed to the volunteer system are given on the following pages.

AMERICAN TRADITIONS AND CONSCRIPTION [1]

Why is it that this Republic of ours in the short space of
150 years has not only become the greatest but the most beloved
land in all the world? We do not boast of our achievements
in conquest. We are not a warlike people. We boast of our
achievements in peace and not in war. The greatness of this
Nation is builded upon that immortal document penned by the
hand of Thomas Jefferson, in which he first announced to human-
kind that all men are created free and are entitled to equal
rights and opportunities, and that all men stand equal before
the law. That was a new doctrine upon the earth. That doctrine
attracted the emigrant from every land under the burning sun.
Those emigrants and their descendants builded this mighty
Republic in the short space of 150 years. Most of them came
to this land of equal opportunity, the land of the free, to get
away from laws similar to the one we are now asked to impose
upon their descendants—a soldiers' conscription law forcing the
citizen of this free Republic to join in bloody warfare with
other nations in a war-mad world.

My father came to this land of the free from Germany a
little before he reached the age when Germany would have
conscripted him as a soldier and forced him to devote the best
years of his life in training for a soldier's job—to kill and shoot
other people. I dare say most of the other immigrants came
here for the same reason—to get away from military dictatorships.

The would-be power lords of Europe are now engaged in
their usual occupation of war. The military dictators in Europe
are in a struggle to see who shall boss the people of that part
of the world. These military dictators were made possible
only because of universal compulsory military training laws.
They were created through the power of enforced conscription.
While we are at peace with all the world and have no quarrel

[1] By Senator William J. Bulow of South Dakota. *Congressional Record.* Vol.
86. August 22, 1940. p. 16450.

with any foreign people and while our sovereignty has not been threatened by anyone, we are asked to abandon our time-honored tradition of a free people and force all our citizens into compulsory training. We are asked to pass a conscription law and adopt the same policy which has made dictators possible in Europe and for centuries has bathed that continent in human tears and human blood.

We are told that we must enact a conscription law to keep our government out of totalitarian hands. If we pass this universal compulsory military training bill the days of the Republic will be numbered, and our boasted freedom will soon pass into historic memory. Pass the conscription bill and create a mighty military machine among a free people and we shall have dictatorship. Pass the conscription bill and we shall have an army Frankenstein which a free people cannot control. Pass the conscription bill and it will bring on totalitarian government, and dictatorship will soon be here.

THE NEED FOR UNIVERSAL SERVICE [2]

The selective service system is democratic in the sense that all are treated alike. The rich man and the powerful man have no more rights than the poor man or the indigent one. A great lottery determines who shall or shall not go. That same lottery determines who shall go first and who shall go last. Personalities have no part in the selection or the induction. Under the volunteer system, those without funds or without jobs, without place or position are naturally the ones to volunteer. In other words, the poor volunteers come to the support of the rich and poor alike. That is wrong. The force of economic circumstances ordinarily forces the poor man to enlist.

Furthermore, voluntary enlistments cannot fill the need of either the Army or the Navy. The Army got 16,177 3-year volunteers in June last; 23,345 in July. It could doubtless fill

[2] By Congressman Emanuel Celler of New York. *Congressional Record*. Vol. 86. September 4, 1940. p. 17379.

out its Regular forces to 375,000 by ballyhoo and expensive advertising. But keep this in mind—the primary objective of peacetime conscription by the selective draft method is not to create merely a standing army. We wish to assure the United States a huge rotating reserve of trained men to be called in an emergency, to be called out quickly in wartime. That is why Congress has been asked to select 400,000 draftees by October 1, and another 400,000 next April. Give these draftees a year's training. They are then to be returned to private and civil life and are to be replaced by another class of draftees. The National Guard, which has recently been called, will be used to train the draftees. We can rely upon such an army of draftees properly trained within the proper time.

The history of our previous wars indicates that reliance cannot be placed upon volunteers. Washington bitterly complained about the inadequacy of this system. He recommended that the states organize their militia for home defense, and after they were trained, they were urged to join the Continental Army. He could never get sufficient men to volunteer for enlistment in the Regular forces. Even with offers of large cash bounties, it was found that voluntary enlistment was most unsatisfactory. Washington had to call constantly upon the states for militia to assist in his operations. As a result of the insufficiency of the volunteer system, the American Army was constantly in danger of final disaster. For example, Washington reported from Morristown, N.J., on March 14, 1777, that he had but 1000 Regulars and 2000 militia, whose engagement expired that same month, to face over 20,000 British in and around New York. Because the central government lacked power to raise an effective army, the war dragged out for seven years, during which the Americans employed a total of almost 400,000 men, while the greatest strength of the enemy in any one year was but 42,000. The conclusions that Washington drew were as follows: First, the only effective troops were those enlisted for the duration of the war; second, the method of voluntary enlistment was not able to supply adequate men. After the Revolutionary War, Washington proposed to the first Congress a true selective service. He failed to get Congress to heed.

He wanted Congress to raise an army and classify men by age and physical fitness—to segregate the fit men between 18 and 25 years of age into separate units and to give them special training by selected instructors. He thus hoped to develop an effective citizen army. We are developing such a citizen army by the current bill.

Jefferson and Madison, after Washington, made the same proposals, but to no effect.

The mistakes of the Revolutionary War were repeated in the War of 1812. We employed all told 527,000 men, while the enemy never had over 16,500 in the field against us at any one time. The war dragged out futilely for three years. A Regular Army of numbers adequate to win the war was authorized but could not be recruited. Even when bounties were offered, the volunteer system broke down. Conscription for the national army was then proposed, but the old prejudice in favor of the state militia was too strong and it was decided to rely on it again. The states accordingly turned out their levies—undisciplined mobs under untrained officers. The old weaknesses were again demonstrated. The action at Bladensburg, in defense of the national capital, illustrates perfectly the working of the militia system. Four thousand four hundred men were drafted a day or two before from their fields and shops, and obediently answered the summons. But, they fled at the first shot. The result—the Capitol building burned and in ruins. The White House was so smeared with smoke that, after the war, it had to be repainted. It was repainted white, and ever after has been called the White House. . . .

THE LESSONS OF HISTORY [3]

What light does our own history throw upon the question? The United States has fought six wars: the Revolution, the War of 1812, the Mexican, Civil, Spanish-American and World Wars. In four of these we relied upon the volunteer system. In one, the World War, conscription was applied from the beginning. In one, the Civil War, both the volunteer and the conscription methods were used for raising armies. What lessons can be drawn?

Did the volunteer system work during the American Revolution? The question is, perhaps, irrelevant, for the only alternative known at that time was the mercenary army. The French Revolutionary and Napoleonic armies were the first to practice conscription—and that is, of course, one explanation of the ability of France to fight the whole of Europe for so many years. The volunteer system was the only one available to the United States during the Revolution, but the most purblind patriot would not argue that it worked well. Americans were fighting for independence, and in defense of their own soil against invaders, yet from a population of some three million Washington was never able to raise an army of more than some twenty thousand, and usually he had about half that number under his command. There were, of course, other armies in the field, but the total number of men under arms at one time was never more than forty or fifty thousand. Finland, with a population but little larger than that of the American states at this time, was able to put into the field an army of almost four hundred thousand men. It was not the American volunteer army, but the fortitude of Washington, French aid, British blundering, and distance that brought victory to the American cause.

[3] By Henry Steele Commager, Professor of History, Columbia University. From "The Conscription Issue: Past and Present." *Scholastic.* 37:11+. September 16, 1940. Reprinted by permission.

Neither the War of 1812 nor the Mexican War throws much light on our problem. Conscription had already been adopted by European countries, but neither of these conflicts was on a sufficiently large scale to require an experiment with compulsory service. Yet the War of 1812 certainly is not without its moral. A nation of over seven million people furnished an army of around thirty-five thousand soldiers. New England opposition to the war and the reluctance of New Englanders to enlist placed the burden of the war on the other parts of the country and illustrated some of the inequalities of the volunteer system. The Mexican War was fought largely by the regular army, aided by some twenty thousand volunteers. Those forces proved, in the end, adequate for the job of subduing Mexico.

But it is the Civil War that best illuminates the problem of the volunteer versus the conscription system. Both North and South started with the volunteer system, but the South, greatly overmatched in manpower, quickly resorted to conscription—and this despite the theories of States' Rights. No war was ever marked by greater patriotism, loyalty, devotion to a cause, than was the American Civil War; none ever called forth greater sacrifices. Yet all this was insufficient for the tasks at hand—the Southern task of winning independence, the Northern task of maintaining the Union. One year after the Confederacy had inaugurated conscription, Lincoln turned to this plan as the only way to make the superior manpower of the North effective. The Civil War draft was perhaps the most ill-conceived and worst-managed experiment of its kind ever undertaken, but for all its faults it was effective in increasing the size of the Union army.

The Spanish War was a minor affray, easily handled by the regular army and the 150,000 volunteers whom McKinley in mistaken zeal called to the colors. The World War, however, was clearly of a different character. In Flanders, in Poland, in Lombardy, millions of men—most of them conscripts—were locked in mortal combat, and manpower was all-important. The

French and German armies had been built up by conscription; the English for two years relied upon volunteering. The French and German systems were successful; the English system was a failure, and was abandoned for compulsory service. All this was clear to President Wilson and his advisers—democrats, all of them, men who cherished liberty and who were ready to embark upon a crusade to save democracy. The day after the United States declared war, Wilson sent to Congress a message calling for conscription, and after five weeks' debate the proposal was enacted.

What conclusions can be drawn from this American experience? Does it support the contentions of those who oppose conscription? On the contrary, our history would seem to support the contention that conscription is the most effective and the most democratic way to do an unpleasant job—that of mobilizing human resources for national defense.

THE NEED FOR CONSCRIPTION [4]

How many men are needed to defend America? Opinion on this subject varies widely and the dispute is couched in excessively bitter terms. Major George Fielding Eliot, who favors conscription, believes in a permanent standing army of 750,000 with adequate reserves. But General George C. Marshall, Chief of Staff, has at last told the country what the army believes is needed. To protect the Western Hemisphere, he says, we should require 3,000,000 or 4,000,000 men. To protect the Northern Hemisphere and the Caribbean, we should need somewhat less than that; General Marshall did not give a figure because he says 1,200,000 is as many men as the army can handle in the near future. We can't furnish supplies and weapons for a larger number; we can't train them, and if we tried to, our present army organization would be destroyed.

[4] From "Do We Need Conscription?" *The New Republic*. 103:294. September 2, 1940. Reprinted by permission.

Can we get a total army of 1,200,000 men within a few months by the voluntary system? It is possible that we could, but it is not absolutely certain; and if we are in any danger from Hitler at all, we cannot afford to gamble on uncertainties.

There is a further question involved here. At present a large part of all our recruits are unemployed men who would join the army as a substitute for a job. It is a question whether a hired army composed of men who couldn't find other work would be the best possible defense force, and we need the best possible or we are wasting our time. For the same reason, we are not impressed by the argument that raising the pay from $21 to $30 will bring a rush of recruits. We doubt whether $9 patriots are the kind of men to save this country if it needs to be saved.

THE MEANING OF CONSCRIPTION [5]

Today it means a country prepared for any eventuality. Today it means a country undertaking total defense. Today it means not only the conscription of a few to serve in the country's military forces but it means a complete understanding of personal economic considerations—the complete organization of our country.

In the assembling of great numbers of men together the risks are not simply military risks. Undoubtedly in the World War, more American soldiers died as the result of faulty preparation, as the result of not having the right kind of medical treatment, as a result of not having the right kind of clothing, as the result of not having proper housing facilities, and because of lack of foresight on the part of those who were providing for the training of these men, than were killed by German bullets.

It is because of experiences of this kind that those of us who were responsible for the training of great units now see

[5] By Senator Elbert D. Thomas of Utah. *Congressional Record*. Vol. 86. August 20, 1940. p. 16144-6.

the need of building the personnel of our national defense on the basis of training, training, and everlasting training; and then, when the time comes for actual warfare, there will be no doubt about the outcome.

It was not until September 1917 that the first draftees were called in. Therefore keep in mind those days, because we cannot do any better, we cannot work any faster, and we should not work any faster unless we are faced by some acute peril.

There were two registrations in 1917, the first on June 5 for men between the ages of 21 and 30, and the second on August 31 for those from 18 to 20 and from 31 to 45. From the various drafts there was a total number of persons who registered running up to 23,908,596. I give these figures because it is only from a study of them that we may obtain a comparison of what actually took place then with what will undoubtedly take place in the next mobilization.

In the first draft there were 9,500,000. From both drafts, during the whole period of the war, when we had in the neighborhood of 4,000,000 men under the colors, only 2,787,000 men came in as the result of registration and draft. Therefore during the war 1,300,000 men came under the colors under the old voluntary system. It is upon those basic facts that I think we ought to study the actual effect of the present draft measure and see how it will work out.

The entire concept of mobilization has changed since the World War, and even before, and I think that as the result of the present war it will change once more. One would not go back before the Franco-Prussian War of 1870 for ideas of modern mobilization. We find with respect to the theories in regard to mobilization in the late war, that ideas changed with circumstances, and, of course, that will always be the case.

Most persons have a notion that war is a static thing. If there is anything that is not static it is war. Most persons have the idea that governments go forth and fight without change.

If there is anything that brings about changes in government, even the best organized and the most stable, it is, of course, the exigencies of war. . . .

Conscription may be defined as merely exaction by the state of military service. That is the sense in which it is used. It has been used in society from the most primitive time down to the present. It has been a technique which has been used for the evolution and development of a state, really growing around the notion of militarism; and there is no use dodging that principle. However, only one state built its state theory upon that principle of militarism in and of itself, and that was Prussia. Probably the same can be said of the Empire of Germany, which inherited its ideas from Prussia. To make a great contrast, the concept or theory of conscription brought about a tremendous democratization of the people in Japan. So those who argue that this technique will do this or do that must go further in their argument and say where it will do it, how it will do it, and when it will do it, because the history of conscription furnishes examples of practically everything.

The theory of the conscription notion is interpreted by some as the most democratic way to carry on. I myself would not use that kind of argument, because it immediately leads into difficulties. In the first place, the democracy or democratic idea is not defined. But the theory, as it is accepted in the bill, is probably something like this: There is in the conscription system a leveling, a community of citizenship, which arises from the basic conception that military service should rest not upon ardor, upon the mercenary motive, upon caste, or feudal obligation, but simply upon the duties of membership in the political association, for the maintenance and defense of which an army is organized. I believe that definition will fit the ideas and the ideals of conscription as it has been resorted to in our country; and if it is resorted to again it will be the dominating and underlying principle.

Since 1919 we have known of this theory in regard to total mobilization, and it is to an extent upon this theory that the Selective Draft Act has been built. The necessity of understanding the people, the necessity of weighing the responsibility in regard to the carrying on of war, the necessity of knowing what the worth of an organized nation is to any army at the front—these are things which have produced the modern theory in regard to mobilization.

THE EFFECTS OF CONSCRIPTION [6]

. . . If conscription is urged on the grounds of dire military necessity, as the alternative to national extinction or the shirking of plain obligations, I have personally not a word to say. If the case of military need is manifest, adopt conscription, knowing it to be a real danger to freedom but a danger faced with open eyes as the alternative to still greater dangers. It is necessary to say, however, that that question is often begged by the assumption that a state is always in dire military need and that it is always a wise policy to attain maximum military strength at whatever social and political cost.

But as a matter of fact, conscription is advocated not on the ground of military need so much as on that of its educational and moral supremacy to the voluntary system; as a means of assimilating the alien, of attaining general national integration, of correcting our materialism, spiritualizing our democracy, democratising our plutocracy, of heaven knows what. . . . I suggest . . . that if during the last few generations England had had conscription the operations of that system would have resulted inevitably in checking the liberal tendencies of English political development and strengthening the reactionary and imperialist, by limiting freedom both of discussion and institution and by curtailing popular right; and would have made English political

[6] By Norman Angell (Ralph Norman Angell Lane), English writer and pacifist. From "The Relevance of Conscription." *New Republic.* 6:345-6. April 29, 1916. Reprinted by permission.

influence in the world very much less beneficent than happily it is.

I will hint at the grounds of that belief . . . by recalling the outstanding facts of a certain recent incident of English history: the Boer war and its sequel.

That incident illustrates, I think, two opposing forces in English political development—in the development of western democracy, indeed: the forces which brought on the war and the opposing forces which dominated the post-bellum settlement. Because, of course, the final settlement which has given us a loyal and united South Africa was the work of pro-Boers who bitterly fought the policy that precipitated the war and who in large degree reverted its object. But so complete a victory of liberal forces would have been impossible if conscription had obtained in England. That system would have strengthened incalculably those reactionary forces which played so large a part in the war itself. Let us see why.

Although the Boer war is not a page of history upon which Englishmen like to dwell, I imagine there are very few who would seriously challenge the view that there entered into its motives very ugly elements of capitalist exploitation, a Prussianisation of English temper shown in a crude desire of domination, excuse or justification of things like the Jameson Raid, a refusal to see an "enemy" point of view, a systematic vilification of the Boer character, and finally, in the conduct of the war itself, methods which the Englishman, who after the war became the British Prime Minister, declared curtly to be "methods of barbarism"—farm burning, concentration camps, etc.

Now, not merely had this lapse into Prussianism ranged the opinion of most of the civilized world against England— certainly as much as it was against France in the Dreyfus case —but what is much more to my point, most English Liberals fought the whole policy and tendency of the war. The pro-Boer agitation (in which Mr. Lloyd George was perhaps the most rabid and violent figure) did not, it is true, stop the war, though it shortened it; but it produced a reaction against the Prussian temper so great that the pro-Boers, electorally triumphant after the war, virtually restored to the Boer Republics their independence under the guise of responsible colonial government; and to the bitter anger of English junkerdom allowed the Boer element to become once more politically dominant throughout South Africa; so that within a year or two of the close of the war the virtual ruler of South Africa was the man who had led the Boer forces in the field against British arms.

But that conversion of the British people, and their revolt against their own government, would have been impossible under conscription.

The war, which lasted nearly three years, called from first to last for nearly half a million men, drawn not only from the regular army, but from militia and irregular forces. Presumably those who offered their services for the war did not share the views of the pro-Boer party of the day. So that the situation I have previously described of the Prussian conscript who is shot for refusing to kill Belgians for the offense of defending their country . . . did not arise.

But what would have been the position of English soldiers under conscription? That system would of course take no account of political opinion. While the pro-Boer might be taken to the front, the pro-Chamberlainite might have been left at home. Young Liberals and non-conformists were reading in their *Daily News* or *Nation* or *Manchester Guardian* or in the books or articles of the Chestertons, or James Bryces, or Hobhouses, or Herbert Spencers, or William Watsons or Steads; or hearing speeches by the Lloyd Georges, or Morleys or Burns's, or by labor leaders, Hardies or Macdonalds, or by pastors or even by bishops (several of them), that the war was a monstrous wickedness, tainted at its source, carried on by methods of barbarism. Inflamed by all this these young men would, under conscription, have been sent to the veldt to kill Boers, burn

Boer farmhouses and drive Boer women and children into concentration camps.

Would they, in such conditions, have done those things? I can answer personally for at least some, they would have flatly refused. We now know—the 1905 election taught us that—that pro-Boerism had gone much deeper than was generally supposed. The refusal would not have been isolated and sporadic, for though pro-Boerism presented what was at the time a minority, it was a passionate and convinced minority. And that minority—the editors, writers, bishops, professors—would certainly, some of them, have supported that mutiny and encouraged it.

What would you have had the conscription authorities do? Shoot the young conscripts and let the forces—the pro-Boer agitation—really responsible for their mutiny, continue unchecked? Let the conscript choose whether he should go to war or not? Then that is the end of conscription in England. And would the military authorities accept surrender to sedition in wartimes?

There was only one thing, under conscription, to have done: suppress the pro-Boer agitation. For conscription to have worked at all in the Boer war would have meant a very thoroughgoing censorship of newspaper opinion, suppression of public meetings, control of university professors and religious teachers, and the suppression of the speaking and writing of the men who have since ruled England and guided her policy.

It would have suited the government of the day, of course; notably Mr. Chamberlain. He would not have needed to answer Lloyd George or the other very violent pro-Boers. He would have sent them to jail. Incidentally, such a step would have been very popular just at the time.

But such a course would have altered not only the subsequent history of the South African settlement, but of all English politics. The discredit which fell upon the authors of the Boer war and finally swept them from office and so completely checked the Prussian temper and tendencies, was due largely to the educating influence of the pro-Boer agitation. The movement which accounted for the landslide of the 1905 election was largely a moral movement, a realization of the true character of Chamberlainite and Milnerite politics, due largely to just that agitation during the war which conscription must have suppressed.   The system could not have worked if it had tolerated it.

If today Germans were free from conscription there might be some hope of a political heresy, corresponding to that which arose in England during the Boer war, raising its head; some hope of the assertion of the right to criticise the policy of war; to take, if need be, the enemy view.   Such a heresy might save Europe, civilization.   But, again, it is incompatible with conscription.   Any system which menaces, even in small degree, the right to criticise the state's action, a right which alone can enable a people to keep their vision clear and save it from the moral fate of Prussia, should not be lightly adopted.

THE C.I.O. POSITION [7]

The Congress of Industrial Organizations stands second to no one in its desire for effective national defense.   It has, therefore, pledged itself to the fullest cooperation with proper defense measures,

In the establishment of adequate national defense, however, it is just as essential that unsound and unwise proposals be defeated as it is that proper measures be taken.   In the excitement of a period of crisis measures are sometimes advanced so fundamentally in opposition to our national democratic traditions that their proponents would not dare propose them at any other time.   It is our belief that peacetime military conscription is just such a measure.

[7] A statement dated August 14, 1940, opposing peacetime conscription, by John L. Lewis, President of the Congress of Industrial Organizations, presented on the floor of the Senate by Senator Rush D. Holt of West Virginia. *Congressional Record*. Vol. 86. August 22, 1940. p. 16429.

The very genesis of the measure for peacetime conscription is open to serious question.

1. The proposed bill was drawn up under unofficial auspices by private citizens, although no measure could be more affected with the public interest.

2. The bill was launched by a group of prominent New York corporation lawyers and other wealthy persons. Neither these persons nor the Congressional sponsors of the bill have been notable in their support of legislation for the welfare of the common people of this country.

3. The measure has not been formally requested of Congress by the President of the United States, the responsible head of preparation for national defense.

4. At their recent national conventions both of the major political parties gave the proposal for conscription consideration, but neither saw fit to give endorsement to the proposal.

Briefly, these are the reasons which have impelled the C.I.O. to oppose the pending measures:

1. There is a better way to recruit a proper army for defense than conscription.

Voluntary enlistment under terms which have real concern for the needs of the individual would quickly provide a suitable army. The period of enlistment should be shortened to one year. The pay should be raised at least to compare with that of the self-respecting workman. The right to return to private employment should be protected. Provision should be made for the continuation of social security protection during the period of such enlistment. Private debts should be either assumed or suspended. Officers' commissions should be more freely open to enlisted men, so that an army career is open to men from the ranks. Under such circumstances the most effective and loyal kind of an army could be raised, with much less cost to the nation than the enormous expenditures necessary for conscription,

2.   Military conscription now would establish the principle in this nation that the lives of our young men are less privileged than the profit rights of dollars.

Today the nation is watching the shameful spectacle of our Government yielding to the imperious demands of corporate industry for vast tax concessions and enormous loans as a precondition to manufacturing arms. The same interests who thus strangle our national defense call loudly for the forcible conscription of our young men. They claim in one breath that no dollar will be turned to the defense of our nation without a fat and untaxed profit being assured, while almost at the same moment they call upon our young men, most of them workers, to cast aside their liberty and sacrifice their ambitions or suffer punishment as a felon. It would be a terrible day in American history should our young men be forced to the draft while industry is free to lay down its ultimatums to the government.

3.   Forced military service in peacetime would be an alarming departure from the basic principles of our democracy. It is the first step toward the break-down of those free institutions which we seek to protect.

Citizens who become subject to conscription lose a substantial part of those civil rights and liberties which distinguish a free democracy from a totalitarian state.

Such conscription would further establish in the minds of the young people of the nation the idea that voluntary loyalty to the nation is no longer a necessary virtue. It would introduce them to the principle of compulsion, a principle native to the Fascist state and alien to our own.

4.   The production of equipment for an army has lagged far behind the enlistments into the military service.

Already there are more men available to the Army and the National Guard than can be equipped for some time to come. The present speed of enlistments is far more rapid than the provision of equipment. From the point of effective defense, an efficient, loyal, and highly trained army, highly mechanized, is many times more efficient than a sullen, ill-equipped, poorly trained, conscript army of three times the size. Conscription now could be an enormous waste of money and manpower.

5. The entire fabric of the nation, both industrial and social, would be torn by conscription. The dislocations in industrial production and in community life caused by conscription would take years to heal.

Therefore, the C.I.O. is opposed to provision for peacetime conscription as a measure inimical to the most effective kind of national defense and alien to the democratic way of life.

RAILROAD BROTHERHOODS ON CONSCRIPTION [8]

The undersigned chief executives of the organizations representing engineers, firemen, conductors, trainmen and yardmen employed on the railroads of the United States have this day given consideration to the provisions of the proposed compulsory peacetime draft or conscription bill which contemplates the inducting into the military and naval service of the United States in the immediate future, some hundreds of thousands of citizens of this country for a period of training.

We refer to the Burke-Wadsworth bill now before Congress for consideration and feel that you should be made acquainted with our views, which we are confident reflect the views of the membership of these organizations of men employed on American railroads.

[8] Memorandum sent to the Senate and House Committees on Military Affairs by the Railroad Brotherhoods, labor unions of railway employees, with a total membership of nearly half a million men, and signed by A. Johnston, Grand Chief Engineer of the Brotherhood of Locomotive Engineers, J. A. Philips, President of the Order of Railway Conductors of America, D. B. Robertson, President of the Brotherhood of Locomotive Firemen and Enginemen, A. F. Whitney, President of the Brotherhood of Railroad Trainmen, and T. C. Cashen, President of the Switchmen's Union of North America.

The memorandum was presented on the floor of the Senate by Senator Rush D. Holt of West Virginia. *Congressional Record*. Vol. 86. August 22, 1940. p. 16428-9.

We are in general agreement with the prevailing sentiment in the United States that every support should be given to adequate measures necessary to the protection of our democratic institutions against attack from the force of dictatorship, both within and without our country. However, grave doubt exists in many quarters with respect to the wisdom of enacting a peacetime conscription bill when it is believed other adequate measures are available. Such proposal borders closely on the principle of dictatorship, and we hold the view that regimenting our people is un-American and unnecessary.

Patriotism is not the monopoly of those who are feverishly urging this conscription bill. We may rightly assume that all citizens are patriotic and if given the opportunity and impressed with the necessity for their doing so, they will volunteer their services in defense of our country.

At present there is a vast army of unemployed, thousands of whom would be desirous of enlisting in the military and naval service if given an opportunity to do so, but they are so circumscribed by technical military and naval physical requirements that many of them are precluded from voluntary enlistment. Consideration should be given to assisting them in removing minor physical defects so that they may be acceptable as volunteers.

Compulsory military service in time of peace is the very antithesis of freedom. It involves an infringement on the very principles of democracy which it is invoked to defend. It imposes upon the individual a mandate to give service which he may not be in position to render without serious sacrifices on the part of himself or his family, or both, and this at a time when there are thousands of other individuals who would be glad to avail themselves of the opportunity to serve if such opportunity were not denied by the restrictive rules observed by the recruiting service.

The youth of our country who are inducted into the military and naval services under the principle of conscription and who are made to serve will quite naturally acquire the viewpoint that forceful means should be adopted in all the affairs of life as an avenue to achieve desired ends.

While you are giving thought to the Burke-Wadsworth bill let not the hysteria of the moment sweep you into supporting such a drastic and ill-advised change in the American way of life. Democracy means that the state exists to serve the individual. The program at present contemplated will cause hundreds of thousands of our youth to become war-minded and will, if carried out, establish the fabric of a giant war machine, which experience teaches us cannot and will not be permitted to rust in peace. "War games" inevitably lead to war. The voluntary enlistment principle confines and restricts the dissemination of war-mindedness to actual necessities through the longer term of service and, above all, preserves the principle of democracy in its strictest sense.

These organizations are wholeheartedly in accord with the establishment and maintenance of an adequate national defense, and their membership will not be found wanting in any support of such proper measures, but we are convinced that under present conditions the regimenting of our people according to the contemplated military pattern is unnecessary and is an infringement upon the civil liberties which they may reasonably expect to enjoy.

We trust that your committee will not favorably report the Burke-Wadsworth military conscription bill.

SHOULD SERVICE BE UNIVERSAL?

DISCUSSION

When the Selective Service Act of 1940 was passed, it provided for the training of approximately 900,000 men each year for a period of five years. Each man inducted was to be given training for a period of one year, after which he was to be placed in a reserve component. At the end of the five-year period, an army reserve of from 4,000,000 to 4,500,000 men would have been created, in addition to the Regular Army of 250,000 and a National Guard of equal size.

The amendment to the Selective Service Act passed on August 1941, however, apparently changed completely the purpose of the measure. The amendment extended the period of training to two and one half years for men already drafted, without at the same time providing increased facilities for training additional draftees. So instead of providing for a long-range training program to create a powerful reserve of manpower, the nation apparently is building a huge and highly trained draft army for the present emergency only. From a program which approximated universal military service, our government has returned to the selective service system of 1917.

Naturally, this change is the result of present conditions abroad. But in planning for the future, after the existing emergency has passed, our military leaders must face the question of which type of permanent preparedness policy should be followed—one based on sporadic training of selectees in time of emergency, or one based on the idea of universal military service for all young men on the attainment of military age. The American Legion advocates the latter method; its leaders argue that if the 700,000 to 800,000 able-bodied young men who reach the age of 18 each year are given a year's military

training, the United States will always have available a reserve
force of six or seven million trained men between the ages
of 21 and 30, making unnecessary the costly and dangerously
slow procedure of training conscripts after the emergency arises.

Should such a plan be adopted, and every able-bodied
young man required to report to the Army for a period of
military training, two major questions arise: (1) At what age
should training be required? (2) How long should the training
period be?

The present law provides for training of men between the
ages of 21 and 28; originally it included men from 29 to
35, but men over 28 are now excluded from the draft. Many
military leaders favor training at an earlier age, not only because
young men of 18 or 19 are more pliable and consequently
more easily trained, but because service at that age would
interfere less with the business of earning a living.

As to length of the training period, the present law, too,
provides for service for 30 months—two and a half years.
Originally, however, when the plan was apparently to create a
military reserve force, length of the training period was set at
one year. And in a recent article in *Collier's,* General Johnson
Hagood suggests that an even shorter period of training would
be adequate. He breaks down the time required for training
in the following manner: 10 days to learn the essential details
of operation of one weapon, and to perform simple field duties;
four weeks to learn company drill and operations sufficiently
well to take the field; and from six to twelve weeks to learn
coordination with the regiment and be ready for action.

Of course, what General Hagood has in mind is training
of an essentially military nature; he does not include the mechanical training required for mechanized forces or for men who are
to keep aircraft fit for service, nor does he include the thousand
similar functions performed by soldiers in wartime which do not
relate directly to fighting. But perhaps such functions can best
be taught in schools, completely separate from the required

military training period. In fact, some experts believe that even the military procedures might well be taught in connection with the young man's regular school work, over a period of two or three years, rather than in a full-time training period of six months or a year.

These matters, however, are details in the program. The major question is still whether any system of universal training is necessary or desirable.

THE AGE OF TRAINEES [1]

Personally, all other things being equal, I myself would like to see these young men taken for training at the age of 21. But there are practical difficulties in the way, and I think if we adopt the system that it would be wise to fix the age at 19. The young man at 19 is more pliable, perhaps, and it would not interfere with the continuation of his college work, but would take him at the end of his high school course. The point I want to make is that it is not a question of fighting qualities, it is not a question of eagerness to fight, nor ability to learn; but the men are just a little bit more mature and perhaps a little bit stronger physically.

A PRACTICAL TRAINING PROGRAM [2]

The practical question which comes up is what would be the best military system for the United States to adopt to insure two things. The first is to insure having in time of war an adequate number of highly trained professional soldiers. The second is to have universal military training for all young men in time of peace. This, so they may start civil life with the

[1] By General John J. Pershing, Commander in Chief of the United States Armies during the World War. From a statement made before the Committee on Military Affairs, U. S. Congress, October 31, 1919. *National Defense Hearings*, pt. 1. p. 378.

[2] By Henry J. Reilly, Brig. General, Officers' Reserve Corps. From *Are Our Youn Men to Have a Chance?* Pamphlet published by the Civilian Military Education Fund, Washington, D.C. 1940. p. 20-1. Reprinted by permission.

benefits accruing them from such training and be ready, should war come, to defend their country with the minimum loss of life and limb, the minimum expenditure of money and victory within a short period of time.

Probably, in general, the French Republic, through its military system, indicates the best route to be followed. They have two classes of soldiers. The first is the professional soldier who spends his life in the army. The second is the ordinary citizen who wants to spend his life as a civilian but who recognizes that he owes military service to his country in time of war and, therefore, should undergo military training in time of peace. This, so he will have the maximum chance as a trained soldier to survive the war and, for the same reason, give his country the maximum chance to be victorious. . . .

Following this general idea, there would be no need to materially change our present military setup in order to establish compulsory universal military training. After deciding the minimum amount of military knowledge necessary, each boy could be given the choice as to where he would acquire it. He could get it in one continuous period in the Regular Army, Navy, or Marine Corps, or in a number of periods in the National Guard, ROTC, CMTC, or CCC. . . .

THE CHOICE BEFORE US [3]

If our army is to be only the A.E.F. over again, its value is certainly to be questioned. But the very circumstances in which it is being created insure important differences.

The conscript army of 1917 was improvised after war had been declared. With surprising efficiency considering the pressure of events, but hastily none the less, two million men were selected, trained, and put under arms. The raising of this army was a temporary break in a normal national life in which military affairs were happily remote from the ordinary citizen.

[3] By Freda Kirchwey, editor, *The Nation*. From "There Is No Alternative." *The Nation*. 151:85-6. August 3, 1940. Reprinted by permission.

After the war armament expenditures were sharply reduced, the army was demobilized, and the United States washed its hands of the affairs of Europe.

Contrast the situation today: France disastrously defeated in the field and Hitler lord over continental Europe; Britain, with no unconquered allies except its colonies and the dominions, facing imminent assault. No one knows whether Britain will be able to resist or will be overwhelmed with the loss of empire and fleet. But, at best, we cannot realistically hope for an early defeat of Hitler. Churchill's warning after Dunkerque that a successful withdrawal must not be confused with a victory applies to England's present situation. A successful resistance will also not be a victory. The political and military dominance of Nazi Germany, together with the spreading power of Japan in Asia—these are the controlling characteristics of the world of 1940. The creation of a strong army is not a temporary emergency measure; it is part of a long-range program necessitated by a world situation which is likely to grow worse. . . .

As long as Nazi despotism rules Europe and threatens the world, so long must the word and hope of peace be banished from our minds. Even today the United States is no longer at peace. It is living in a state of war preparation which will last until fascism has been defeated. Hitler's successes and further ambitions have thrust upon us an unwelcome but inescapable job of total preparation. Out of nothing—speaking relatively—we must create a war machine, not as an emergency improvisation but as an integral part of our national life in the years to come. . . .

If a small, well-equipped army were sufficient, conscription would never be necessary. On the other hand, if, . . . a conscript army is required in case of war, it should most certainly be created before the actual fighting begins. That is the real lesson of 1917. For such an army must not be improvised. Its construction and equipping are a long job, especially today, when . . . the intricate machines of modern warfare demand a high proportion of technically trained soldiers. . . .

The choice lies between an army based on universal service and a greatly expanded professional army.

THE AMERICAN LEGION PROGRAM [4]

The American Legion launched its program for making the emergency peacetime draft permanent as the cornerstone of a future continuing national defense policy, with the opening of the first session of the 77th Congress, January 3, 1941.

United States Senator Morris Sheppard of Texas, chairman of the Senate Military Affairs Committee, introduced the American Legion Bill, S. 243, in the Senate. At the same time Congressman Andrew J. May of Kentucky, chairman of the House Military Affairs Committee, brought out a companion bill, H.R. 1411, in the House of Representatives.

Known as the Sheppard-May legislation, these twin American Legion bills propose two amendments to the present conscription law:

1—Ages of men selected for service to be fixed between 18 and 21.

2—Universal military training to be made a permanent policy of the government.

The national legislative committee of the American Legion asked Senator Sheppard and Representative May to introduce these two measures simultaneously in both houses of Congress.

The authority for the action of the national legislative committee in sponsoring the Sheppard-May legislation was based on three sources—two resolutions adopted by national conventions of the American Legion, and a formal approval by the national executive committee.

[4] From "Why 18 to 21 Universal Military Training?" Publicity release from National Publicity Division, The American Legion, Indianapolis, Indiana, January 20, 1940. Reprinted by permission.

The 2nd national convention of the American Legion in Cleveland, Ohio, September 27 to 29, 1920, set the keynote for all national defense programs of the last two decades when it adopted the following resolution:

The examination of young men called under the Selective Service Act demonstrated a high percentage of physical disability and also illiteracy among both native and foreign born, indicating the necessity for a system of compulsory universal training of young men, which should tend to obviate this deplorable condition in the future.

Therefore, we recommend the adoption by the Congress of a system of compulsory universal training, which shall include physical training, educational training, and Americanization, as well as efficient military training to form a foundation for future extended military training in time of war.

Twenty years later by the time the 22nd national convention of the American Legion had met in Boston, Mass., September 23 to 26, 1940, our country had resorted to the first peacetime conscription of its manpower as a result of a eleventh hour awakening to the perils of its two-decade long neglect of national defense.

The 22nd national convention declared unanimously:

The American Legion has for the past 20 years consistently advocated selective service, now legislated by the Congress, as sound in democratic principle and essential to the adequate defense of this nation, and we believe it is logical that our military manpower should be assured its proper supply by the appropriate federal control of supply agencies.

We also commend the United States Congress for its adoption of the Selective Service Bill, and urge that this legislation *be extended to provide a permanent system of universal military training.*

On the recommendation of Warren H. Atherton of Stockton, Cal., chairman of the national defense committee of the American Legion, the national executive committee at its meeting at national headquarters in Indianapolis, Ind., November 21 and 22, 1940, adopted the following resolution:

Whereas, the Selective Service Act, recently enacted, is a temporary measure to recruit the armed forces of the United States and does not make provision for the training of all young Americans *as they reach military age*; and

Whereas, for 20 years the American Legion has urged the adoption of universal military training as conducive to the making of loyal citizens and the creation of adequate trained reserves; and

Whereas, the national convention at Boston (1940) again urged universal military training as a vital defense need, now, therefore, be it

Resolved, that the national legislative committee of the American Legion is directed to make every effort to secure legislation requiring service and training of every American youth *as he becomes of military age*.

By unanimous vote also, the national executive committee of the American Legion at this same meeting approved and adopted the entire report of National Defense Chairman Atherton. This report went into minute detail on the entire national defense situation.

Reviewing the progress of national preparedness, Chairman Atherton declared:

Now the defense committee wants to impress upon you that this matter of defense has not been solved or taken care of on a long-range program. We have not as yet any long-range, continuing plan of defense. We are apt to be carried away with the thought that we have appropriated great sums of money, far beyond anything we have been accustomed to think about in connection with national defense, but those appropriations are for the purpose of meeting this emergency.

So far as anything that has yet been enacted into law, the situation in which we find ourselves now can recur in five years or can recur in ten years, just as it has recurred over cycles of some 20 years, ever since the birth of our nation. When an emergency arises and the storm hits, we think about fixing the roof. We start to get ready, start to prepare, and by the end of the war we are in pretty good shape. Then we declare peace and abandon our plans for armament, just as has happened in the last two decades. We go from perhaps the strongest and best prepared nation on earth in 1920 down to one of the weakest of all major powers in 1940.

The present draft act is not the law for which we have been asking and contending for 20 years. The Draft Act is an emergency measure to recruit the armed forces of the United States at the present time, and it is sufficient for that purpose. By its own terms, it expires in five years.

Chairman Atherton in his report emphasized the necessity of the American Legion's standing up now to get a "continuing, reliable, high standard of national defense, not the on-again-off-again kind that makes us strong once in every 20 years."

He pointed out that objectives advocated by the American Legion for two decades, namely: an adequate army with modern equipment, a two-ocean navy, the strongest flying forces in the air, and training of American youth, were about to become realities.

> Our function should change with changed conditions. . . . We should now bend our efforts to having present emergency measures amended to provide permanent defense.
>
> The Draft Act is only a temporary measure to recruit and train an army now. By its own terms it expires in five years.
>
> We should move now to change the Draft Act to a universal training law.

Chairman Atherton pointed out to the national executive committee that the ideal age for training young Americans for national defense was when they came out of high school or reached college age.

At this period of their lives, the drafting of young men would cause less disruption of the nation's economic life, because they are less likely to have acquired responsibilities which at later ages they will have accumulated.

Specifically Chairman Atherton recommended, and the national executive committee approved, the following:

> We must see that the Draft Act is amended so as to provide for a long-range plan of universal military training for young men who come out of high school or reach college age, allowing them a bracket of four or five years at that age, in which to take their year of training.

These were the arguments, and this was the recommendation which guided the national legislative committee of the American Legion, after further consultations with War Department officials, in selecting the age bracket between 18 and 21 as the ideal period for universal military training, in the committee's bill to amend the Selective Service Act and make it permanent.

In concluding his recommendations on the amending and making permanent the emergency peacetime draft act, Chairman Atherton listed five benefits that would accrue to the nation, as follows:

1. Universal training will, within a few years, create so great a body of effective reserves that this nation will be forever safe from attack.

2. When every young American who reaches the age to enjoy the right to vote, to contract, to inherit property, to own property, to engage in business, to be entitled to the protection of his person through law, to free speech, to freedom of religion, to choice of occupation, to unemployment insurance, to social security, to workmen's compensation and to the thousands of other benefits and privileges conferred by American citizenship, has earned those rights and privileges by training to defend them, he will have a greater appreciation of their worth.

3. National discipline will reduce the commission of crime.

4. National health will be benefited.

5. Unemployment will be reduced.

A NATIONAL SERVICE PROGRAM [5]

I agree to the idea that Americans as a group of people need to learn more about what they should give to their nation, and that we have taken too many things for granted—all of us I mean, not just young people; everybody has taken too many things for granted about our country and has not thought enough about what we needed to give to it. But on this matter it seems to me again that the bill falls short. What it is going to do is to pick out certain people and put them under the Army for a

[5] By Congressman Jerry Voorhis of California. *Congressional Record*. Vol. 86, September 3, 1940. p. 17318-9.

period of "training and service," as the bill puts it. We are told that is more democratic, but I am not sure, for you select certain people to do a tough job for the rest of the people. And if I read the testimony correctly these will be mostly selected from among the unemployed who have had the very least opportunity of anyone in the past few years.

It seems to me that what would be a democratic proposition would be if we said that everybody in a certain age group should give a year of service to the United States of America and in so doing we gave a certain amount of choice as to the kind of service they should give and some consideration to their own abilities and opportunity for development. We should require it of all—this year of service—and those who preferred would go into the Army—and I would pay them more than the rest—and some would be doing work like the CCC and some learning mechanical training, some in the Coast Guard, some in public health work, and so on; but everybody would have to do something.

I believe the Army would get enough men to have the necessary trained reserve and all these men would have an experience at some sort of orderly, health-building service to their country. But you would not be doing the one thing that I am afraid of, and that is you would not be adopting what I do not think anyone can deny is the central feature of European dictatorship. Adoption of the power to draft men as a permanent policy seems to me to be the central feature of these dictatorships. I want to use it as sparingly as possible—for an emergency, maybe; but as a permanent policy I am dead against it. I shall ask unanimous consent to insert as a part of my remarks the text of a bill I have drafted which embraces the program I have spoken about, and which I consider as an intelligent approach to this problem, one that has some consideration for the people affected, one that takes into account the capabilities of the men, and one that gives a reasonable freedom of choice as to type of service but which requires training and service from all at some time in their lives and which would offer special inducements to those going into the armed forces. Such a program would provide a balanced program of defense training in all its aspects. I believe the schools and colleges could and should be properly tied into such a program. . . .

Under this proposal that I sketched very briefly that could not happen, I may say to the gentleman, and at the same time the program I outlined would be administered by a civilian group. It would be a national service program in the true sense. It seems to me we could meet the national emergency other than by a draft bill, such as this one is at present. We could make it a real emergency measure, if there is a real emergency. We could do the fair thing by the men in the Standing Army; and we could have a national service program of benefit to the nation and to those participating in it. We could do all this without the things I fear in this bill. But I think we should be very careful, in our approach to this problem, that we do not establish such a peacetime draft as a permanent policy for the United States.

There follows the text of the bill to which I have made reference in my speech:

Be it enacted, etc., That the Congress hereby declares that the defense of the United States and the preservation of its integrity and its institutions demands the broadening of the opportunities for constructive work and training for American youth, the up-building of the nation's health, the conservation of human and natural resources, and the continual maintenance of a body of citizens trained for participation in all the branches of defense activity, including that of the armed forces.

Sec. 2. It is hereby declared to be the policy and purpose of the Congress to establish the general principle that all male citizens of the United States shall engage in some form of service to the nation for a period of 12 months at some time during their lives.

Sec. 3. It is further declared to be the policy of Congress to recognize the particular abilities and characteristics of individual citizens, to enable them in so far as possible to perform the service and acquire the training for which they are best fitted, and to promote the full employment of American youth in work beneficial to the nation, its agriculture and industry, and to themselves.

At the time of registration each registrant shall indicate a first, second, and third preference as to the type of service he desires to perform and shall also indicate the year during which he desires to perform such service: *Provided,* That such service shall be performed during some year between the ages of 18 and 24 for each registrant required to register under this act. . . .

Men during their period of service shall receive $25 per month, plus necessary travel expenses from their home to the point of assignment, together with maintenance during the period of their service: *Provided, however,* That men choosing assignment to any branch of the armed forces of the United States and assigned to such service shall receive $30 per month.

The President is authorized, under such regulations as he may prescribe, to establish the method of registration provided for under section 2 and section 3 of this act; and such regulations shall provide for a method of registering the preferences as to the type of service of each person so registered, with proper provisions to assure that registrants will not be permitted to serve in any agency in which the service would injure their health; and to further provide a system of educational examination boards, to assure that persons selecting service under any agency requiring technical or educational training for effective service have such technical or educational training as will make the service of such persons of value to the nation. In the case of persons engaged in courses of study, training course, or work of a nature essential to the national defense or the welfare of the nation, the Commission, through the local national service boards shall have power to designate such study, training, or work as national service and to exempt such persons from other such service.

The Commission is hereby authorized to establish, under the active control of a civilian agency having experience in the field, and after proper negotiations with and approval by representatives of the nations involved, service camps in any or all South or Central American nations where such camps might aid in the national policy of friendship and good will to neighboring nations. All persons registered would be eligible for such service: *Provided,* That the Commission carefully investigated the individuals requesting such service to make certain that only those registrants who could aid in the national policy of good will to neighboring nations were assigned to such service.

The following agencies are hereby designated as national service agencies:

1. Civilian Conservation Corps.
2. Civil Aeronautics Authority.
3. National Youth Administration.

4. Public Health Service.
5. Soil Conservation Service.
6. United States Army.
7. United States Army Corps of Engineers.
8. United States Coast Guard.
9. United States Coast and Geodetic Survey.
10. United States Forest Service.
11. United States Marine Corps.
12. United States Navy.

Congress shall from time to time add to the above list of national service agencies the names of such other agencies as in the opinion of the Commission should be designated as national service agencies.

THE ADVANTAGES OF A DEMOCRATIC ARMY [6]

There is endless talk in these days about "preparedness." Both political parties and both candidates for the Presidency advocate a larger Navy and a larger Army. On preparedness and Americanism the Republican platform uses the braver words; but the Democratic Party has voted—with more or less reluctance—the largest appropriations for the Navy and Army that have ever been voted, and also made the most earnest attempt ever made to convert the state militias into a national force. As to the defunct Progressive Party and its leaders, it shouted louder than either of the others for warlike preparation, and, indeed, appeared to advocate war against piteous little Mexico; but its principal doctrines related to social and industrial improvements at home, and it has had no chance to put those doctrines into practice through legislation. Under these political conditions at home and in the present fearful state of Europe, it is important that the American people, and particularly the public men who undertake to lead the people, should consider, first, for what uses the United States needs a navy and an army; and secondly, the sort of navy and army which the United States should prepare. . . .

[6] By Charles W. Eliot, President Emeritus of Harvard University. From "Shall We Adopt Universal Military Service?" *World's Work.* 33:16-24. November, 1916.

Why should the American people make this formidable change in their national habits and their international policy? First, because the industrial and commercial interests of the nation have completely changed since the Civil War, and can no longer be preserved and promoted in isolation. The country cannot keep its existing machinery running, or sell its surplus foods and raw materials, unless foreign markets are open to it, and are freely developed. The United States, having become an industrial and commercial world power, needs to have all the seas and oceans of the world open for its foreign trade in times of peace, and so far as is practicable in time of war also— open for both its imports and its exports of foods, drinks, drugs, raw materials, and manufactured articles. . . .

Secondly, steam and electricity have done away with the physical isolation of the United States. The oceans are not barriers, but highways which invite the passage of fleets, pacific or hostile. The security of America can no longer be trusted to the width of the Atlantic and the Pacific. . . . The only available insurance is a Navy powerful in every respect, and an Army in reserve visibly strong in numbers and visibly prepared for immediate service.

If the principle of universal military service should be accepted and acted on in the United States, several important consequences would immediately follow:

1. The country would always have to call on a trained force for all the duties and services which the Regular Army now performs, and this force could be increased by telegraph and telephone to any desired extent up to the limit of the reserves. Within ten years these reserves would be formidable in number. It would probably be desirable to maintain a special force for a service of two years in the Philippines, the Panama Canal Zone, and other outlying regions; but this force should consist of young men who volunteered for that special service after they had received the universal training at home, or the better part of it.

2. It would no longer be necessary to maintain any state militia, provided the governors were authorized to call on the national War Department for any troops they might need for local service. But if any state preferred to do so, it might maintain a local volunteer force made up of young men who had already served their first period (sixty to ninety days) in the national army.

3. The nation would be always prepared for defensive combat with any military Power which might assail it for purposes of conquest or ransom; and, being prepared, would probably be safe from such attempts.

4. In case of rebellion or outbreak of any sort within the country itself, a national force could be promptly put into the field to subdue it.

5. All the able-bodied young men in the country would receive a training in the hard work of a soldier which would be of some service to them in any industry in which they might afterward engage. They would have become accustomed to a discipline under which many men cooperate strenuously in the pursuit of common objects. They would have mastered the use of some instruments of precision; and would have learned much about personal and public hygiene, and the means of preserving bodily vigor and utilizing it to advantage.

6. The defense of the country would be always in charge of a Navy and Army neither feudal nor mercenary, neither drafted "for the war" nor professional in the sense that its members mean to spend their active lives in the service, but on the contrary composed of all the able-bodied youth of the nation, acting under a universal sense of obligation or duty, but also willing to serve the country in a hearty cooperative spirit out of love of freedom, justice, and all that makes "home."

7. In case of war, large or small, long or short, the great waste of lives and money which has taken place at the beginning of every war in which the United States has been engaged since the government was organized would be avoided, because

the government would have at call any desired number of competent officers and well-trained men. In case of war alarms the country would not be obliged to summon untrained militia, or to resort to such crude and unsound methods as Plattsburg camps and college regiments. . . .

If the United States sees reason for maintaining any army at all, it will be wise for it to maintain a democratic army, in which all able-bodied young Americans should serve for several short periods, and then be held in reserve for a long period, its officers being selected from the ranks by their instructors and commanders during the prescribed periods of service, and educated as now at the Military Academy to serve for life as teachers of the successive levies of raw recruits, or held in reserve with liberty to follow civil occupations. A few thousand non-commissioned officers would also be kept in the service permanently, or for considerable periods, to serve as instructors to the raw levies and as non-commissioned officers of any force the country might need for sudden and sustained service. . . .

Given universal service, it would require only six or seven years to build up an American army fit to perform all the present functions of the Regular Army and of the militia in the several states, and also to meet the exigencies of an attack on this country by a great military power. . . .

It is a grave conclusion to come to, that a great democracy whose primary object is the promotion of the public welfare and happiness must arm itself to fight, and must teach all its young men how to fight—which means how to kill and wound other men with whom individually they have no quarrel, to destroy public and private property, to disrupt homes and extinguish families, to interrupt commerce, and to waste on a prodigious scale the accumulated savings of generations. . . . For the nations that already possess a good deal of freedom, and mean to have more, there is no other way to security and peace than to organize and use their own forces with greater skill and more devotion than the nations despotically ruled exhibit.

HOW LARGE AN ARMY? [7]

It is acknowledged by almost everybody that the only efficient way to raise a great army for modern war is by compulsory universal service. Every nation confronted with this task has used this means, whether the government concerned be autocratic, democratic or somewhere between. . . . The primary reason for universal service, whatever else may be said for it, is dire necessity. The ultimate test of victory is manpower; nothing less than the military effort of a whole population will suffice. Campaigns for volunteers are too slow and uncertain in recruiting the necessary numbers.

Volunteering suffers two additional disadvantages which alone would be enough to send it into the discard. First, an army must receive long and intensive training before it is called upon to fight efficiently in the modern manner, and it is impossible to stir up enough interest in a recruiting campaign while a nation is still at peace, though that is the time when the training should be given. Second, there is much more in proper war organization than getting the necessary number of men under arms. It is getting the right men in the right places, and refraining from putting uniforms on the men who would be more valuable in the equally important functions of industry and transport behind the lines. In order to mobilize a nation it is necessary to put through the sieve the whole generation of fighting age, so that there may be sifted into separate compartments those who ought to stick at their jobs, those who are unfit for service, and those who are better fitted for special duties than for the front line. Universal service is the only possible means of putting system and order into a military machine of ambitious size. . . .

[7] From "Universal Military Service." *The New Republic.* 103:6-7. July 1, 1940. Reprinted by permission.

The question before the United States . . . is still a question of how large an army we shall want and how soon we ought to try to get it into shape. If what we need is what is at present authorized—a highly skilled and mechanized force of something less than a half-million men, it is not too large to be raised by ordinary recruiting methods from our great population, and it is scarcely large enough to be a danger to our institutions. To put every young man through intensive military training when we expect to utilize only four or five per cent of those between twenty and twenty-four (who number above 10,000,000) would be excessively wasteful. Even an army of a million or a million and a half would scarcely seem to warrant universal training, though it might justify selecting those for training through the method of universal registration. And no wildest estimate holds that we shall need a force larger than this, or could equip it soon if we did—unless, indeed, we are preparing to challenge Hitler on the other side of the Atlantic and the Mikado on the Yangtze. . . .

With these considerations in mind, it seems to us that the Burke bill for universal training . . . is ill adapted to the situation. It is almost a carbon copy of the measure used in the last war; it is unnecessary for anything except the task of raising and training a military force of millions; it contains no hint that its authors have anything like a realistic view of the present world or of the needs of this country. . . .

A PLAN FOR AMERICA [8]

Much has been said and written against the volunteer system during the past five years. Undeniably it is undemocratic. If all are to participate in the government, all should defend or be prepared to defend the government against attacks since the government is the people, is the means by

[8] By J. B. W. Gardiner. From "What Kind of Military Training?" *World's Work*. 37:549-52. March, 1919.

which the voice of the people finds expression. There is as much logic then in the assertion that the defense of the country should be borne by a volunteer soldiery as there would be in the claim that the expense of running the country should be provided by volunteer taxation. Both are ridiculous. The President realized this and realized further the failure which was inherent in the volunteer system when in his war message to Congress in April 1917, he cast the volunteer idea aside and pleaded for universal service as the only feasible means of putting into the field against Germany the man power of the country. In other words, when the cloud of war came upon the horizon our first act was to cast into the scrap heap every military measure on our statute books and to replace them by a universal service act.

This raises a question, therefore, that we must ask ourselves and then answer: If a given military system is of such character that its failure in an emergency is a foregone conclusion, if when the nation is threatened the people accept without question its utter inadequacy, is it logical to retain such a policy as the means of preserving our national life? It does not seem possible then that the President and the Secretary of War can again advocate or support the volunteer system without stultifying themselves. The adoption of universal service as the fixed military system of the country would seem inevitable.

Many reasons have been given in the past why this system should be adopted. Our experiences of the last two years have served only to emphasize, to crystallize them. The draft proved to us that there is a great work remaining to be done in America —a work which will affect the youth of the country for all time. In the first place, our young men must be more thoroughly Americanized. Much has been said of the great number who registered for the first draft, and this fact has been pointed to as an evidence of the patriotism of our men. But the test, it seems to me, is not how many registered, but how many expressed a willingness to go to the front by not claiming exemption. This number was only about 25 per cent of the total registration. There were, moreover, more than a quarter of a million clear-cut slackers—men who failed to register at all—and the fact that they did not register lest they be sent to the front is good evidence that they were front-line timber without legitimate exemption claim. It is evident then that Americanization is needed. Men must be taught that there is no such thing as a privilege without a corresponding duty; and that if they want all the privileges of living under our government and participating in all that government offers, they have a duty to perform toward that government, a debt of honor to pay. And the training camp is the best possible school to accomplish the needed result. . . .

Physical training should begin at an early age. Just what this age should be is open to debate, but the soundest medical authorities consider it about twelve years. It need not be, should not be, strenuous, consisting for the first two years in calisthenics and the simpler forms of "setting up" exercises. Fifteen to twenty minutes a day of such exercise would be all that would be needed. This would mean a minimum of about ninety hours a year. As the boys grow older, both the time and requirements should be made more rigid, involving elements of military discipline, elementary target practice, and in the later stages a few days in camp. By the time a boy who had had this training reached eighteen he would be a healthy human being, immeasurably better morally and physically than our present product, and with a respect for authority which is now generally lacking. For this reason, his value as a productive unit in our national life would be greatly enhanced.

On reaching the age of eighteen he would then become available for military service proper. Because of attendance at school, dependencies, occupational requirements, or other reasons which might preclude such service at positive periods without such heavy personal sacrifice as could not be reasonably demanded, it should not be required that he go immediately into service. There should be a period—as between eighteen and twenty-three—during which he could serve, the time being as far as practicable, selective by the man himself. Certain exemptions would have to be provided for, of course. But these should be very positive and definite. . . .

Just how long this period of service should be has been a subject of much debate. In discussions that were held previous to 1917 there was a wide difference of opinion—ranging from nine months as the minimum, to two years. But those of widest experience in the intensive training of the summer camps—General Woo, for example—contended that six months of such training would be sufficient. The experience which we have gained through the war shows that beyond all doubt six months' training under proper auspices—that is, with an adequate number of capable instructors, and a proper supply of modern arms and equipment, an advantage which we have not yet possessed—will produce excellent results. A great many of our draft men went into action against the Germans within less than six months after they were drafted. The same was true of the men of the other belligerent nations. Only in the beginning of the war, when officers were scarce and when there was little or no equipment to work with, was the period of training extended to a year. . . .

What would this scheme of training mean in numbers? Every year about 1,100,000 men in this country reach the age of eighteen. The draft examinations indicated that only about half of these would, during the first two or three years, be available for service. The others would be exempt, either on account of physical defects or other causes specifically provided for in the universal service law. The effect, however, of the preliminary training would soon be felt, the percentage of those available would steadily increase until at the end of five years—when all the youth of the country had had the advantage of the physical training provided for the twelve to seventeen year old classes—this percentage would reach its maximum, which would be about eighty. Thus, during the first two or three years, between 500,000 and 600,000 men would be available, and after five years 800,000 would be called annually. . . .

It will be recalled that the ages between which the six months' training is to be taken are from eighteen to twenty-three. But what will happen after a man reaches his twenty-fourth year? He should at that age enter a reserve which would be properly classified for future mobilization. When this mobilization would occur and what its purposes would be would, of course, be left to the President. It might be because of a threatening war, an insurrection; it might be only for training purposes, but it would have to rest upon a wise discretion of the Chief Executive. The main point is that from twenty-four to forty-five the reserve would be subject to call whenever in the opinion of the President the welfare of the nation demanded it. Under this plan we would have, after this training of the citizens had been going on for eight years, a trained force of 4,000,000 men less the normal loss from death, or a net force of at least 3,500,000. This force would be distributed over the country on a basis of population. It would be a well balanced force in that it would contain the proper proportion of the various arms and, if proper use is made of the war material and manufacturing facilities which we have acquired in the present war, it would be well equipped in every particular. . . .

From the foregoing, it would appear that we would be building up for ourselves an enormous annual military budget which would be steadily augmented. This however is apparent, not real. Our men while in training should not receive pay, any more than our school children should be paid for attending the public schools. They should not be put to any expense, but neither should they be rewarded.

A complete plan for universal service would involve much more space than is available at present. All that is now attempted is to put forth a basic plan for universal training, a plan which is sound and is known to be sound since it is supported by the weight of the experience of all the Powers—including ourselves—in the Great War.

TRAINING FOR AMERICA'S FUTURE [9]

We are witnessing one of the great convulsions of history, such as man has endured every century or so in the past. No man can tell how it will end. But for some time to come Americans will know what it is to live dangerously, as our ancestors used to do.

We need clear thinking and firm decision. We have made a beginning by appropriating some billions of dollars to produce new weapons. But weapons alone are not enough. It would be folly to overlook the brilliant skill with which the Germans handle their equipment. Thorough training is the greatest of their "secret weapons." Americans must now decide how we are to train the skilled men to handle our new weapons of defense.

The apparatus of the modern army includes most of the apparatus of modern life: telephone and radio, photography and light, planes and motors, transport, communication, and repair.

Consequently, young men cannot be given effective military training without also being trained in useful civilian skills. Some picture military training in terms of the cantonments of 1917-18. Although, of course, the men would always have to live as soldiers, training today is a very different matter. Part of it will be in the shops where the mechanical equipment is made and repaired. We can enlist the cooperation of the entire industry of the United States in supplying training facilities.

[9] By Senator Henry Cabot Lodge, Jr., of Massachusetts. From "Every Boy a Soldier." *American Magazine*. 130:16-17. September 1940. Reprinted by permission.

Germany was favored by the fact that she was the most mechanically minded nation in Europe. America starts with more general mechanical knowledge than Germany ever had; our problem is to apply a sufficiency of this to military science.

For some time I had been thinking along these lines.

In May, while the Germans slashed swiftly through the supposedly impregnable defense lines in northern France, I was serving as a reserve officer in our Regular Army maneuvers in Louisiana. What I saw there, excellent but tiny against the European background, made me realize the imperative need for an expansion of our army so that it would be large enough to make a major effort immediately—without the tragic and paralyzing delays which so impeded the Allies.

An expansion of the army raises the problem of industrial mobilization so that the weapons may be produced. It also raises the question of procuring the manpower to furnish the needed increase. Some suggested that the increase should be obtained by voluntary enlistment—from many standpoints a desirable method, if it will bring results and bring them fast enough. Others suggested militarizing the CCC: it seemed to me that to this there were many objections, the gravest of which was that it would single out boys for combat service simply because they were in moderate circumstances financially.

A far better system, more democratic and more efficient, would be a system of universal military training. To me this was the preferable plan, and I believe I was the first in this Congress to urge it. What I have in mind is quite distinct from a draft to enlarge the Regular Army, or even to train men of all ages for the immediate emergency, necessary as this is today. It is, rather, a long range plan of peacetime military training; a preparation of youth for the new world we are living in. I would like to explain my reasons, because such a measure would defeat its own purpose in America unless it had the general consent of the people.

In my opinion the time has come when every able-bodied young man, "rich, poor, and middling," should be trained to aid in the defense of the country.

I consider this an obvious necessity for the national safety. I believe, from my own experience, that it will be a definite benefit to the young men themselves. And I am convinced that, properly administered, it will nourish the spirit, health, and comradeship of our democratic American institutions. Discipline which we freely impose upon ourselves is the opposite of, and the best protection against, a dictatorial or Fascist discipline imposed from outside or above.

First, as to the military necessity. Since the World War our Regular Army has stressed quality rather than quantity. It has been a laboratory for the development of military science. It has kept abreast of military knowledge. The method of the "blitzkrieg" was pretty accurately forecast to me by American officers as far back as 1933, when I was serving a tour of duty with the mechanized brigade at Fort Knox—though I think the scale and precision of it has startled us all.

The idea was that this small but expert army could be rapidly expanded, in case of war, so that in three months we would have a protective force adequate to repel any attack.

Three months—that seemed pretty fast. Now it seems absurdly slow. A masked, modern, surprise attack on some remote coast of our continent may not give us three months', or three weeks', or three days', or three hours' notice. Our Regular Army, much larger than now, must be ready to roll with a speed comparable to that of a fire company answering a five-bell alarm. Part of this army will be ready to move by great transport planes, carrying along not only artillery, anti-aircraft, and supplies, but even light tanks.

Back of the ever-poised Regular Army, however, we must have a citizen army and reserves, trained in all the hard and complex skills which the new war of machines demands.

It is for this supporting army and reserve that we must resort to the training which only universal service can supply. That training should be given, in my opinion, between the ages of 18 and 19. Some may feel that this is too tender an age for the severe arts of the soldier. But that is the age when a youngster is best adapted to the physical and athletic training required. It is a time when, usually, he has not settled down to regular work, and so his life trade or profession is not interrupted. It is a period when he most easily learns difficult mechanical skills—skills, incidentally, which may be of great value to him in earning his living. And he is young enough to take a certain sporting pride and pleasure in the hardships which go with military training. Those who go to West Point and Annapolis generally begin their strenuous training at 18.

It is estimated that slightly over a million boys reach the age of 18 during each year. Of these, perhaps six or eight hundred thousand would measure up to the standards of physical fitness for training. Each boy would be given, so far as possible, a choice of the service he desired, whether in aviation or in mechanized divisions, the Navy or Marine Corps; whether in photography or radio or motor repair; whether as a pilot, driver, or mechanic.

As I say, I think the conservation work of the CCC should be separate from military training. Boys could serve in the CCC before age 18 or after age 19.

Some who want universal training consider it "a dreadful necessity." I do not see it so. A necessity, yes. But for one who loves his country it is honorable to spend a year in training for its defense. In recent years all of us in America, talking about our rights, have tended to forget the duties which accompany and make those rights possible.

Even if the country were in no danger of attack, I would consider general military training valuable to the individual and to the nation.

During the last eleven years that I have served in the army maneuvers, I have noticed the steadily rising requirements in individual initiative, judgment, and technical skill, among officers as well as the enlisted men.

For example, when tanks are released for their mission, they almost immediately get out of the close control of the regimental commander. Every tank is an independent unit, commanded by a sergeant, a corporal, or even a private, who goes on to achieve his mission as best he can. These tank commanders must acquire a sense of generalship and a full understanding of the military objective, yet they are enlisted men.

In the mechanized regiment with which I served, every man, whether a driver or mechanic or radioman, must know the intricate mechanics of at least four weapons.

During the recent maneuvers I saw young men sitting under the trees in Louisiana forests doing trigonometry and logarithms to calculate the location of "enemy" artillery. These men were not college graduates nor commissioned officers. They were enlisted men.

Following a torrential downpour of rain in Louisiana, our mechanized brigade found lowlands turned into soupy bogs. I saw a force of men, in two hours, throw a bridge across these bogs which safely carried the rumbling 10-ton tanks. The bridge was built by enlisted men. . . .

I saw the complex and specialized engine of a tank completely disemboweled; and there, in a little clearing under a pine tree, an operation was performed on it which in our civilian life is done only in a factory. This was done by enlisted men.

Those are just a few examples. But they show the variety of skills required.

Not long ago, in the *American Magazine,* Mr. William Knudsen wrote that if he were a youngster again he would be a mechanic. He pointed out that, even if a man were later to work at a desk or a profession, an early training in skilled manual work was a valuable contribution to rounded character and straight thinking. A year of the new kind of military training would give somewhat of a foundation to most young men.

Apart from mechanical skills, proper military training will give schooling in neatness, alertness, discipline, sanitation, and self-care, first-aid to self and others, efficient working habits, administrative direction of troop or company, and most importantly, the development of a rugged physique.

In the old days military training was too often a matter of dreary drilling in barrack towns, "spit and shine," boredom, repetition, and a good deal of loafing. Such training is useless today.

We still need a certain amount of drill, of course. But the emphasis now is on speed and movement. We don't want a "standing army," but a rolling, flying, striking army. That means a great deal more time devoted to maneuver, to large-scale work over open country. Too many of us know only the concrete highways. The boys must learn the character of the fields and forests and rivers of this country we are to defend.

They must know not only the iron "innards" of their tank, mobile howitzer, or armored car, but how it will behave in mountains, in tidewater sand, in canebrakes; in sleet, blizzards, and steaming summer heat. If European troops can fight from Mediterranean shores to the arctic cliffs back of Narvik, ours must be ready from Alaska to the Panama Canal.

Or perhaps we should amend that to "from Greenland's icy mountains to West Indies' coral strand." And right here I think we ought to make it clear that we are not training these boys to fight in Europe. It should be our declared national policy that we are to defend this continent and its essential outposts; to make that defense so strong that no successful attack on us will be possible.

The better we do this training job, the less likely it is that we shall have to fight. If we don't do it, and attack comes, it may be a long and bloody business to repel it, with hundreds of thousands of our youth going bravely to the slaughter which poor training invites.

But what, it may be asked, will this universal training do to our democratic way of life? Will it lead us down the road to fascism, to totalitarianism? To my mind it will have the contrary effect.

In the first place, there is no contradiction between preparedness and democracy. The very men who founded our republic were trained to gun and saddle. Their marksmanship, physical endurance, and knowledge of the country were superb.

Military training, properly conducted, would not hurt our democracy. Rather it would knit and strengthen it. In the last twenty years there have been rifts and cleavages of spirit. Class has been set against class. Farm and city have grown suspicious of each other.

Now, of course, military training won't *cure* all that. But at least it will bring all our young men together in a common purpose on which all are agreed—defense. It will get this country, all classes and sections, acquainted with itself again.

It was not until I had my military training, working under difficulty and hardship with men of every background, that I really appreciated the texture and quality of our people. That meant a lot to me, and made me proud, and I think every youngster should have that experience and privilege.

If this training is to be a democratic process there must be no loopholes by which youngsters with money or pull can escape their year of duty. All who are physically qualified must serve, whether Pop is a sharecropper, a corporation magnate, a WPA worker, or President of the United States. And serve under the same conditions, without any special privileges or luxuries.

The creation of such a system of training will not be cheap or easy. It will take fairness, constructive imagination, and good will if we are to make this a vital force for the health as well as the defense of our country.

Thus defended we can proceed, with good heart and without foreign interruption, to make this country, in all its freedom and variety, an even better place to live in for all its citizens.

UNIVERSAL TRAINING AND PREPAREDNESS [10]

The first object of a rational military policy is to establish security against invasion. That object of itself may demand universal military training in countries whose geographical position exposes them to sudden hostile incursions. Switzerland and Belgium are cases in point. France, Germany, Poland, Russia are all in this position. England is not in such a position; she never had universal training, and in spite of her war experiences, refuses to provide for it in the future. Neither is Japan, and if she maintains universal military training, it is for the sake of having large armies for use on the Asiatic continent. Least of all is the United States exposed to invasion. Before the war there were hair-raising warnings in circulation of the dangers of a sudden hostile landing on our coast. But the Gallipoli fiasco exhibited the difficulties of invasion from a sea base. As for an invasion through Mexico, what vital point could a hostile power strike, even if it could operate over a desert communication line of a thousand miles? Invasion by way of Canada would imply that England had fallen into the hands of madmen ready to risk the complete dissolution of the Empire. We are not secure by geography against the shelling of our ports or against attacks even inland by aircraft. But these are dangers that will not be warded off by men trained through six months to the use of arms and to habits of discipline, but by the rigorously pro-

[10] From "Universal Training and Preparedness." *New Republic.* 22:70-2. March 17, 1920. Reprinted by permission.

fessional forces of the navy, the coast defence and the air service.

If we need such vast armies as universal training would provide us with, it must be, as in the late war, for service on other continents. But where do we find, at present, or where can we contemplate in the near future a hostile force which might require the use of millions of American soldiers? . . .

We can see no need, within ten years at least, for such masses of men as universal service would provide. We see a real need for an efficient navy, for a large and thoroughly trained and equipped air service, for a regular army large enough to furnish effective contingents for service abroad if our statecraft commits us in any measure to the maintenance of the present status of Europe . . . if we adopt universal military training, it must be for the sake of preparedness against contingencies lying beyond the next decade.

But even so, it is often argued, military training would be worthwhile. Train the present generation, who will not have a chance to fight, and it is more certain that the next generation, who may have to fight, will be trained. There is force in this argument. Effective preparation for war requires long antecedent preparations, if only in the matter of creating a tradition of discipline and command. Yes, but are there not other directions in which antecedent preparations are yet more imperative? We shall not, as a nation, specialize ourselves to war. We shall not spend unlimited money and energy on preparing for war. It behooves us then to spend most freely where the longest antecedent preparations are required.

Now, whatever may be said of the insufficient training of our officers and men in the late war, that was not our greatest weakness. We had to draw on our Allies for guns, we had to rely on them for the aircraft which we meant to contribute in overwhelming force, but hadn't the time. If we had entered the war early, before our Allies had worked out a superiority of gun power and an air service capable of disputing control with the Germans, and before the submarine problem had been in some measure mastered, we should have paid for that weakness by horrifying casualty lists.

We cannot count, in future, upon finding allies who will make up our deficiences. We ought to fix on the principle that we shall not send an American army anywhere until we can provide it with the guns and aircraft without which an army is led blindfold to the slaughter. Let us not prate over ten million men trained to arms. They belong in the same museum with Mr. Bryan's million men springing to arms between sunrise and sunset, unless they are properly backed by the professional military service which cannot be improvised out of a universally trained manhood, but can only be built up through many years of persistent effort. If we are going to be prepared, let us provide for those services first.

But they are terribly expensive. A hundred million does not go far in the aircraft realm, as most taxpayers now know. That is why Congress is starving this branch of the service. A hundred million soon disappear in the equipment of ordnance plants, in the provision of submarines and antisubmarine craft, in the development of the machinery of chemical warfare. . . . But universal service would cost little, and its incidental benefits would be worth the cost. So its advocates urge.

That, however, is a point worth investigating. What is the minimum cost at which we could give all our young men a respectable course in military training? We take it that nobody supposes that less than four months—few would say less than six—would answer the purpose at all. We take it also that nobody supposes that a brief training period, given once for all, fits a man for soldiering through the ten years of maximum liability for service. Annual or at least biennial periods of intensive drill, extensive maneuvers for the training of both officers and men, would be imperative. . . . Well, one million men six months in barracks, with eventually five million assembled for three or four weeks of drill and maneuvers—what would it cost? Certainly not less than a billion a year. . . .

America could afford to spend a billion dollars a year on universal training if she thereby placed herself in a position to execute properly a well defined, democratically approved international policy. She has no such policy, as yet; when she has one, she will need far fewer soldiers than her aggregate young manhood, and far more highly developed special services than she now has in contemplation. Financially considered, the outlay on universal training would be mainly waste. From the point of view of real preparedness, it would be worse than a waste. If we vote a billion for universal training we are not likely to appropriate adequately for any other part of our preparedness program. We shall repose a fatuous confidence in our ten million trained men, instead of facing the facts squarely and making provision for what we really need when we need it.

THE DEFENSE WE NEED [11]

Congress can appropriate endlessly and still not give us the kind of national defense we need now. The days of great massing of foot soldiers has passed. What we need now is machines and still more machines. Airplanes, tanks, combat cars, anti-aircraft guns, anti-tank guns, rapid-fire rifles, and things of that sort. That is what we need in vast numbers to give us an impregnable national defense system. You do not have to be an expert on military affairs to see that.

Old methods of warfare are so obsolete that it is reliably reported that 60,000 Germans with mechanized equipment overran France's army of more than 2,000,000 men in just a few days. That proved that men are only incidental in modern warfare—it is more machine against machine than it is man against man. . . .

[11] By Congressman Anton J. Johnson of Illinois. *Congressional Record.* Vol. 86. September 3, 1940. p. 17308-9.

We need no such army as conscription will bring.

Wars are no longer fought by masses of men. They are fought by instruments mechanized and motivated by powers other than human.

When Napoleon Bonaparte had finished his course, was on his way to St. Helena, with Elba and Waterloo behind him, with ambition atrophied, with the question of empire turned into dirty rags, with his France a great sepulcher of epauletted marshals and musket-bearing soldiers, it was found that commune after commune had no young or middle-aged men to do the work of rehabilitation. All had been conscripted; most of them had died for the greatness of France and for a burning candle of glory that had died in a flickering flame.

Conscription of men—masses of men who tilled the soil, who went about the daily business of the smith and the shop-keeper—the conscription that had taken the sons from the family and put them in the army of which they knew nothing, had been the strong arm of the despot from the day that power vested in one man had spread blood on the soil of the Eurasian continent.

TRAINING THE DRAFTEE

DISCUSSION

Nothing is more vital to any consideration of universal military training than *"how* shall the draftee be trained?" Numerous suggestions have been offered, and even more possibilities can be found.

For the most part suggestions center around those institutions which we already know: the army cantonment, the school or university, the CCC, the CMTC, and the ROTC, not to mention branches of the Regular Armed Forces.

The army cantonment suggests itself as a likely training point because it is created primarily for that purpose, and because there a trainee can gain more intensified training in a shorter period of time than anywhere else.

However, such a program would be expensive, possibly more so than expanding the CMTC or the ROTC organizations for everyday instruction. Certainly more so than mere instruction in military science in schools and universities, regular classroom work.

The Army itself is possibly the least attractive in that it would be an unstable mixture of professional and amateur soldiers, with the result that the professional soldier would be primarily an instructor. The disastrous consequences of such a program are readily apparent.

Still, some method must be chosen, if compulsory military training becomes a reality. A number of persons, both army men and civilians, have suggested the seemingly logical plan of permitting the trainee to decide for himself both when and where he receives his instruction—with the proviso that he take it as part of his educational training in some high school or college.

Several factors influence the thinking of military leaders along these lines. Among them is the attitude of educators and psychologists throughout the nation. Professor of Educational Psychology S. L. Pressey of Ohio University states in regard to schooling, that studies in the field of retentiveness of the subject matter learned in school show a heavy loss within the first year or two after a subject is studied. Yet the teacher may change this result by increasing the amount of time the student is permitted to participate in that field of learning. But most psychologists will agree that, from the standpoint of future use, knowledge learned under field conditions, in camps, in the CMTC or ROTC summer camps, would prove far more beneficial and more likely to be remembered than mere study of the same principles in the classroom.

That the better educated the trainee is in advance, the more readily he will grasp the fundamentals of military science is the substance of a statement by Professor W. B. Pillsbury of the University of Michigan. He concluded that the man with the best background, with a truly well-rounded training will on the average learn faster and more easily in any field than the man with no training or whose training has been limited to one field alone.

While these statements may be disputed, experts agree that the most useful training is that which is acquired through actual experience. So it is probable that even a short length of time serving in the field will be more beneficial to the trainee than a much longer period devoted to the study of textbooks and military manuals.

A YEAR'S TRAINING PERIOD [1]

It is suggested that we could not train our soldiers in 12 months. In the last World War young men were trained and

---

[1] By Congressman John M. Robison of Kentucky. *Congressional Record,* Appendix. Vol. 87. August 15, 1941. p. A4269.

put into service as officers in 3 months and thousands upon thousands of young Americans were put into the battle line before they had been in the service for as long as 4 months. If we can train and make officers in 3 months we certainly ought to train privates in 12 months. Sergeant York, the great World War hero, had only been in the service a little over 10 months when he performed his great feat of heroism on Flanders field.

After the World War under the Treaty of Versailles, Germany was not permitted to have more than 100,000 men in her army. She had short periods of training. She would train one group for a short period of time and let them out and place them in the reserve and then call in another group, and in this way Hitler did much to build up his mighty war machine. If we train 900,000 each year and let them out and place them in the reserve and then call in another group we would have a great reserve force of trained men in this country able to defend this nation in case we were attacked. No good reason has been offered or can be offered for keeping one group of young men in for 2½ years or longer. If a young man is so inept that he cannot receive all the training necessary to become a good soldier in 12 months he should be turned out because of his lack of aptitude for training and get somebody in his place who has the intelligence and aptitude to make a good soldier.

THOROUGH TRAINING NEEDED [2]

There is also another factor of utmost importance that we must consider. Modern armies must be technical as no army before has been. It is necessary that soldiers have complete familiarity with tanks, new types of armored cars, new types

[2] By Congressman William H. Larrabee of Indiana. *Congressional Record.* Vol. 87. July 24, 1941. p. A3821.

of guns; some of them such as anti-aircraft guns and long-range field rifles requiring the highest degree of skill to operate—a skill that is not easily developed in a year of training, especially when it has been difficult to obtain implements and materials as quickly as they should have been placed at the disposal of the Army officials.

Coupled with training in the skill of operating these defense machines is the requirement of skill in mobility—the skill to move the machines quickly from one field of operation to another. . . . Our defenders . . . must be skilled in moving at a pace that no other army has ever moved.

We are told, and the information comes from those best qualified to know, that we need an army, skilled in these defense tactics, of about 1,000,000 men. . . .

To the highly skilled army of 1,000,000, we are best advised, we should have another 2,000,000 trained men that could be called in for grave emergency, to repel an actual attack or invasion attempt, should such arise.

Those opposing a large army say that Hitler conquered France with about 12 panzer units comprising some 200,000 men supported by some 3000 pilots of attack planes and dive-bombers. That may all be true, but at the same time many thousands of other men were in constant training, or were on guard at other borders. Hitler had no such expanse of land as that of the United States to guard, and it is also known that he managed to rotate his troops, replacing the worn and injured men at the front at intervals with well-trained, fresh troops quickly transferred from quiet guard spots on other borders.

We will do well to learn our lesson in modern warfare from those who have been successfully prosecuting modern war abroad and be so prepared that aggressors will have no desire to attempt to lodge an attack upon us.

EDUCATION AND UNIVERSAL TRAINING [3]

Hitler has compelled us to adopt universal military service. Universal military service gives us a chance to reorganize our program of universal free education. That program has needed reorganization for 50 years. If we are at last driven to it, Hitler will have been, within very narrow limits, a blessing in disguise. . . .

This reorganization is urgent whether or not we have universal military service. With conscription, which we must assume will be with us for a long time, some sort of reorganization of the school system is imperative. When both education and military service are compulsory for the young, they must be adjusted to each other. From the educational point of view the present minimum draft age of twenty-one is just precisely wrong. The student should be drafted at some natural break in his educational career. That is at the end of his sophomore year, at graduation from the junior college. This is the time for him to do his military stint. When he has completed it, he may, if he is qualified, enter upon university work. If he is not qualified, he should go to work.

College students should not be deferred because they are college students. But the draft age should be lowered and enough flexibility introduced into the system to permit the student to serve his country in the armed forces without damage to his preparation for the other duties of citizenship. Nobody can accuse Mayor La Guardia of indifference to the military needs of the country. But early in May he said, "It must be remembered that in addition to military training the country requires the training of its youth in sciences, the professions, the arts, and industry. The army needs not only soldiers but also a large officer corps now and in the future. Educated men are needed by the country even though we are in an

[3] By Robert Maynard Hutchins, President of the University of Chicago. From "Conscription and Education." *Liberty*. 18:20-1. August 23, 1941. Reprinted by permission.

emergency of training or may be confronted with a more serious emergency. In either event, our country, our customs, our cultural life must continue. . . . There is no need to interrupt education. Irreparable damage is being done at this very moment by taking young men who would have entered colleges, and by interrupting the college courses of other young men who might never again have an opportunity to continue their studies. That is not only unnecessary but cruel and destructive."

In view of the variations in the ages at which students reach the end of the sophomore year, the individual should be permitted to take his year of service at any age between eighteen and twenty-two, inclusive. It can be provided that he must in no event enter upon military service later than the end of his sophomore year, or he may choose his own time, in which case he would be well advised to choose the end of his sophomore year.

MILITARY SERVICE AS EDUCATION [4]

It is our American habit if we find the foundations of our educational structure unsatisfactory to add another story or a wing. We find it easier to add a new study or course or kind of school than to reorganize existing conditions so as to meet the need. Manual training schools, trade schools, vocational schools and courses, now pre-vocational schools—and next year perhaps pre-pre-vocational and post-vocational—testify how we manage when it is seen that our system does not conform to the demands of present life. Just now we have discovered new defects and are having another addition to our educational scheme urged upon us. The defects are that our educational measures do not assimilate the foreign born and that they do not develop public-mindedness, a sense of public service and responsibility. Some persons might think that the remedy is to

[4] By John Dewey, professor of Psychology, Columbia University. From "Universal Service as Education." *New Republic.* 6:309-10. April 22, 1916. Reprinted by permission.

improve our existing educational agencies and to make our existing public institutions—including government—more serviceable to the people so that they would arouse greater devotion. But no: let everything else be as it is, and let us add a new agency devised *ad hoc*. Let us have the school of universal and compulsory military service, and the trick is done.

It is a pleasure to acknowledge that there is an awakening to the presence in our country of large immigrant masses who may remain as much aliens as if they never entered our gateways. It is questionable, however, if there is much gain in passing at one bound from seeing nothing to seeing red. Having formerly lulled ourselves to sleep with the word "melting-pot" we have now turned to the word "hyphenate" as denoting the last thing in scares with a thrill. Casting about for some magic, universal military service is to replace the schoolhouse as the melting and brewing pot. In the words of Major General Wood,

> Great portions of our population develop in racial areas, reading a dialect press and controlled in the intervening years by dialect interests. Some sort of community of service must be established in order to develop a proper and necessary appreciation of the duties and obligations of American citizenship. I believe that the best method is by some sort of a systematized military training of a universal character.

Is it then axiomatic that nothing socializes the mind and enables it to think in public terms so much as a service rendered under military auspices, with the accustomed environment of military paraphernalia and by the traditional rules of military command and obedience?

A speech of Major General Wood as reported in a Philadelphia newspaper puts the matter more vividly. "It is a pretty dangerous situation to turn loose in this country all kinds of humanity seen on the docks at Ellis Island, to turn them loose with no sense of responsibility to their new land. They come in racial groups, drift through our schools in racial groups and are controlled by a dialect press. We are doing absolutely nothing to make these people understand that they are Americans, at least in the making." Then with swift intuition comes the remedy. "There is nothing like compulsory military service to accomplish this." I will not ask how much of the ignorance, and how much of the snobbery of those who, having been longer in the country, look with contempt and suspicion upon newcomers there may be in this view, though I suspect that it is safer to idealize with Mary Antin's *Promised Land* than it is to take after-dinner long-distance surveys of Ellis Island hordes. I will not even inquire whether inter-racialism is not a truer definition of America than that provided by even the most cultivated New England provincialism, or whether the melting-pot metaphor is not itself traitorous to the American ideal. It is enough that there is a genuine intellectual and moral problem in connection with the heterogeneously diversified factors of our population.

But the problem is not to reduce them to an anonymous and drilled homogeneity, but to see to it that all get from one another the best that each strain has to offer from its own tradition and culture. If authentic America is not to be a cross-fertilization of our various strains, it had better be a juxtaposition of alien elements than an amalgam of the barracks, an amalgam whose uniformity would hardly go deeper than the uniforms of the soldiers. Admit everything which can be said in favor of the European system of military service, admit that we ought to turn from our previous wholesale glorification, and there is yet something childishly undisciplined in supposing that we could reduplicate its merits by establishing compulsory system on American soil. We forget how largely its efficacy there is due to the prior existence of just the uniformity of tradition and outlook whose absence is the reason urged in support of it here. We forget how real and how constant in the mind of every continental European is the sense of an enemy just over the border, and how largely the sense of cohesion is a common sense of enmity. Shall we deliberately proceed to cultivate a sense of the danger of aggression, shall we conjure up enemies, in order to get this stimulus to unity among ourselves? The tendency of the upholders of the plan of enforced universal service to resort to this appeal, unconsciously gives away their case. To stir up fear and dislike of home countries as a means of securing love of an adopted country does not seem a promising procedure.

But it is not necessary to bring accusations against the policy of military service. The real point is that we find it so much easier to cry up this policy than to remedy those defects in our existing system which produce the evils in question. Any truly educative system must precede and prevent instead of following after and palliating and undoing. Until we have at least made a beginning in nationalizing our system of education, it is premature to appeal to the army, to marching and to sleeping on barrack cots as the best way to remedy the evils of a lack of national mindedness. When Mr. Lippmann suggested nationalizing our means of transportation and communication as a method of securing an integrated and coherent America, some of his critics intimated that his project was too materialistic. Well, the district schoolhouse of some portions of the United States—often those very portions which most deplore the foreign invasion—with its independent district control is a symptom of a spiritual localism which defies a unified America quite as much as does any racial area and dialect press. We might at least try the experiment of making our Federal Bureau of Education at Washington something more than a bookkeeping and essay-writing department before we conclude that military service is the only way of effecting a common mind. When Mr. Roosevelt writes with as much vehemence about national aid to vocational education, national aid to wipe out illiteracy, and national aid for evening and continuation schools for our immigrants, as he now writes in behalf of military service, I for one shall take him more seriously as an authority on the educa-

tional advantages of setting-up exercises, firing guns and living
in the camp.

I can see a vision of a national government which takes an
interest at once paternal and scientific in our alien visitors,
which has a definite policy about their reception, and about
their distribution, which guards them more jealously than its
own sons against industrial exploitation, and which offers them
at every turn educational facilities under its own charge. If
every foreign illiterate had compulsory educational service to
perform, if he had not only the opportunity but the obligation
to learn the English language, if he found conditions of labor
safeguarded in the interest of his health and his integrity as an
economic agent, and if he learned to associate these things in
whatever part of the country he found himself with the United
States and not with the district, township or state, it would not
be long before compulsory service, if it had to be discussed at
all, would be discussed as a military proposition and not as an
educational one. Until we have developed an independent and
integral educational policy, the tendency to assume that military
service will be an efficient tool of public education indicates
a deplorable self-deception. I sometimes think the worst of the
evils connected with militarism, in fact and in idea, is its power
to create such illusions. Military service is the remedy of despair—despair of the power of intelligence.

TRAINING FOR PEACE [5]

Once more a large conscripted army will be summoned for
training. What form is that training to take? We can, of course,
do the usual thing. We can call these young men together, teach
them the workings of certain instruments of destruction, and send
them home again—a year older, and of no greater value to peace-

[5] By John Erskine, professor of English at Columbia University, wartime chairman of the Army Education Commission. From "Train Conscripts for War—and
for Peace." *Educational Record*. 21:441-4. October, 1940. Reprinted by permission.

time society than they were before.   Fortunately there is a proved and workable alternative.

After the Armistice in the last war, while our troops were waiting in France for transportation home, the Army inaugurated a huge educational program, with its own schools, extension courses, and even an Army University.   The purpose was not only to keep the men occupied but to prepare them for jobs when they returned.   The result gave us a wholly new conception of what national training can mean.

In that vast experiment each man had complete liberty to select his studies.   Subjects ranged from automobile repairing to Greek grammar, from sign painting to dentistry. . . .   These educational opportunities . . . were purely voluntary; and yet they proved so popular that the peak found three-fourths of the Army's two million men enrolled.

Mobilization had revealed that such training was a basic need. An appalling number of our young men were not in proper physical condition.   Far more than half the men of the A.E.F. were without adequate training for any trade or profession.   An astounding number of native-born citizens were illiterate; many foreign-born Americans could not read, write, or in some cases even understand, the English language.

The Army showed that these national weaknesses could be corrected.   It showed how rich potentially the manhood of our nation is, and how quickly it responds to regular life and scientific care.   The soldiers in general enjoyed such health as is the rule in no other community.   The total discipline of their life —regular hours, rational diet, and decorum of conduct—so quickened their intellectual capacities that those who taught them wondered at their eagerness and ability to learn. . . .

Everything the Army taught in its improvised schools was useful to the soldier, but twenty times as useful to the citizen.

When we came home we brought with us a vision of adapting this new kind of national training to peacetime needs. But in the years that followed our plans fell on deaf ears.

Now once again the world is in turmoil. Once again we are preparing to mobilize our young men. Those of us who remember the lessons of the last war hope our people will compel, this time, a true national training, training for peace as well as for war. Certainly there is no reason to suppose that the need for such broadened training is less today than it was twenty years ago. Indeed, it appears far greater.

The A.E.F. demonstrated the Army's value as a vast university of citizenship. Let us utilize now what we discovered then. If the compulsory training period is to be twelve months, the first half of that year should be given over to military science and physical development; for the remainder of the time, at least half the day should be free for general study. In establishing the curriculum it is absolutely essential that each man . . . be allowed complete liberty to select the subjects he believes would be most useful to him. To dictate what shall be studied would be to defeat the broader purposes of the program. If a man looks forward to business, to agriculture, to industry, to art, then his training should help him toward that career. If he expects to attend college, the training should take the place of his freshman year.

The practical studies in trades or professions, offered under army discipline, would teach habits of application at the moment when young men most need to learn them. The average student in college not only wastes the greater part of his time, but is extremely careless in his diet and is far below the proper physical state. Army life provides for every soldier a finer system of physical training than even athletes in college usually submit themselves to.

The most direct advantage in such a plan would be for the neglected majority who at present receive no high school training at all, nor even much elementary education. To insure for them a reasonable start in life would be worth any cost and any effort. In no other way can this vast body of each generation be sought out in the small town, on the farm, in the overcrowded city, and taught the things necessary to each individual case. To care for these young men would be really to train our nation.

I wish every boy in the country could have this year of training just after high school age. What a great opportunity for all our boys to meet for one year on terms of absolute democracy! I should like to see the young conservative bunking in with the young radical. Whatever became of their theories later, they would know each other as human beings. I should like the boys from one section of the country to do their year of service in another section.

Today the illiterate keeps to himself, and the foreign born associates with others of his origin. Both classes thus avoid that social criticism which would urge them toward complete citizenship. Economic and social pressure tends actually to segregate them. Unless some strenuous effort is made to weld these groups into the rest of the country, there is no likelihood of change.

A system of national training which would develop latent powers of the individual would shortly transform our national life. It would be costly, but no more so than our handouts to relieve the unemployed, part of whose trouble comes from our failure to give them in the first place a suitable education. . . .

Under the stimulus of national danger, we must look forward to new horizons of national advancement. We must bring men together for training in the *total* defense of their homes—against possible enemies on sea or land, and against disease, ignorance, and incompetency. Such an effort would not only make us invincible in war, but would immeasurably strengthen and enrich our nation in peace. It is the great opportunity of our generation. We must not let it pass.

THE ARMY GOES TO SCHOOL [6]

When the first raw conscript soldiers drifted in last fall at Fort Jackson, S. C., Major General Henry D. Russell, in com-

[6] From "Education: The Army Goes to School." *Time*. 37:69. May 19, 1941. Reprinted by permission.

mand of the post, was appalled at the number of them who could neither read nor write. Before long he had on his hands some 600 total illiterates. General Russell got in touch with WPA. Result: At Fort Jackson last week elementary classes, taught by WPA teachers, were going full blast, and an Army education program had spread from coast to coast.

In World War I, 25.3 per cent of the first 1,500,000 U. S. citizens examined for the Army were illiterate. The average soldier had only half completed the seventh grade of grammar school. No figures were available last week on the number of illiterates in the draft, but the average soldier has finished his third year of high school.

But modern armies require a much better-educated personnel than was needed in 1917, and there are still too many igno-ramuses in uniform to suit Army leaders. So WPA, which has taught some 2,000,000 illiterate citizens to read and write in the past six years, last week had 82 teachers on the rolls in 16 Army camps. Some of their activities:

WPA has published an elementary textbook, *First Days in the Army,* for soldiers learning their ABC's. . . .

Candidates for appointment as flying cadets (who must have the equivalent of two years of college credits) learn algebra, trigonometry, history and other academic subjects at a number of Air Corps bases.

At Fort Des Moines, Iowa, non-commissioned officers study shorthand.

Ohio's National Guardsmen are taught to read maps.

All commissioned officers in the Air Corps (about 10,000 men) have signed up to learn Spanish. . . .

At four defense bases in Puerto Rico classes in English have been started for island recruits.

Classes are usually held in mess halls or recreation buildings. But at several Southern posts, including the Savannah, Georgia, air base, soldiers assemble at night for instruction at local high schools which by day are filled with giggling girls with socks and sweaters.

THE VALUE OF MILITARY TRAINING [7]

Half the boys of the 1939 graduating class at New Hanover High School, Wilmington, North Carolina, had taken two years of military training. They were compared with the other half who had not taken any military training. In general, and so far as observed, military training attracted a superior group of boys; offered no interference with their more rapid development along mental lines; and afforded definite stimulation to extrovert adaptation, participation, and conformity.

If the experience reported herein is confirmed by other studies, the conclusion may be justified that a limited amount of R.O.T.C. work accomplishes what military men have claimed for it and what certain others have frequently questioned. Military leaders have asserted that a certain amount of discipline is good for youths; certain other people have deplored strict discipline, arguing that it destroys initiative and warps personality development. The experience in the present case supports the military view and is contrary to the latter view.

A general hypothesis is suggested: Drill in specific compliance with formulated requirements, in certain restricted areas of life, and for a limited portion of time in any day or week, may be a wholesome element in a person's development and possibly in his mature life.

SCHOOL MILITARY TRAINING [8]

. . . Several study commissions and survey groups have published reports during the past twenty-five years which show the extent to which military preparedness claims usually made for school military training are and must be discounted when they are subjected to careful scrutiny. In 1915 a Massachusetts State

[7] By Douglas E. Scates, Duke University, and Dale K. Spencer, Bradley Creek Elementary School, Wilmington, North Carolina. From "Retroactive Experiment on Effects of Military Training in High School." *The School Review.* 49:205. March, 1941. Reprinted by permission.

[8] By Edwin C. Johnson, secretary, Committee on Militarism in Education. From "School Military Training Reconsidered." *School and Society.* 51:261-4, 267-8. March 2, 1940. Reprinted by permission.

Commission on military training, three of the nine members of which held high military commissions, incorporated the following pronouncement in its report:

It is generally agreed that the military drill which a boy receives in school is of little or no advantage to him from the point of view of practical soldiering.

A similar suggestion found expression in the report of the Sacramento, California, School Survey, published in 1928, as the following indicates:

There are even grounds for debating whether close-order drill is the best type of military preparation. With the changing character of warfare so recently manifested, one might successfully maintain that physics, chemistry and mathematics are superior as military preparation to close-order drill for upper grade high school boys.

And in the report of the Chicago School Survey, published in 1932, the following finding is stated:

It is very difficult to show how the Junior Reserve Officers' Training Corps makes any significant contribution to national defense.

More recently a committee of community leaders, which had opportunity to formulate a report on proposed drill units for the public high schools of Flint, Michigan, came to the conclusion that the alleged objective of military preparedness is not realized in high school drill because the training involves "obsolute, rather than modern, methods," and because it deals "with an age group which is incapable of absorbing the complex, technical details of modern warfare." The committee's report declared:

Parade-ground formation, platoon movements and squad drills are, from the standpoint of modern warfare, about as practical as a study of the science of slingshots.

As if conceding the soundness of the above conclusions, some people will respond with the contention that secondary school military drill is maintained without any intention of training professional soldiers, and that such military values as it may have are an indirect rather than a direct achievement. The chief military value of the drill, they say, is psychological; rather than producing a complete and well-trained soldier, it merely gives the pupil a bent in that direction; it merely provides a psychological climate—a state of mind—favorable to the development of future soldiers. . . .

In summary, the record clearly indicates that neither the military nor the non-military justifications popularly made for school military training are new or novel in American experience. They have been advanced often and urgently enough in the past to have caused many competent leaders to appraise their merits. In short, it appears that the weight of informed opinion, especially as it is reflected in the published findings and reports of such commissions and survey groups as have been referred to, contradicts most of the claims advanced by the proponents of school military training. The plain fact is that the evidence available for supporting school military drill in terms of its contribution to national defense is both scanty and of highly dubious quality. That available for its support in terms of educational or nonmilitary considerations is even less extensive and certainly less sound in quality. Need more be shown to demonstrate the validity, even in 1939, of the position to which the federation committed itself ten years ago?

THE HIGH SCHOOL AND DEFENSE [9]

Without giving the matter much thought the average citizen associates our expanding national defense with a vivid image of close-order drill or of men marching in military formations. Naturally, we think that to prepare for home defense is to shoulder arms.

[9] By Calvin P. Stone, professor of Psychology, Stanford University. From "The Role of the High School Curriculum in National Preparedness." *School and Society.* 52:366-7. October 19, 1940. Reprinted by permission.

This idea is not entirely wrong, for soldiers, aviators and sailors are among the more obvious features of national preparedness. Nevertheless, the idea is wholly inadequate because it fails to embrace the thousands of essential activities of a nation that must precede and accompany the training of a soldier, aviator and sailor if these instrumentalities of national defense are to be of any consequence whatever in defending the homeland. Moreover, it is an idea that may give rise to no end of fuzzy thinking with respect to educational policies in our high schools during the present year throughout the United States.

Strong pressure is certain to be exerted on school boards to install cadet training in the high schools, giving various pretexts such as: The community should do this for the sake of national preparedness; it will give the boys a feeling of pride and worthiness to wear military uniforms; it will make them straight and strong; it will arouse and nurture a feeling of patriotism which today is absent; and, above all, it will instill much needed "discipline" in a "cocky" generation of young kids, softened by educational pampering and exemption from the toil that made the parent generation what it is today!

The foregoing pretexts have little to commend themselves to a board of education. The military training required in modern warfare is highly technical in nearly all of its aspects and does not stem from the "About face! Squads right!" type of cadet training so prominent (and so useless for most people) in high schools during 1917-1919. That cadet uniforms may give to many high school students a peculiar feeling of pride and to a few, even, a vicarious sense of worthiness is not improbable. Such experiences were achieved by Hitler's youths who donned the brown shirts and swastika arm bands. Needless to say, we should be playing to a human frailty which requires no nurturing beyond that already afforded by band costumes, athletic suits, "making the team" and class numerals. As for making boys straight and healthy, cadet training is entirely superfluous. We have prescribed and elective programs of physical education and hygiene in the modern high school to serve these functions. Correction of omissions and abuses in these programs may be needed. If so, the necessary steps should be taken now, as strength and good health are highly relevant in preparing high school students for the multiplicity of services required by their country in time of peace and war. If we do not expect military officers to be experts in physical education and hygiene, we shall not be disappointed. As for the last two pretexts, namely, developing patriotism and "disciplining" the high school lads, it is my confirmed opinion, based on twenty-five months of army service, that we are concerned here only with pious hopes for which there is not a jot of evidence favoring their being realized. Land grant colleges have had military training for sixty years, but that training did not make students patriotic. Patriotism, in the broadest meaning of the term, ofttimes causes men voluntarily to undergo military training; but there is no evidence that patriotism grows out of that training. If by "discipline" is meant merely the suppression of the jaunty self-assurance that characterizes a few of our high school lads, the curtailment of independent thinking and self-reliance which both parents and teachers nowadays try to inculcate in children, in short, a kind of goose-stepping, I am convinced that the majority of parents in the United States do not want it at the high school level of education. Even if they did, cadet training would not give it, for the kind of discipline there provided has little spread to other life situations. This conception of formal discipline belongs to Spanish-American War ways of thinking.

In rejecting cadet training for the high schools as a relatively futile and even wasteful gesture in national preparedness, school administrators should not at the same time close their minds to the urgency of revitalizing those parts of the established curriculum which are believed to fit young men for national service in times both of peace and of war. Preparation for, and conduct of, war today utilizes technically trained men and women to an extent never before experienced by nations. There will not be enough technically trained civilians to fill the jobs awaiting, consequently intensive short courses will be required in many centers to correct this condition. These pertain to national defense trades and occupations as well as to the specialized training needed for aircraft mechanics, machinists, auto mechanics, sheet-metal workers, welders and the like. What better kind of training can be given high school students who face this eventuality than that already provided by proper courses in English, mathematics, modern languages, drafting, biology and the physical sciences, and by diverse vocational courses, including agriculture? With the best training obtainable in these subjects the high school graduates who seek employment may be ready to step into places in their communities vacated by those of mature age who have already entered war industries or are called for conscript training. Moreover, this kind of training has the advantage of serving lifetime pursuits as well as those of war, and can be achieved without submitting the impressionable children of the public schools to the omnipresent specter of peacetime military training. Let the school boards hew to the line in peacetime!

A CONSTRUCTIVE TRAINING PROGRAM [10]

No problem now before the United States is more important than the question of national education. . . . We find ourselves facing a special problem of training for national defense. . . .

The principles according to which we would envisage such national training are five. In the first place, the idea of universal service should be expanded so as to include training for all other duties of citizenship besides military and to include training of all prospective citizens, even of those physically unfit for military service. In the second place, the present temporary

[10] By John Erskine, chairman of the Army Educational Committee of the AEF in 1918-19. From *Universal Training for National Defense*. Pamphlet prepared as a report to General Pershing in 1919 and reprinted by the Civilian Military Education Fund, Washington. 1940. p. 7-8, 13-15. Reprinted by permission.

cantonments in the United States, or equivalent cantonments, should be converted at once into permanent training schools for citizenship. In the third place, a permanent educational corps should be added to the Army. This corps should be formed of the most competent experts in school, in vocational, and in the more elementary college subjects. From time to time competent officers in other branches of Army service should be assigned to this corps. In the fourth place, there should be a compulsory training period of twelve months with the colors, from September 1 to September 1, or from June 1 to June 1, or between any other dates which should be found practical, care being taken simply to fit this period into other educational or vocational obligations. This period should be begun between the ages approximately of 18 to 20, perhaps a little earlier or a little later, as experience might prove advisable. Approximately one-half of this training should be for military science and for physical development, the other half for training under military discipline in school, in vocational, or in college subjects. In the fifth place, the citizen in training should be free to elect the kind of civil education he receives, with the exception that training in elementary subjects should be compulsory for illiterates and for the foreign born. . . .

Such a system of training as is here suggested would be very expensive. The items of expense would be buildings and their upkeep, their equipment, the teachers who would form the framework of the educational corps, and the cost of providing subsistence for the men in training. . . .

A system of training so organized would have obvious advantages. In a general way each training camp would become an educational center. More specifically, the annual inventory of our educational shortcomings would point out for our school system the task to which it should address itself. . . .

But the most direct advantage would be for the large majority of our young men who at present receive no high school training at all, nor even much elementary education. To insure for them a reasonable start in life would be worth any cost and any effort. In no other way than by national training, undertaken as a national expense, can this vast body of each generation be sought out in the small town, on the farm, in the overcrowded city, and can be taught the things essential to each individual case. To care for this neglected majority would be really to train our nation.

Perhaps the by-product of such a system of training as is here outlined would be the bringing of the Army into a sane relation with society. Through the fear of militarism which possesses the modern world it has become our custom to support the Army and to admire military science only in moments of extreme need. As a result, the soldier in wartime receives an adulation perhaps exaggerated and in peacetime he is neglected, feared, certainly put to no good use. . . . If we could add to the military function of our Army the constructive kind of national defense, we should be providing a noble and honored career for the man on whom in extreme moments the life of the nation depends; we should be bringing the soldier into constant relation with the social needs of the country he serves, and we should be teaching every youth within our borders that large conception of citizenship expressed for the Anglo-Saxon race by John Milton, "I call a complete and general education that which fits a man to perform justly, skillfully, and magnanimously all offices, both private and public, of peace and war."

THE CITIZEN ARMY TOMORROW [11]

The weapons and whole military character of our new citizen army are being shaped by what is happening on European battlefields. After the fall of France last spring, changes were made ranging from the General Staff, at the top, to the infantry

[11] By Jonathan Mitchell, Washington political commentator. From "The Next Four Years: The Citizen Army." *New Republic*, 104:364-6. March 17, 1941. Reprinted by permission.

squad, at the bottom, and fresh changes will doubtless follow the events in Europe of the next few months. But there are two aspects of the new army about which predictions seem possible. One is the impact that it will have on the young men now entering its ranks; the other is the impact it will have on our society.

After the great reforms of Mr. Roosevelt's first two administrations, many liberals, inside and outside the New Deal, believe that the new army ought to be not merely a replica of the socially unplanned draft of 1917—out of which came, among other things, the American Legion, the vigilantes and the Kluxers of the twenties. They would like to see the army do something for the men in it, and for the country. Often you meet the feeling that the new army ought to have the quality of Washington's troops of 1776-83. The men who endured those seven tremendous years were made into able, devoted citizens, and they ran the infant country for fifty years thereafter.

What can the army do—and what is it likely to do—for the men in its ranks? The army's authorized strength is 1,500,000; it may soon have a strength of 3,000,000. In the present army, about 900,000 are youngsters called under the Selective Service Act. The remainder, about 500,000, are regular troops with three-year enlistments—many of whom have joined up since the selective service law was passed—and National Guardsmen. These two groups need to be considered apart, since the army will treat them very differently.

Through hard military necessity, the hope of teaching a trade to the selective service recruits—or making any systematic effort whatever to develop their abilities—has been regretfully, but definitely, abandoned by the army's high command. Since September 1939, we have heard a great deal about the mechanization of warfare, that what are needed now are trained machinists and engineers, not bayonet wielders. This is only partly true. Of the army's total 1,500,000, about 180,000 men will be in the air corps. Only two American panzer divisions, of about 15,000 men each, have so far been established, although later on we may have six such divisions, or even eight. As airfield mechanics, the army is, quite understandably, demanding men with three-year terms. Its duty is to make ready a fighting force, and it cannot risk giving boys elaborate training and having them disappear back into civilian life.

An analysis of the proposed composition of the army gives a quick view of its opportunities for job experience. Of every thousand men, there will be infantry, 290; field artillery, 141; coast artillery, including anti-aircraft, 131; air corps, 128; medical department, 76; quartermaster corps, 69; corps of engineers, 61; cavalry, 29; signal corps, 29; armored corps, 22; ordnance department, 18; chemical warfare service, 4; finance department 2. The army will contain, as its primary striking force, twenty-seven infantry divisions, and in them one-third of the personnel will be riflemen.

It would give an untrue impression to say that none of the recruits under the Selective Service Act will receive training that will aid them later on. Boys who have a trade when they are drafted will be encouraged to continue with it. At reception camps, recruits are exhaustively classified according to their skills and aptitudes. A boy who had worked in a garage, for example, might be assigned to a tank company, and might leave the army at the end of his year's hitch a proficient mechanic. A restaurant worker might become a full fledged cook. But the army will not systematically undertake to train its selective service recruits.

Against this, the half million three-year volunteers and National Guardsmen will almost all be encouraged to learn a skilled trade. The 12,000 boys now studying to be airplane pilots, the 150,000 men being trained in ground crews, will, it is predicted, permit an enormous increase in peacetime air transportation. Air passenger travel will be inexpensive and common; air freight lines will connect remote towns.

At the time the Selective Service Act was approved, various proposals were made to give recruits either academic or vocational education in their spare hours. As the lesson of the Battle of France sank in on our General Staff, however, these vanished in mist. The problem that has arisen needs to be better appreciated. The one-year recruit will have very little spare time. Under newly revised plans, he will go first to so-called replacement centers, which will soon take the place of the current reception camps. If he has sufficient experience to qualify as a specialist, he will be immediately started on advanced training. Otherwise he will remain in the replacement center for sixteen weeks; part of his time will be spent in physical hardening, but mostly he will be prepared for actual fighting. The just issued Infantry Manual makes strange reading for 1917 veterans. It skips over close-order drill, plunging into such problems as when a squad, separated from its company, finds itself in the path of an enemy tank.

This is the conscious result of the French army's defeat. It is now a premise of our General Staff that the French disaster came largely because, during the "phony-war" winter of 1939-40, the troops in the Maginot Line were occupied in elaborate education and recreation projects, while the Nazis were ceaselessly engaged in mimic war. After a recruit leaves his replacement center to join an organized division, he will spend as much time as possible—almost continuously in the summer months—in large-scale maneuvers where all arms, bombers, tanks and artillery will participate.

A recruit's leisure hours, accordingly, will be almost non-existent. Under his daily routine, he must devote himself to his military duties from reveille at six in the morning until dinner mess every weekday except Wednesday and Saturday, when he is excused at noon. Saturdays his regimental or camp team plays another regiment or camp, and he is supposed to cheer it on. The army makes out a good case for the social value of these contests.

This leaves unpreempted the recruit's evenings from dinner until taps, and his Sundays. Every regiment has a change of movies twice a week; in most of the larger camps it will be possible for a soldier to see a different show every night. Human nature being what it is, at least two nights a week must be surrendered to movie-going. On Saturday nights, the soldier goes to the nearest town, and there is no stopping him. This leaves, for possible educational pursuits, three weekday evenings and Sunday. But, for most of his stay in a replacement camp, long days of extremely heavy physical labor leave the recruit dog-tired at night. During his succeeding eight months with the organized forces, never ending maneuvers—in which he may spend days at a time away from his barracks—make planned study very difficult.

For the task, directly or indirectly, of giving recruits a concept of modern democracy, the prospects seem more cheerful, although still uncertain. The army itself is markedly more democratic than in 1917. Army higher-ups admit the change, and say it is due to the high type of three-year volunteer since the depression years of the early thirties. Last summer the War Department purchased punch sorting machines, and recently ran 180,000 cards through them to sample the educational qualifications of our present regular troops. The scholastic level reached was: 0.1 per cent, college post graduates; 1.4 per cent, college graduates; 1.0 per cent, third-year college; 2.5 per cent, second-year college; 3 per cent, first-year college; 29.6 per cent, high school graduates; 8.2 per cent, third-year high school; 11.3 per cent, second-year high school; 10.4 per cent, first-year high school. The remainder, 31.8 per cent, had all gone through grammar school. With such men, army officers say, the Hard Boiled Smiths of 1917 are anachronistic.

It is now the custom throughout the army for an enlisted man to use the first, instead of the third, person. He says: "Did you send for me, sir?"; not, "Did Colonel Belch send for Private

Spelvin, sir?" Off post, enlisted men do not salute officers. By a War Department order, the ceremonies for general officers of other days—eleven guns for a major general, nine guns for a brigadier general—have been dropped. . . .

The primary responsibility for fostering a democratic spirit among recruits rests obviously with the army's morale division and the Joint Committee.[12] They will decide what books they read, what movies, plays and vaudeville shows they see. They will have supervision over the soldiers' forays into the outside world. . . .

It is worth pointing out that, no matter how the present emergency ends, the army is likely to have an increased national influence in the future. With the Atlantic bases acquired from England, and the Alaskan and mid-Pacific islands that are being fortified, we shall need to maintain permanent overseas garrisons that, including the Panama Canal force, will total about two hundred thousand men. Almost inevitably we shall have a much stronger air corps. Where the army was below 100,000 at the beginning of the New Deal, we must expect it to have a minimum of 500,000 henceforth. If conscription is continued into a future peace, as Mr. Roosevelt seems to intend, the army's weight will be correspondingly greater.

The hope that our new citizen army will have the quality of Washington's men of a century and a half ago is by no means certain to be fulfilled, but it is not altogether impossible. From the very circumstance that Mr. Roosevelt is still leader of the nation, that the army's ranking officers are his personal appointees, it is bound to reflect a certain degree of New Deal democracy. A great deal is being done to develop the abilities of the three-year volunteers; not enough is being done for the one-year selective service recruits. However, this is Hitler's fault, not the army's, and an immediate improvement can hardly be hoped for.

[12] Joint Army and Navy Committee on Welfare and Recreation.

THE ARMY OFFICER AS A TEACHER [13]

For sixteen months during 1934 and 1935 I was a constant visitor to two dozen CCC camps in New York state; I was serving in the dual capacity of field supervisor for the camp educational program and liaison officer between New York TERA and the Civilian Conservation Corps. One can learn a good deal about CCC from hundreds of camp visits and conversations with army officers, educational advisers and enrollees. One discovers, for example, that it is impossible to generalize accurately about the corps program, its accomplishments and failures, on the basis of acquaintance with a few camps. The amount of variation between camps, in regard to location, work projects, personnel, educational and recreational program and morale is surprising. Conditions in one place are frequently totally different from those in another camp only three or four miles away. Nevertheless, out of a welter of varying experiences, I find that a few rather well-defined impressions emerge. The clearest of these impressions has to do with the failure of the social education, or citizenship training, program in the CCC.

The educational program for CCC boys was inaugurated in January 1934. All during the following spring the "educational adviser" began taking his place in camp as a civilian member of the company commander's staff. Practically all of the advisers were, and still are, college men of some ability and enthusiasm; they pitched into the life of the camps. Sometimes it was harder to "sell" to officers than to enrollees; many officers considered teachers "the bunk," like Y.M.C.A. men, chaplains and reformers in general. Other advisers got first-class cooperation from their officers and have put on outstanding programs. Some advisers, of course, met obstacles of one sort or another, lay down on the job and accomplished little.

[13] By S. Stansfeld Sargent, former CCC educational field supervisor. From "The Army Tries to Teach." *The Christian Century*. 53:565-7. April 15, 1936. Reprinted by permission.

At the start the United States Office of Education put out a little "Handbook for Educational Advisers in the CCC Camps." In it were set forth six well-stated aims of the program, of which number three reads as follows: "To develop as far as practicable an understanding of the prevailing social and economic conditions, to the end that each man may cooperate intelligently in improving these conditions."

The handbook was approved by the Secretary of War and circulated to all the camps. The program began to get under way. Socially minded leaders everywhere welcomed the great new venture in adult education which was to reach hundreds of thousands of our young men through the cooperation of military and civilian personnel in the camps. Before many months had rolled by, however, some observers came to realize that, despite much good work in the fields of vocational and recreational and even cultural training, the amount of real social or civic education taking place was infinitesimal. Why?

One of the cardinal principles of adult education is that an educator, besides imparting knowledge and skills, should teach his students to be critical, to think for themselves. From the social standpoint we must have intelligent, informed, critical citizens if democracy is to survive. Moreover, this type of education is best carried on in the small informal group whose members are at ease and free to question and comment. But sad to say, education of this sort is quite foreign to army men—and the army controls the life of boys in the CCC. This attitude is a direct result of military training. The watchwords of army life are discipline and unquestioning obedience to superiors; it is unheard of to criticize a "higher-up" or to ask him how he arrived at a certain conclusion.

Now this may be all very well within the army. Indeed one may argue that it is essential there. But it is a state of mind which renders army men incapable of understanding how citizens should function in a democracy. From many observations, I can say definitely that army officers do not understand the objectives of informal adult education, or worse still are opposed to them.

The typical army officer is conservative, if not reactionary. His mission is largely to preserve the status quo, so he resents criticism of the government and of the existing order. His job is reasonably secure and most of the time he lives apart from the economic and social hurly-burly with its inconsistencies and injustices. He distrusts reformers, planners and social scientists, setting them down as cranks and radicals. He customarily sees eye to eye with captains of industry and men like William Randolph Hearst, who defend vigorously our status quo which is so profitable for them. On my visits to CCC camps I have noticed that Hearst papers, with their sensationalism and super-patriotism, are far and away the most popular news sheets with the officers—and the boys too. On one occasion I remonstrated with a commanding officer over a bit of inspired jingoism which he had quoted to me. He informed me: "I don't care what you say. Hearst has the right idea."

Men such as this captain—many better and some worse—control the lives of the two hundred boys in their respective camps. Realization of the aims of the educational program depends upon them. An adviser can do little unless his commanding officer backs him up.

I do not mean to disparage the commanding officers or their lieutenants in the camps. They are personally good fellows who like their boys and have their welfare at heart. Time and again the "C.O." lends his boys money, goes to bat for them if they get into trouble, and thinks up new ways to make them happy. He believes they should do their work well and have a good time during free hours. He can see the value of recreation, hobbies, vocational education and, to a lesser extent, of cultural pursuits. But he doesn't want them playing around with self-government, or asking why certain rules and regulations exist. Because of his own army training, he doesn't see much point in developing a lad's individuality; he prefers to have them all conform to the camp social pattern. Interest in "prevailing social and economic conditions" (despite the government handbook) is regarded suspiciously and seldom encouraged. As one officer expressed it to me: "They shouldn't be fooling around with that stuff; it'll put funny ideas into their heads. Too much communism floating around nowadays."

In his recent study entitled "The School in the Camps," published by the American Association for Adult Education, Mr. Frank Ernest Hill makes the following comments in regard to civic and social education in CCC:

> I have observed a tendency both on the part of the corps area officials and camp commanders to discourage frank discussion in the camps. They have in general an almost panicky fear of "agitators," and of books which might stir up uncomfortable discussion. . . . I should guess from the remarks of many officers and advisers (who are sometimes as extreme as the former) that enrollees were severely limited in speech when discussions of social and political matters developed in current event or history classes. . . . Unless there is a change in attitude on the part of officials, the effort to instruct the enrollees in the problems and conditions of modern America will be definitely impeded. That 85 per cent of the men may have little interest in democracy, fascism and communism as world or national forces is no excuse for discouraging them to develop one. Free discussions would also bring into the open and dissipate a certain amount of dissatisfaction which now exists. Discussions of camp government might prove a mutual education to both officials and men. In free political discussions the "agitator" would be much less a menace to camp morale than he sometimes now is in the role of a martyr working under cover.

The dread of "agitators" is great among army officers, but a more inclusive and horrible bogy is "communism." To hear many of them talk one would suppose there are several million Communists in the country, and that revolution will be here by next month at the latest! One officer seriously informed me that 90 per cent of the social workers in New York City were Communists, apparently because some of them refused to encourage boys to join the CCC. A district officer assured me that Cornell University was a hotbed of communism; he had heard some students there call members of the R.O.T.C. "tin soldiers." In one New York state camp the commanding officer asked the educational adviser to remove from the camp paper a section describing Consumers' Research, lest district and corps area officers might consider it communistic. A college educator who was giving attitude tests to enrollees in a camp was requested not to use the word "communism" on his questionaires, lest the word put bad ideas into youthful heads. And so it goes; dozens of comparable incidents might be cited.

The word "communism" is to army men, as to most readers of publications of Messrs. Hearst and McFadden, a scare word which is loaded with emotion; it is applied indiscriminately to critics of things as they are, whether such critics be mild liberals or extreme radicals. Group discussion of public affairs is not encouraged lest some young "radical" have a chance to make "subversive" speeches. (It is easy, however, for the head of the local post of the American Legion, or for a crusading Daughter of the American Revolution to give a patriotic pep-talk to the boys, or place an article in the camp paper.) How much better it would be, as Hill suggests, for any young agitator or Communist in the CCC—there are very few of them—to voice his sentiments in public and thereby provoke constructive discussion, than to propagandize his comrades in private! But army men have never really believed in freedom of speech.

Amusing yet deplorable confirmation of the above statements occured last fall when a new manual for instructors in the CCC was published by the United States Office of Education. It contained a choice section giving the instructor advice on how to avoid dangerous issues in discussion groups. Some of the suggestions were: "Lead the discussion away from that topic." "Refuse to discuss it." "Promise to bring the dangerous issue up at some future time. This will make it possible for the instructor to secure additional information before discussing it, and it also sets up the possibility of the topic being forgotten." A fine realistic way, indeed, to deal with the important problems of our times!

One might be led to ask at this point: Does this attitude on the part of army officers mean that the CCC boys are being groomed to serve as American storm troops? Hardly. Out-and-out fascism means military drill and a degree of indoctrination which is not present in the existing CCC. Yet it is true that army ideology has a considerable indirect influence on the enrollees. If CCC continues and the army remains in control, that influence might conceivably become greater. A high army officer informed me that the pacifists had a lot of "pull" in Washington, and that the army was obeying to the letter all regulations about not giving military training in the camps. "But the boys are getting what we want," he said. " When another war comes along, we can count on them." Certainly the army viewpoint has an effect upon the campers, particularly when the officers are admired and respected by the men, as they are in many camps.

My purpose, I repeat, is not to find fault with the CCC educational program as a whole. Some excellent work has been done and is now being done all over the country. Nor is it my purpose to attack army officers for not having the same enthusiasm for education that a teacher has. It is to the credit of the military personnel that they have come to realize that the program is a measure for the rehabilitation of the unemployed youth in the camps; most officers are cooperating to try to make it a success. My object is to point out as forcefully as possible that the presence of army officers in the camps makes genuine civic and social education impossible. They cannot or will not see that a realistic study of existing conditions, plus a free interchange of opinion about them, is the way of democracy and only proper training for intelligent citizenship.

CCC boys are not being encouraged to study the causes of the very depression which forced them to go to camp. They are learning nothing about the background of the social security program, the reasons for strikes, principles of taxation, legislation on neutrality, revelations concerning the munitions-makers, the present status of the New Deal and dozens of other important subjects. Yet all these are live issues upon which enrollees will vote in the very near future—perhaps this year! Many of the boys have attended high school and a few college. There is a small group in every camp which is eager for knowledge and willing to share it with others. What sort of "citizenship training" is it which steers away from the vital problems of the day?

Army psychology and genuine civic education simply do not go together; they don't talk the same language. CCC has helped thousands of young men in a time of crisis, but we must not deceive ourselves into believing that it provides a well-rounded training for the voters of tomorrow.

HOME TRAINING FOR THE DRAFTEE [14]

On the strength of one year's experience as a frightened buck private in a military prep school we take this opportunity to join the other amateur generals in a discussion of military conscription proposals now before Congress.

We do not hold with the plaintive pacifists who claim that conscription in peace time is a denial of the American way of life and a useless threat to our personal liberties. We think it is much fairer to select young men for military service by lot than it is to put the whole burden on the backs of those who have the patriotism to volunteer. After all, it's everybody's country and its defense is everybody's job.

Moreover, we don't think the volunteer method will bring enough recruits to form an adequate reserve army which could take the field on 48 hours' notice in the event we are attacked from abroad. Conscription is the only sure method of getting enough men in training quickly. The personal liberties such an army will protect are far more important than the personal liberties which conscription will violate.

[14] Editorial in the *Tulsa Tribune*, presented in the Senate by Senator Gerald P. Nye of North Dakota. *Congressional Record*. Vol. 86. August 23, 1940. p. 16518.

But we see no reason why conscription should seriously interfere with the normal lives of those who are called. We believe there should be varying degrees of training to fit the personal circumstances of those who are mustered into service.

To illustrate:

If we fear the blitzkrieg method of warfare, we must develop a blitzkrieg army to combat it. The Germans have a vast number of men under arms, but the spearhead of German striking power (and the secret of German military success) has consisted of a large, well-equipped, and well-trained air force, working in close cooperation with small but equally efficient mechanized ground forces called panzer divisions. In short, these new weapons have taken over on a magnificent scale the old functions of horse cavalry: i.e., speed, surprise, and the ability to demoralize the enemy behind its own defense lines. The Germans have made little use of the regular infantry which comprise the vast bulk of the Nazi Army, except to occupy and police captured territory and to repair and maintain supply lines.

If we intend to build an army along the Nazi lines it is obvious that the personnel for an air force and for highly complicated mechanized divisions must come from our regular enlisted services. The handling of such weapons requires full-time training and study. This is no job for conscripts. Besides, it will be years before we have enough tanks and other mechanized equipment to keep our Regular Army busy. So far we have just one completely mechanized division. The rest are on order.

Our National Guard could presumably take over the ordinary garrison duties of the Regular Army and aid in the training of conscript troops.

The idea of taking conscripted recruits away from their homes and their jobs for periods of training lasting from nine months to a year in central training camps seems silly. If these troops are not to be used as combat fliers or tank crews there is no reason why they couldn't be trained on home camp ground two days a week without disrupting their home life or losing their jobs.

It shouldn't be difficult to train infantrymen. After all, any young man with a modicum of sense can learn how to assemble and operate a Garand rifle in eight days, and he should be able to handle a Springfield rifle in an hour. He could master a machine rifle or a machine gun in two weeks. He doesn't have to be locked up in an Army camp in order to find out how to put up a tent or roll a pack. There is no reason why he should waste his time going through the complicated drill formations and arm manuals that are of no use except on the parade ground.

There is a lot of lost and useless motion in our traditional military training. Drill sergeants have always spent more time training an army for pageantry than for fighting. There is no reason why a new recruit couldn't be taught in three weeks to handle all the equipment an infantryman will ever need. After these basic lessons the conscripts could concentrate on fighting formations and tactics. One year of week-end training close to home should turn them into pretty fair combat soldiers. No homes would be broken, no jobs lost, no farm or factory production crippled.

Why isn't it just that simple?

OFFICER TRAINING IN BRITAIN [15]

War, with its demand for thousands of men trained to lead troops, and the "Belisha army reforms" have unseated a generation of old British army tradition. Numerous schools, called Officer Cadet Training Units (OCTU), have been established throughout Britain to produce army officers en masse. The former Secretary of State for War, Leslie Hore-Belisha, democratized the officers corps and provided, among other things, that all candidates must serve at least six months in the ranks of serv-

[15] By Larry Rue, special correspondent for *The Chicago Tribune*. From "Britain's New Army Officers." *The Chicago Tribune*. April 27, 1941. Part I, p. 16. Reprinted by permission.

ice units before being allowed to qualify for selection to be trained in an OCTU for a commission. This has put an end to the "Old School Tie" monopoly and has converted Sandhurst Royal Military College, Britain's West Point, into just another OCTU. . . .

Any able soldier is entitled to selection for the OCTU. All he needs is a recommendation from his commanding officer. Each OCTU has about ten groups of forty cadets in training. A new group enters every two weeks as another group is graduated. This allows for continuous progressive training by the same officer-instructors who pass the classes on in stages. Each group has an officer who "nurses" it through the course from beginning to end. Each 20 cadets share a batman (orderly). They continue to receive only the pay they received before entering the school, and in case of all who do not have a private income this is a hardship. When they pass out as second lieutenants their pay is only 11 shillings 6 pence a day (about $2.32), out of which they must pay at least 3 shillings (about 60 cents) to meet mess costs.

The OCTU course has been shorn of everything except the subjects vital to the prosecution of the war. The instruction varies from two to eight months, depending upon the branch of the army. It is divided into 667 periods of study as follows: Tactics, 226 periods; weapon training, 82; company command, 64; map reading, 55; field engineering, 54; drill, 48; physical training, 43; military vehicle training, 40; organization and military law, 28; special lectures, 16; and anti-gas training, 11. Each of these main subjects is further subdivided. For instance, organization and military law is split into more than 20 subjects.

A successful cadet receives only a temporary commission, and his performance, until he reaches the rank of captain, at least, determines his promotion.

Large British forces have engaged the enemy in so few actions that it is still too early to compare the work of the working class officer with his "Old School Tie" colleague.

MILITARY TRAINING
AND THE INDIVIDUAL

DISCUSSION

The subject of military training and its effect on the trainee is often overlooked, but still is vitally important. Upon his morale and his willingness rests the entire success of the training program. Should he be opposed to it, perhaps even rebel, the compulsory service plan would be a total failure. So the viewpoint of the draftee and the effects of training upon him must be considered as much as any other factor.

This is especially true in a program of selective service, where the student, the farmer and the laborer are dragged off to the army at $21 per month for undetermined lengths of time, while their colleagues may be passed over or get highly paid jobs in defense industries.

Leaving family and friends and job is never easy, but when a nation prepares for war certain hardships must be met. The test of compulsory training lies in the reaction of the individual to that training and to the hardships it entails.

EFFECTS ON PERSONALITY [1]

The brutal logic of events during the past few weeks has swept away many illusions long cherished by those who call themselves liberals or progressives. Pacifism has become a luxury which we dare no longer enjoy; few of us who fought armament bills in the past have come out against the President's recent unprecedented defense program. The fate of France with its Popular Front reforms has even raised the question of how far

[1] By Maxwell S. Stewart, professor of Economics, College of the City of New York, and associate editor of *The Nation*. From "Conscripting America." *Nation*. 151:86-8. August 3, 1940. Reprinted by permission.

we dare go in ameliorating working conditions when faced by potential enemies whose strength is based on a slave economy.

This revision of judgments has not been wholly free of hysteria. In the rush to secure our national defense, in the shortest possible time, we have taken action that would have seemed fantastic a year ago and that may seem equally so a year hence. Some of it has little relation to a rational defense plan. The gravest example of this mass hysteria, to my mind, is the general support which has been given to proposals for peacetime compulsory military service. Conscription in wartime is regrettable but necessary; it also may be necessary for a country with hostile armies on its borders. But the dangers of conscription far outweigh its utility for a country possessing the peculiar defense advantages of the United States.

That these dangers have not been more clearly pointed out is probably due to the fact that they are largely intangible, and are recognizable chiefly to those who have had the misfortune to pass through a period of rigorous military service. My protest against conscription grows out of personal experience and observation in the last war; prior to my enlistment in the Marine Corps in 1918 I shared most of the popular misconceptions regarding the value of military training. (The training given to marines during the last war, however, was in every way superior to that given the conscript army.)

Theoretically, compulsory military service offers certain advantages. It is said to develop strong bodies, a valuable sense of discipline, self-reliance, and a worthy spirit of patriotism. There is a tendency to idealize it as a means of building citizens. On the first point there is little room for argument. Military training, like any other form of organized exercise, is beneficial physically. The more intensive the training, the greater, under most circumstances, are the physical benefits. Sloppy, half-hearted training which leaves the recruit with hours of time hanging on his hands may actually be detrimental physically.

As to the other supposed gains, the effects of military service are the reverse of those claimed.

Take, for example, the matter of discipline. No one will deny that intensive military training involves strict discipline. Discipline is indispensable for effective military operations. A certain type of discipline as enforced in the last war was far better training for life under a dictatorship than in a democracy. It was anything but a conscious, self-imposed discipline. No effort was made to explain its purpose. Obedience was expected to be unquestioning. Every detail of the soldier's life, including much of his recreation, was controlled from above. Individual initiative of any type was distinctly not encouraged in the ranks. It was a prerogative of officers. Absolute discipline is of course necessary in war. But I maintain that the efficiency it creates is gained at the expense of those qualities of human personality most essential to a democracy. It is sheer hypocrisy to pretend, as do the military minded, that discipline "builds men." Its purpose is to create not men but robots.

Nor does military training build self-reliance. A soldier may be accustomed to hardships, but he is not practiced in bearing responsibility. His food, clothing, shelter, and employment are provided by the government. As a result, civilian life with its uncertainties and lack of security becomes rather terrifying. I have known able young men who have reenlisted in the army year after year because they lacked confidence in their ability to cope with civilian problems. And I can testify from personal experience to the deadly, enervating effect of having decisions made by superiors. It is particularly unfortunate that military training should usually come just at the period when boys are attempting to escape from the sheltered life of childhood and take their places in the world. For it definitely impedes, if it does not altogether block, that process.

Equally demoralizing for the developing personality is the dull routine of military life. Wholesome recreation is almost completely lacking. To be sure, there is a certain amount of supervised athletics, and some "uplift" recreation is provided by the Y.M.C.A. and the Salvation Army. But the average young soldier wants to get away from supervision and uplift in his free time. He wants, if possible, to use his scant leisure as he chooses. He would like, above all, the companionship of young women of his own kind. This is rarely possible. So, at best, the average soldier idles away his spare hours in desultory talk or in playing cards or shooting dice; at worst, he spends his time, at least before pay day is too far in the past, in bars or brothels. Often he can literally find nothing else to do. Good current books or magazines are rarely available. Nothing is provided to appeal to the intellectual or artistic interests of youth. The effect is particularly bad in the case of pampered youngsters who have never learned to stand on their own feet. And how many young men of eighteen to twenty-one are really fortified against the dull monotony of military life?

For years our jingoes have lauded military training as a means of developing a sound patriotism. Pacifists have opposed it on the ground that it tends to create a military mind-set, that it makes killers out of otherwise normal young men. Actually, it develops neither patriotism nor militarism, as millions of former service men can testify. The average soldier in the ranks comes to dislike or despise his officers, and soon his resentment is extended to the government which is responsible for the injustices and petty inconveniences of military life. Our conscript is not patriotic; he is cowed and submissive though inwardly seething with rebellion. This attitude may, as military men insist, make a good soldier. It does not make a good citizen.

I have reserved for the last what seems to me to be the most serious indictment of military training, especially in peacetime, namely, that such training conduces to inefficiency and sloth. Nowhere in civil life would inefficiency be so generally tolerated, or rather encouraged, as it is in the army. This is quickly realized by the soldier in the ranks. Seeing inefficiency on all sides of him, he rapidly becomes cynical regarding his own duties. Finding that only suckers work, he shirks at every opportunity. This is distinctly not the attitude that I should like to see inculcated in American youth.

The inefficiency which characterized our wartime preparations in 1917-18 is sometimes blamed on the necessity for speed. It is pointed out that nearly five million men were trained, fed, and equipped within about eighteen months. Under such circumstances little attention could be given to standards of efficiency. Most of the officers were either uneducated army men from the ranks or inexperienced men drawn hastily from civil life. But I suspect that conditions would be even worse if an extensive program of military training were launched today. Control would rest in the same military caste as before, and my experience with this caste suggests that without the compulsion of war, morale would probably be lower than it was in 1918. Moreover, the peacetime conscript is not likely to take his job as seriously as the man seeking knowledge that may save his life. In the last war it was difficult to make the average soldier see the value of close-order drill. In peacetime the traditional routine makes even less sense.

Some sober-minded persons who advocate universal military training in spite of its dangers give two arguments more weight than they deserve. One is that conscription is a means of getting rid of the military caste that has held the services in its grasp for many generations. Only a draft army, it is asserted, can be truly democratic, because it alone allows no distinction of class. The idea appears on the surface to make sense, but unfortunately it finds little support in the experience of the democratic countries of Europe which have had conscription. The Swiss army has frequently been held up as a model of democratic efficiency. Yet a recent study shows that even in Switzerland a highly disproportionate number of the officers come from well-to-do families with rightist political leanings. The same seems to have been true in France. In this country conscription would probably only place more power in the hands of the present military caste.

Even more persuasive is the argument that universal military training is necessary if we are to avoid the slaughter of untrained youths in the next war. This belief seems to me to be based on misreading of history. Insufficient training was not responsible for American young men being sent to certain death during the last war. Few men were sent to the front without an adequate number of weeks of training. It was simply the wrong kind of training. Practically the entire period in camp in this country was given over to close-order drill and parades. Little or no attention was paid to maneuvers simulating actual combat conditions. Many a man was sent to France before he had ever handled a rifle, but this was not for lack of time but for lack of rifles.

The experiences of the last war, moreover, can scarcely be used to illuminate America's present defense problem. For under any conditions that can be foreseen today manpower is of relatively little importance. Experts are generally agreed that a rational defense program for the United States requires: (1) a two-ocean navy, (2) an enlarged air force together with greatly improved anti-aircraft defenses, and (3) a small but highly mobile land force. A well-equipped, well-trained army of 300,000, with a National Guard of about the same size in reserve, could meet any conceivable defense demands. Such a force would have to be highly trained technically. The doughboy of the last war must give way to the technician, skilled in one specialized duty. This implies a professional army with a relatively long period of enlistment. Conscript armies may still have their place in the land fighting of Europe, but they are ill suited to the peculiar defense needs of this country.

In the light of these facts Senator Burke's plan for universal military service seems fantastic. His bill looks forward to the training of all men between the ages of eighteen and sixty-four, men between twenty-one and forty-five being subject to call for active service. To provide these tens of millions of men with even the most fragmentary training would place an enormous strain on our military equipment and personnel. And in modern warfare poor training is little better than none.

If war comes, conscription may become necessary as a means of mobilizing the entire force of the nation against the enemy—conscription of economic resources as well as of manpower. The nature of the training to be given will depend on the source of the attack. Presumably more attention would have to be paid to education in industrial technique than to purely military training. Let us arm to the limit against Nazi aggression. But let us not think that we are safeguarding ourselves against attack by teaching our men and boys to do "squads right" and "squads left" under the totalitarian discipline of an army clique.

NO WAR PSYCHOLOGY [2]

Military training does not make students war-minded, it is revealed by a three-year study of the attitudes of 587 college students toward war. Dr. George J. Dudycha, professor at Ripon College, concludes from his survey that compulsory military training for college men apparently has little effect on their attitudes either toward or against war.

Moderately or strongly opposed to war are the majority of students whose attitudes were measured by Dr. Dudycha. Only a few, 5.6 per cent, were moderately favorable and none were strongly favorable toward war. Women tended to be more opposed to war than men, but they seem to become somewhat less opposed as they pass through four years of college.

Those junior and senior men who voluntarily elected to pursue the advanced courses in military science continued, for the most part, to be moderately or strongly opposed to war.

[2] By the Society for the Psychological Study of Social Issues. From "Military Training in College Fails to Change Attitudes." *Science News Letter.* 37:172. March 16, 1940. Reprinted by permission.

When these men taking advanced work in military science were compared with those who did not continue this course, little difference between the two groups was discovered. There were only approximately 5 per cent more men opposed to war among those not continuing courses in military science than among those who did. In general, this study indicates that those men who take four years of military science in college do not materially change their attitude toward war and that those who do not take advanced military science become slightly more opposed to war as they pass through college.

"These results," Dr. Dudycha observes, "probably are unsatisfactory to both militarists and pacifists. People who favor compulsory military training often claim that knowledge of military training leads to an abhorrence of war. Those who are unalterably opposed to such training, on the other hand, argue that this knowledge leads students to be more war-minded. Neither point of view is supported by the results that have been obtained. Consequently the issue of compulsory military training in American colleges should be decided on other grounds than its supposed effect on students' attitudes toward war."

TRAINEES: FOUR MONTHS LATER [3]

Four months have gone by since the first trainees, fresh from the pavement and from the farm, came to this camp for one year's training. One third of their enlistment is up.

Their lives are completely changed. They stand straighter. The thin ones have put on from five to twenty pounds. The obese have lost their excess. They are tough. They can hike fifteen to twenty miles, with pack, in almost any weather, without dropping by the road. They can sleep under the stars without getting sniffles.

[3] By Meyer Berger, feature writer for *The New York Times*. From "Trainee: Four Months Later." *New York Times Magazine*. April 6, 1941. p. 4-6. Reprinted by permission.

They walk lonely posts for hours, sharply cutting the turns in the dark from sheer military habit. Their reflexes are alert to sharp command. Their hands come up in brisk salute when bars, oak leaves, eagles or gold stars cross their line of vision.

Once familiar noises have receded from their memories—the subway's roar, the traffic hum, factory and office clatter, the insistent ring of the office phone. Ears are attuned, now, to bugle call, to the whimper of wind round the tent or barrack wall, to the steady tramp of marching feet, to the brassy song of regimental band.

Only the more emotional still eat their own hearts with nostalgia. Only the more ambitious anxiously look toward the day when they take up civilian careers so rudely snapped by the Selective Service Act.

Mostly, despite the grumbling, the men seem to have taken to the new life. They complain about camp fare, but their improved physical shape does not justify the complaint. They rant about hard work, but they never felt better.

Their bitter petitions worry anxious parents and solicitous friends. Actually, though, they are healthy signs. Invective and complaint, old soldiers assure you, have been characteristic of the breed, standard for military men since Joshua's legions bivouacked at Jericho.

Critics contend that current trainees lack the fire and the spirit of the 1917 army. They seem to overlook the fact that the new soldiers have not been inspired by fighting slogans and screaming posters; that they have not been fired to combat mood with atrocity stories. Their bayonet-practice dummies have not been invested, as World War dummies were, with positive enemy identity. This seems to make a difference.

This is still a peacetime army.

For most new men, especially city types, reveille was a major curse. Few of them had ever known the dawn. Their teeth chattered and their limbs shook until scalding coffee broke the ague at morning mess. They have overcome these daybreak shakes.

First call sounds at 5:45 A.M. when the sun is maiden pink on camp water towers, on barracks and tent walls. Ten minutes before the bugler blows the soldier in charge of quarters has been down the company street, sadistically turning his fellows out of their warm cots.

The company cook and the K.P. detail, up for three hours already, have sleepily walked through the street to the mess shack to prepare the morning meal. The night fire detail and the guards have not been to bed at all. The fire detail has kept the stove fires going.

At 6:15 A.M., before the sun has cleared the scrub pine of the fort horizon, the men are through morning mess. They hurry back to straighten their cots, to sweep the tent or barracks, for a really honest wash and shave. The tent fire, banked all night, is alive again.

At 7:45 A.M., if the schedule calls for drill or problems in the field, the trainees line up with rifles in the company street. Greatcoats cover their blue denim drill clothes. Canvas leggings keep the wind from their shins. They have gloves for cold days; arctic caps to protect their ears and their necks.

It is Spring now. The soldier has shucked his Winter flannels and his jerkin. The morning wind has less bite. He holds his head higher as the company tramps down a regimental avenue to a sharp "Hep! Hep!" an added section to the khaki serpent winding down the camp road to the drill field.

(Back home, at this hour, Mom is putting on the coffee. The kids are stealing another ten minutes' sleep before school call. Back in Hunts Point or Flatbush a fellow could indulge his Spring fever. Not here. "Hep! Hep!")

On the drill field heavy outer things are neatly mounded next to each soldier's position. The men go through fifteen minutes of setting-up exercise. They drill. They rest a while. They hear military lectures on rifles, machine guns, concealment, skirmish.

At 11:15 A.M. they start back for the company street. Noon mess call sounds at 11:45 A.M. At 12:30 P.M. the serpent winds down the road to the drill field again or strikes out across the reservation for a long hike.

At 4:30 P.M. the company hears recall shiver across the New Jersey plain. The men move back toward their tents or barracks. They are tired. Their lungs are filled with fresh air. Their faces are brown with wind and sun. Except for possible details, the work for the day is ended.

Shadows lengthen in the company street. Men lie on their cots awhile, relaxed, but they must be out of their denims and into their good woolen khaki before retreat sounds at 5:10 P.M. They must be shaved, their good boots shined when they go out to the line.

They salute the descending colors. A momentary hush falls over the broad camp area before the band plays "The Star-Spangled Banner." The last notes quiver; die away. The sun moves toward the horizon with little purple clouds as flankers. . . .

Evening mess is over at 6 o'clock. Soon barracks and officers' quarters come bright with lighted panes. Then night closes on Fort Dix and the evening winds start whispering.

From 6 o'clock until 11 P.M. each soldier's time is his own. He may lie on his cot and dreamily listen to radio music. He may write letters in his tent or strike across the plain for the hostess house and write them there.

He may play cards or checkers. If he is fortunate, and so inclined he may get a chance at the billiard table in the hostess house. If he wants to read, the post library has some 6000 to 7000 volumes. It will get special books, if he asks for them.

Some one may launch a conversation in the tent, or in barracks, about the old job back home. It's more likely, though, to be something about girls and dates. It may be rumor of regimental transfer to some romantic spot far away. The soldier has a childish love of rumor.

The talk languishes. Abundant fresh air works narcotic miracles. Men who never got to bed in the city before 1 or 2 A.M. turn in early. Their sleep is sound. They do not hear the tent canvas bellying and slapping in the wind. They are used to it. After four months it is a kind of lullaby for them.

Sometimes there are night problems. The men are jarred out of deep slumber at 2 A.M. or at midnight. Swearing and grumbling, they sullenly get into their denims. They go out under the stars, move off down the road past sleeping units, to attack some mythical foe ten or twenty miles away.

There are details that break routine. Kitchen police duty, guard duty, coal duty, loading food at the commissary, cleaning out the hostess house. This work is done, in many cases, by young men who have never put hand to broom, coal scuttle or kitchen tools. They learn to bear it with complete resignation.

In a tent in Company A's row in the Seventy-first (New York) Regiment you break in on John C. Vance. He is tall, solemn. He sits on the edge of his cot, dog-weary after a day in the field. He is an aristocrat in blue denim.

Vance was graduated from Yale in 1935, from Harvard Law in 1938. He is a junior member of a Wall Street law firm with a name a yard long. He lives—when he's not at Fort Dix—in a wealthy district in Westchester County.

He says the most difficult thing for him was reveille. Waking on Winter mornings, before night had left the sky, seemed strange. The strenuous exercise and drill; the long hiking in all kinds of weather—these were tough on a young man who never had gone in for such things.

Private Vance is philosophical about it now. He grins a little. "You miss not being free to come and go as you please," he confides. "I guess you miss that more than anything." Somehow you slowly lose interest in what seemed to be vital topics—international situations, things like that.

You think you'll catch up on your reading, but you don't. "You're too tired at the end of the day." You may go to a movie at the camp theatre, but it's a long hike to the theatre. You lie around the tent and relax. You get caught up in the little company squabbles. The time slips away.

You leave Private Vance and move across the reservation to the old red barracks where the provost marshal's men are billeted. You talk with Private Thomas J. Slattery, who was the first New York City cop inducted last fall.

As Patrolman Slattery, five years on the force, he walked a lively beat near Grand Central Station—Forty-second Street, between Lexington and Fifth Avenues. About a year ago, one morning, at 3 o'clock, he caught three hold-up men carrying loaded pistols.

He'd like it here, all right, if it wasn't for the money part. As a cop he was ready for his $3,000 a year. As a soldier he gets only $21 a month. "That's hard on the mother," he says. "I keep worrying about that."

Getting up at dawn is nothing new to Private Slattery. He did that when he worked the 8 A.M.-4 P.M. tour in front of Grand Central. Discipline doesn't bother him. He got that, just the same, in police school and as a New York cop.

The work he does here is something like the job back in Manhattan. He investigates petty crimes; teaches other M.P.'s how to track thieves, how to handle camp traffic, how to report accidents on the reservation.

He's healthy here. Sticks pretty close to his 204 pounds. He likes it all right. He misses his friends and family, though he gets up to Manhattan every second weekend, on pass. If it wasn't for the money angle he'd have no kick, d'ya understand?

Sergeant George T. Richardson in the Personnel Section in the Seventy-first Regiment has put on almost thirty pounds since he came into the new Army. He was about that much under normal when he was inducted.

He wants to get out as soon as he can, to pick up his job at Sinclair Oil, in Rockefeller Center, where he left off last Fall. He had charge of credit identification cards in the East for the company. He hears from the boss and the fellows at the office.

His work at Fort Dix isn't too different from his civilian job. He feels he won't get rusty, anyway. He'd like to be back in civilian life to continue his studies before his mind gets too set for study. He's 25.

The sergeant is tall, blond and personable. He makes social contacts easily. He has dates in Trenton, is invited to some of the best homes for Sunday dinner. People living near the camp have been extremely hospitable.

He thinks conscription is all right, but it might be better if they took younger men—kids just out of high school, say. "A year in the Army for a fellow right after he gets out of high school would give him a settled viewpoint," the sergeant says.

Private Frank Tufano worked on *The Sun* in New York. He lived in Flatbush. He thinks a year in the Army will be a good thing. He likes it. "I'm not sore," he assures you. "I figure maybe I can work up to a rating here, and better pay."

He misses the gang back in Flatbush, but he has made new friends in the Seventy-first. "We have a lot in common," he tells you, "because we're all from New York City." Private Tufano has one astonishing habit; he goes for hikes on free Sundays.

"I've done things out here that would have killed me in civilian days," he discloses. "I do a fourteen-mile hike with combat pack, but I can stand it now. I'm plenty toughened. I got through the Winter with fewer colds than I ever had before."

Private Tufano has put on five pounds. He resented having to have his hair cut down to the one and one-half inch maximum imposed by Army regulations, but he's used to it now.

"It's for my country," he says philosophically.

These are the four-months soldiers. Some of them love the life. Some of them don't. Some feel mentally cramped here. "A mental vacuum," one college man called it. On the whole, though, the men have benefited; and, physically, the results have been all that Army men hoped for.

CONSIDERATION FOR THE CONSCRIPT [4]

Little has developed to disprove the belief that the draft act, when introduced, was a political measure regarded as essential to the third term and not a then necessary part of the military program. The opinion that it was intended, at the time it was proposed, to help create the war atmosphere in which a change of administration could be pronounced imprudent and unwise, has not been altered by subsequent events. The army could not take care of the men already enlisted. What was needed was the production of material, but that sensible program would not have stimulated the political drama of the war in the United States.

The draft act as a military measure was badly conceived, as is conceded. It created a maximum of civilian disturbance with a minimum of military benefit. The proposal now is to revise it with a better understanding of the future needs of the American army. The *Tribune* has been an advocate of military education for many years. This newspaper supported such education for American youth at the end of the other world war and had in mind the various benefits which would come to the young men so trained as well as to the country they might be called upon to serve.

Apparently it is now recognized that military training should come to the young man at the time when it will fit most appropriately into his schooling and into his preparation for the future—when it will be the least disturbing to his personal economy. The *Tribune* has emphasized the value of the training given in the high schools and the colleges.

[4] From "The Conscripts." Editorial. *Chicago Tribune.* April, 1941. Part I, p. 16. Reprinted by permission.

The age range in the present conscription act was bound to cause economic dislocations. The various draft boards would act on varying interpretations and rulings which would result in inequality of treatment in different districts.

If the permanent policy of the United States requires the military training of American youth, it should be recognized that the young men are entitled to consideration. Countries which have used conscription for many years have, when they have been wisely guided, taken their conscripts when there would be the least interference with their preparation for civilian life.

It can be argued, and the *Tribune* has argued, that the physical checkup necessary to the service can be made to contribute to a raising of public health standards and of physical fitness, that the schooling can be a valuable aid to national morale, and that it can be so diversified as to add the individual's mental equipment as well.

MEN AND MORALE [5]

What everybody should know is that if we come in armed conflict with the expanding forces of fascism, victory or defeat depends on the kids. Fighting in Stuka bombers and speedboats and fast tanks has to be done by kids. At thirty, in 1940's army, you are an old man, just as you are in the ring or in any other violent competitive sport. The weakness of Hitler's army was once supposed to be that so many of his warriors were 17 and 18 years old. That turned out to be his strength, not his weakness.

Kids only fight when they feel like it. They are more emotional than their elders—or rather, their emotions play a larger part in their decisions. There were young men in Gamelin's army and whether the High Command did or did

[5] By Ralph Ingersoll, editor, *PM*. Editorial titled "The Kids." *PM*. July 29, 1940. p. 8. Copyright, 1940, by The Newspaper PM, Inc., New York. Reprinted by special permission.

not sell them out, they could have fought a lot harder if they had felt like it. They were up there in the air and out there in their tanks. But obviously they didn't feel the same way about fighting as the young Nazis. If they had, their defeat would not have been a matter of only a few weeks.

Now, if the kids are the ones who are going to do the fighting, and the vital thing is how they feel about it—how do they feel about it?

What's extraordinary to me is how little interest is being taken in this right now. When you think of the enormous importance of the answer, the bickering over whether the group called the Youth Congress does or doesn't speak for Youth, with a capital Y, whether it has or hasn't officers who are members of the Communist Party, and whether its manners are good, indifferent, or bad—all these things become as childish as the children themselves are so often accused of being—and only a Gene Tunney could get so excited over the wrong thing.

For the truth needs neither Gallup polls nor F.B.I. investigators to discover. The truth is that if you are an American boy between the ages of 16 and 26 there is only one question for you: "What can be worse than what I've got?" If this nation has had 10 years of insecurity, these kids have had a lifetime of it—and they have a lifetime of it ahead of them.

It isn't that they've read too many books about how horrible the last war was, or talked to too many Communists about how wonderful the next world will be, but that they have been brought up in a country that has nothing to offer them except more education than they are allowed to use and a boring year or two in a CCC camp. And they know by instinct, if nothing else, that they're worth more than this.

They also know—and no politician's speeches are going to kid them out of it—that the deal they've been getting isn't worth being killed for. They didn't have to read any Hemingway or Dos Passos stories about the horrors of war to catch on to that simple fact. The right to listen to the radio plugging consumer products you can't buy, to borrow pop's car on Saturday night, is not worth getting your head blown off for.

I said in an editorial here that I didn't like the idea of kids being conscripted before they knew what they were conscripted for. It doesn't matter what I or anyone else likes. The truth is that we could conscript the kids by the million, give them the finest guns in the world to shoot and if they didn't like being in the army, didn't feel they had anything to fight for except the right to be jitterbugs, they'd get shot down and rolled over just the way the young men of France were shot down and rolled over.

For no matter how war changes it's always the same and unless you are an Italian shooting at spear-carrying Ethiopians with a machine gun—if the arms are anywhere nearly equal, the side that knows what it's fighting for is the side that's going to win. That's the side that scares hard while the other side scares easily. And if you are too scared to look down the sights you're not going to hit anything even if you have the finest gun in the world in your hands.

The first problem of arming America is not storing ammunition dumps, but interesting ourselves in the kids who will use the ammunition. For what kind of a country are they to fight? What's in it for them? What do they need and want and dream of? We must think about these things and act on them. And the promises that we make, we must be prepared to keep. For one does not break one's promises to a million armed young men twice.

MISCELLANEOUS

FORTUNE SURVEY—1939 [1]

Question: Would you favor a term of compulsory military service for all young men of eighteen or nineteen?

Answers:
Yes 31.3%
Yes, if necessary 11.6
No 48.8
Don't know 8.3

Age and sex groups differ hardly at all in their opposition to conscription. The War veterans, however, once mostly conscripts themselves, would favor it for all young men either now or if necessary, by 51.1 per cent. Opposition is uniformly greatest among the three upper income groups, falls away to a half-and-half division among the poor. No group, however, shows much more or much less than a third giving unqualified approval to compulsory military service.

By occupations there is this distribution of opinion: Labor of all kinds and the unemployed seem more ready to accept the idea of military service than any other classes, and professional people and white-collar workers are the most opposed. Incidentally, opposition is 10 per cent greater among people having a close relative of military age than among others. Furthest apart among all breakdowns are the parts of the country that seem most consistently to represent, respectively, isolation and intervention, as follows:

	Southeast	Northwest Plains
Yes	40.9%	18.6%
Yes, if necessary	12.8	9.0
No	35.2	66.9
Don't know	11.1	5.5

[1] From "Would You Favor a Term of Compulsory Military Service for All Young Men of 18 or 19?" *Fortune.* 20:116. December, 1939. Reprinted by permission.

The people expressing themselves as opposed to general military training for young men gave these reasons for their opposition:

Don't believe in compulsion............... 21.6% ⎤
Not democratic—un-American—free country.. 11.6 ⎥
Too much like dictatorship—like Germany... 11.5 ⎬ 47.7%
Too much like Europe .... 3.0 ⎦

Not necessary, no immediate danger......... 19.7 ⎫ 23.6
Plenty of volunteers .... 3.9 ⎭

Creates war spirit, makes youth war minded.. 11.0

Too young .... 8.0 ⎫ 11.8
Interferes with education and career .... 3.8 ⎭

Other 6.8

Don't know 2.0

Apparently the most obnoxious thing about the idea is not militarism, nor a strong belief that training is bad, but the idea that compulsion is un-American.

National opinion on the subject of compulsory military training for young men would seem to suggest that if we are to enlarge our armed forces, for which there is a mandate, it must be done through voluntary enlistment. Even the opponents of conscription are for increased armaments by about 80 per cent or more. But there is one alternative that has sometimes been mentioned, although it has not been widely discussed by the general public:

Would you favor giving military training to the CCC boys?

	Total	Men	Women	Under 40	Over 40
Yes	64.2%	67.2%	61.1%	63.1%	65.2%
Yes, if necessary ..	9.3	8.9	9.6	9.6	8.9
No	20.5	20.3	20.8	21.7	19.5
Don't know	6.0	3.6	8.5	5.6	6.4

By class and occupation the variations upon these answers are too small for notice. By geography there is the old difference observed before between the Southeast and the Northwest Plains

—a difference of about 15 per cent, with the Southerners the most in favor of beating axes into rifles.

The people who answered "no" or "don't know" to this question were asked if they would favor CCC military training if it were not made compulsory, and 68.4 per cent of them said "yes." Adding these to the 73.5 per cent who are for militarizing this organization anyway, with or without qualification, the figure comes to 91.6 per cent of the population—all of which goes to show that against a strong libertarian mistrust of regimentation, there is a strong determination that we shall be better armed, and a willingness to find the manpower to that end where it is freely available.

GALLUP POLL—1940 [2]

Do you think every able-bodied young man 20 years old should be made to serve in the army, navy or air force for a year?

Young men and women both were asked. The response: Yes, 68 per cent; No, 32 per cent. The majority explained they favored preparedness for the defense of democracy; were for preserving peace by impressing the world with our military strength; thought universal training prudent in view of our prospect of standing alone in a hostile world. The minority feared regimentation under a dictatorship, doubted that there was any likelihood of invasion, or asked why only boys of 20 should be allowed to serve. The young women were the more outspoken and critical in the minority group.

The boys who are going to be drafted voted just like their elders on this question; our national poll of adults on conscription had also been two to one in favor. It is interesting to note that on every other question where direct comparison is possible, the young people voted just like their elders. Nor was there any significant variation of results in the replies

[2] By Dr. George Gallup, head of the American Institute of Public Opinion. From "American Youth Speaks Up." *Reader's Digest.* 37:52-3. October, 1940. Reprinted by permission.

to any question when broken down either by educational, economic or geographical lines.

Under selective conscription, will you, personally, have any objection to spending a year in some branch of the military service?

Only young men were asked this question. And 76 per cent of the boys questioned answered No! "If I'm likely to be called upon to fight, I'd rather know how," was a typical comment. . . .

COMMON SENSE ON CONSCRIPTION [3]

"Conscription" has an odious and ominous sound. Its connotations are bad. But compulsory school attendance is a kind of conscription. . . . It is not entirely inconceivable that some sort of plan by which every boy and girl in the country would have to go through a year of some kind of training and service related to the general welfare might have beneficial results. This we say never losing sight of the fact that the army itself has estimated its needs for an adequate *defense* force at only 45,000 men.

THE COST OF OUR MILITARY PROGRAM [4]

The total amount of wealth in the entire United States is roundly only 300 billion dollars. Our federal government has in the last ten years spent almost a third as much money as the total value of all the wealth of our country!

The debt at the end of 1941 will be about 50 billion dollars. By the end of 1942, it will be about 60 billion. Congress only since last January has appropriated and authorized to be spent 23½ billions. This would be enough money to buy all of the property in Ohio, Indiana, Illinois and Wisconsin.

[3] Excerpt from editorial titled "Shall American Youth Be Conscripted?" *Christian Century.* 57:845. July 3, 1940. Reprinted by permission.
[4] By Frederick C. Smith, dean of the Graduate School, University of Tennessee. From "The Federal Debt," a talk given over the Mutual Broadcasting System. *Scribner's Commentator.* 9:102-3. January, 1941. Reprinted by permission.

People should also realize that the heavy additional costs of defense are not be merely temporary. This is to be a permanent program.

How much will the conscript army and the two-ocean navy add to the taxpayers' burden?

The new program calls for a standing army of perhaps no fewer than 1,500,000 men. Certainly no fewer than 1,250,000 men will be added to the number in the armed forces we had in 1939. On the basis of previous army costs it has been estimated that it will cost to maintain this added force roundly 4½ billion dollars a year.

It has been reliably estimated that the upkeep and maintenance of the two-ocean navy will add about 1½ billions. The interest cost on the increased debt that is involved in this program will add 425 millions. This totals approximately 6½ billion dollars, which will be the added cost of the conscript army and two-ocean navy. . . .

If we add the costs of all federal programs to those of the state and local governments, the annual bill to the taxpayers of the United States is 22 billions of dollars. . . . Farmers, laboring groups, small salaried employees and the other low income groups will have to pay more than 18 billions of this.

THE NEED OF SPEED [5]

The United States Army today is at a crossroads of development.

In training camp and in halls of Congress there is being formulated a new military policy for this nation, one which may outlive the war and last into the peace. It is a policy that, like Topsy, is "jest growin'," under the imperative necessity of emergency, and hence it is a policy which is not clearly

[5] By Hanson W. Baldwin, *New York Times* military and naval expert. From "Emphasis In Army Swinging to Speed." *New York Times*. July 1, 1941. p. 14. Reprinted by permission.

defined and perhaps may never become the military policy best suited to this nation.

Today that policy is being hammered out between the hammer and the anvil of two conflicting schools of tactical thought. There are those of the conservative school who still hold that the infantry and artillery are the backbone of any army; there are those of the opposite pole of thought who believe that the spearhead of any army must be the plane-tank combination with which the Germans have overrun Europe.

This is the fundamental cleavage in the Army today; it is a cleavage between speed and security, a cleavage between the French school of tactical thought, which believes in rather carefully graduated maneuvers, and the new German school which believes in risking much to gain much quickly.

Today, the nation has twenty-seven infantry divisions; eighteen of them "square" National Guard divisions formerly with actual strength of about 18,700 men each; nine of them Regular Army "triangular" divisions of about 15,000 men each. There are two horse cavalry divisions of about 11,125 soldiers (who have a large mass of mechanized equipment), only one of them completely organized. There are four tank or armored divisions, two of them fully organized, of about 12,080 men and about 400 tanks each. There are other smaller units, such as a horse cavalry brigade, corps-reconnaissance regiments (half-horsed and half-mechanized) and corps and army troops of all kinds.

Staffs have been set up, although they are not at full war strength, for four armies and nine corps, but neither corps nor army troops are fully organized yet.

Only one of the twenty-seven infantry divisions which form the vast preponderance of our field forces today is classified as a motorized division; and this division, the Fourth triangular, is as yet incompletely motorized.

The GHQ Air Force is not attached to any field army, but is under the new Deputy Chief of Staff for Air, Major General

H. H. Arnold. It has, however, no dive bombers, although some are on order; and it has only a handful of attack planes and other types most useful for coordinated operations with land forces. The Army today, therefore, has only a relatively small part of its striking strength, which at present is about 1,413,000 men, earmarked for the plane-tank team.

However, plans for the next fiscal year represent a considerable modification of the tactical program envisaged when the present expansion program was started. The four armored divisions are to be increased to six (there are to be at least eight eventually); there are to be twenty-five GHQ tank battalions instead of the ten originally planned; five more of the Army's triangular divisions are to be completely motorized, and experiments will probably be conducted with a view to development of other mechanized units. Dive bombers are to be procured; the recent reorganization of the Air Corps has given the air forces greater autonomy and opportunity for development and air officers will share in the command of various task groups.

The gradual progress away from the static concepts of war to the dynamic concepts of today has been and will continue to be a hard one, but it is also marked in other ways. After the recent Tennessee maneuvers Major General Frederic H. Smith, commanding the Seventh Corps, suggested that the present "square" infantry divisions (formerly Guard divisions) were too cumbersome, and their transformation to smaller and more easily handled "triangular" divisions might be helpful.

The process of training has probably gone too far to make any such transformation an easy one now, and the square divisions, if their offensive and defensive capabilities are built up with new weapons and they are thoroughly vitalized with good staffs and good leadership, can play an important part in modern war.

But they are not organically equipped or organized to play that part today. More and more anti-tank guns have been added to their arms as maneuver lessons showed plainly what should already have been learned from the battlefields of Europe, and now more and more anti-aircraft guns, particularly perhaps of the 40-millimeter Bofors type (the first of which has just been turned out in this country after a remarkably short preparatory period) must be added to the division.

The infantry must also have its own artillery, as the Germans do; artillery on wheels or tracks, artillery which does not have to be unlimbered to be fired, but can move under its own power. The infantryman, too, must move more and more on wheels; he must have a greater and greater variety of equipment and he must be trained in special task forces.

All these developments, although some of them are bitterly opposed by the old line, are on the way; new weapons, particularly mechanized weapons and self-propelled mounts, are being devised and developed.

These things are all heartening evidences of progress; evidences of the modernization, in tactical concepts and thought processes, as well as in equipment, of the United States Army. But that modernization is progressing far more slowly than it should because of the limited vision of too many of our officers and the inefficiency of others.

It can be materially speeded up, in the opinion of many officers, by three major measures:

1. Authorization of the War Department (such authorization was requested of Congress on Friday) to remove unfit officers without the red tape and interminable delays now required.

2. Elimination of the arms, and perhaps of some of the services, in the Army. An officer is now commissioned in the infantry, cavalry, etc.; this tends to create over a period of years restricted vision and cliques which are a bar to coordinated progress. The War Department is making a study of this now.

3. A general shift of Regular and National Guard officers, so that none of the National Guard divisions will remain, as

they have tended to do, Guard divisions; no Regular division
remain "Regular." There is too much sectionalism in former
Guard outfits; when possible, especially in units drawn from
small towns, officers should not come from the same localities
as their men. The officers and men should be reasonably inter-
changed, so as to produce in reality an Army of the United
States.

THE PACIFIST VIEW [6]

President Wilson's proposal to make conscription illegal in
all countries affiliated in the League of Nations, lately taken
up at a European committee including persons of international
prominence, stirs echoes both of approbation and distrust in
this country. Citizens of fourteen countries signed the manifesto
calling up "men and women of good-will" to help create everywhere a public demand which "will induce governments and the
League of Nations to abolish military conscription." Curiously
enough, there are no American signatories to this plan, first
put forth by the American War President. Nevertheless,
"America is agreeable," says the *Syracuse Post-Standard,* and
the signatories of the original petition announce that the publication committee will be glad to receive further signatures. The
men behind the movement include such figures as Norman
Angell, H. G. Wells, and Bertrand Russell, of England, Henri
Barbusse, Georges Duhmel and Romain Rolland of France,
while Germany is represented by Prof. Albert Einstein and a
number of men with military titles, led by General Von Deim-
ling. The keynote of the plea, as reported by the London
Bureau of *The New York Times,* is found in three paragraphs
running:

We call for some definite step toward complete disarmament and
the demilitarizing of the mind of civilized nations. The most effective
measure toward this would be the universal abolition of conscription.
We therefore ask the League of Nations to propose the abolition of

[6] From "An Attack On Draft Armies." *Literary Digest.* 90:14. September 18,
1926. Reprinted by permission.

compulsory military service in all countries as a first step toward true disarmament.

It is our belief that conscript armies, with their large corps of professional officers, are a grave menace of peace. Conscription involves the degradation of human personality and the destruction of liberty. Barrack life, military drill, blind obedience to commands, however unjust and foolish they may be, and deliberate training for slaughter undermine respect for the individual, for democracy and human life.

It is debasing human dignity to force men to give up their lives or to inflict death against their will or without conviction as to the justice of their action. The State which thinks itself entitled to force its citizens to go to war will never pay proper regard to the value and happiness of their lives in peace.

The manifesto was published simultaneously in most countries of the world, including the United States, and is said to have the backing of a number of humanitarian organizations, here and abroad. It concludes with an appeal for more signatures. The *Springfield Republican,* known for its sympathy with the League of Nations and other disarmament projects, explains and comments:

The demand is based both on the danger of war from the accumulation of great reserves of trained soldiers and on the bad effects of barrack life, military drill, blind obedience to commands, and deliberate training for slaughter as "undermining respect for the individual, for democracy and human life." It will be easy in most countries to get a long list of signatures to such a protest, but the recent higgling of the experts at Geneva over the theoretical refinements of disarmament shows how difficult it will be to accomplish anything worth while.

The impracticability of the idea suggests itself to some of our publicists, who comment on its "rash idealism." The Springfield *Union,* observing that the prospect that " the nations of the world can be induced to abandon conscription is, of course, exceedingly small," demands:

When they can not be brought to abolish chemical warfare, against which public sentiment is admittedly overwhelming, how can they be induced to abandon conscription, against which there is no such one-sided sentiment?

For several weeks members of the preparatory commission on disarmament have been sitting at Geneva. They have made little progress, and this for the plain reason that most nations prefer to increase, rather than decrease, their military effectiveness. As long as that attitude persists among nations, what shall we say of the futility of a manifesto of this sort?

But the general idea has been good American doctrine through generations, retorts the Hartford *Times,* and "the attitude expressed in it is one which most Americans before the war held as a matter of course." So much was this true that:

We regarded ourselves as superior to European nations because we had no obligatory military service in time of peace. Immigrants came to this country to escape such obligations in their own countries, and we regarded them without disfavor.

Twenty years ago any American would have assented to the proposal to outlaw conscription, and political aspirants would have been obliged to agree to something very much like it. The war, with the success of the draft law and the general clamor for universal peacetime service, changed all that, and now one is on the defensive if one suggests that compulsory drilling of college students is unnecessary and perhaps unjust.

As a matter of fact, an agreement to end military peacetime conscription in Europe would go far toward eliminating the state of fear and mutual distrust which dominates the international scene. Perhaps, in view of the relaxed state of mind in most European countries— except when the United States is concerned—this is not too much to hope for.

The main obstacle is the lack of security that a disarmed nation feels, believes the Philadelphia *Evening Bulletin,* a point which the many and important signatories of the manifesto seemingly overlook. The Philadelphia editor continues this criticism:

Only a League that was a real superstate, able physically to defend its members from any possible attack, could induce its members to forego the right of self-defense to the extent that this committee asks. For the petition goes further than to ask abolition of universal military service which keeps a whole nation constantly in arms for purposes of possible aggrandizement. It strikes at a fundamental power of every State, which it must retain unless it abdicates to a superstate, to demand that in the emergency of war all its citizens shall serve it under arms, if they are needed.

This right exists in every State, whether it is exercised or not. That every citizen on call is bound to defend his country is as fundamental American doctrine as it is the doctrine of healthy nationalism elsewhere. What the League can do, and ought to do, is to help its members to cut the number of men actually kept under arms to a minimum and to help create such a feeling of international security that training may as a matter of fact be restricted to those who voluntarily seek it.

That is the present practise in the United States as well as in Great Britain. But these free and non-aggressive nations must maintain unimpaired the right of the State to summon every son to its defense and the duty of the citizen to respond. That right is the guaranty by reason of which the maintenance of great standing armies is avoided.

DEMOCRACY AND PREPAREDNESS [7]

During the World War, I served on the Oregon Appeals Board for the selective service. As a member of that board I classified and reclassified many who had appealed from the local boards. My service on that board convinced me that the only democratic and equitable method of securing defenders was through the operation of a selective service plan. Many people believe that the volunteer system is the proper one; that that is the only fair way to secure brave, intelligent defenders of our country. I appreciate the fact that the volunteer in military service is unquestionably the better soldier at the start at least. I am, however, firmly convinced that, while the volunteer system in emergency takes the bravest and the best, the strongest and the ablest, there are countless others just as fortunate in enjoying the great inheritance of this country, and just as capable of defending it, who stand back and let the more patriotic volunteer make the sacrifice for their advantage. Each should have an equal interest in doing his part in defense of

[7] By Congressman Walter M. Pierce, of Oregon. *Congressional Record*. Vol. 86. September 5, 1940. p. 16560-1.

the country under which his liberties are guaranteed in times of peace. During my service on the Appeals Board I discovered that some men and families make all sorts of excuses and resort to all kinds of subterfuges to keep some greedy, timid, or lazy and worthless renegade from doing his part. The man who has not enough character and gumption to join the ranks and to fight, if necessary, to defend America is not worthy to enjoy the advantages of American institutions.

Certainly our only hope of preserving our privileges under a free government rests in the willingness of all our people to unite in giving to the defense program all that each can offer. American ideals have been wrought out of the anvils of bitter conflict. We may have the wisdom and foresight to retain our independence and our privileges without fighting battles. We know we cannot maintain them if we are meekly submissive, weak, and defenseless. Our colleague from Illinois expressed it concisely yesterday when he said that it was better to train without fighting than to risk fighting without training. If we should be forced to fight in an extreme emergency, we must not throw into the front lines, unprepared, the finest flower of our youth. We must prepare a cross section from all those who are enjoying the privileges of American citizens—the greatest privileges enjoyed today by any people on the face of this earth.

I resent the propaganda which declares that we cannot preserve democracy in the world by abandoning democracy in the United States. Just how would these misguided citizens prepare democracy to fight for its own preservation? Do they expect an unorganized mob to face the onslaughts of the most highly trained and mechanized army the world has ever known? I hold that it is not inconsistent for democracy to accept discipline and leadership.

Our democracy is not an undisciplined, headless mob rushing hither and yon. It is a disciplined, devoted citizenship with orderly procedures, meeting events as they arise. Our men and women willingly face their responsibilities. They are not craven, nor rebellious. They know our country and our Government have not attained perfection, but they also believe that we are going forward in the hope of reaching our goal. Any action is consistent with democracy if arrived at through democratic processes.

THE PRICE OF PREPAREDNESS [8]

The first response of the American people to the war danger was to sanction the appropriation of huge sums of money for the Army and Navy, along with an increase in taxation. Necessary and natural though this was, it would be folly to think that making the nation secure is merely a matter of spending money. The price is sure to be more inclusive than that. What political sacrifices will it involve?

There is a current belief that a nation cannot successfully fight fascism without itself becoming Fascist. This belief is exploited in two opposite directions—by those who would keep out of war at any cost, and by those who want some kind of Fascist dictatorship. It is supported by a simple and persuasive logic. The essence of fascism is total concentration on war or on preparation for it. The essence of democracy is peace, individual freedom and good will. Democratic states are therefore certain to be beaten by Fascist enemies. They are too inefficient, divided and good natured to survive in a war culture. The only way to preserve democracy is to remain at peace, and the only way to win a war, if fighting cannot be avoided, is to go Fascist. Recent history is cited to confirm this conclusion.

But it is, for us at this moment in world history, a defeatist conclusion, and perhaps the strongest ally of Hitler and Mussolini. It leads a large number of people in this country, especially young people, to oppose not only entry into the war— a policy which may well be justified on many grounds—but anything like adequate preparation for resistance. This road,

[8] By George Soule, editor, New Republic. From "The Political Price of Preparedness." New Republic. 103:166-8. July 29, 1940. Reprinted by permission.

as European experience clearly shows, leads straight either to defeat in war or descent to voluntary vassaldom. The conclusion also prepares the way for a large number of other people to exercise their naturally Fascist tendencies by using the emergency as an excuse for a sapping of democratic rights and processes. When any proposal of this sort is made, many of those who would normally object shrug their shoulders and say, "Oh well, this is what we must expect when we go in for militarism." Once convinced that democracy cannot defend itself by arms, we either lose it by weakness against the aggressor or toss it away in the process of defending it.

Defeatist or not, the conclusion may turn out to be true. Many, including this writer, have pointed out the peril in the past. But there is no reason to think that descent into fascism is inevitable, or that there is no point in preferring a successful war of defense to submission. Democracy may indeed be betrayed by those who are always ready to turn its energies to military preparedness against illusory dangers. But there is a profound difference between a fear of unreal peril, used to enforce unprovoked aggression, and defense against a real attack. The first is a neurotic symptom, of the kind that we recognize as Fascist; the second is a wholesome and necessary act.

The difference at heart between a sick fascism and a healthy democracy is not that one is combative while the other does not have and never employs any fighting power, but that in the first case aggression is neurotically reinforced and is used inappropriately, while in the second case it is called for only in the presence of actual danger. It is risky to speak of nations as if they were individuals, but something like this is true at least of separate persons. The man who sees enemies and conspiracies everywhere and devotes his life to intrigue and murderous combat is insane. But the healthy man is not one who represses his aggression so rigidly that he will not and cannot fight under any circumstances. Nor is he incapable of returning to peaceable life when the fighting is over, just because he can be combative when assaulted.

I am not one of those who is so bemused by semantics that he thinks all words are deceptions and there is no reality. Fascism and democracy are both genuine entities, and the second is infinitely preferable to the first. Nevertheless the two words are commonly used by persons who understand neither. If we are to know in any positive sense whether we must sacrifice democracy in order to prepare to fight effectively, and if so to what extent, we shall have to get down to cases. . . .

A navy and a small army may be maintained by voluntary enlistment, but if, as is possible (and the plans of the administration are already laid on this basis), we shall need to organize an army of 2,000,000 seasoned men, with adequate reserves, it will be necessary to resort to conscription and compulsory military training. . . . Thorough training is necessary far in advance of any possible hostilities in modern warfare. The chief hesitation in embarking at once on such a plan is the doubt whether efforts to equip a great army might not interfere with the desperate need of Britain for those munitions we can now make.

Are conscription and compulsory service undemocratic? Norman Thomas has recently testified that they are Fascistic. That, it seems to me, is an inexcusably loose employment of words. Our Revolutionary War was, to be sure, fought with volunteers, many of whom deserted and went home whenever they felt like it, though Washington disciplined his men with far more brutal measures than would now be permitted. Long before fascism was ever heard of, Abraham Lincoln resorted to conscription in the Civil War. That measure was undemocratic in one important respect, because it allowed people with money to buy their way out by hiring substitutes. Conscription was employed by us in the last war, as by almost every other nation then and since, no matter what its form of government. Compelling men to serve in the army in time of war or threat-

ened war is undemocratic if one means by democracy un-
restricted individual liberty. It is the essence, however, of the
type of democracy that emphasizes the welfare of the community and equality of obligation. Recruiting an army by force
is tyrannical if the decision to do so is made by a tyrant, but
if it is voted by a democratic government it can scarcely be
called a dictatorial measure. Gallup polls have already indicated that a large majority of the citizens favor the proposal,
even in families containing men of military age. And a majority of men of military age themselves favor it. In these critical
times, if the controlling principle is to be supremacy of the
classic rights of individuals and minorities rather than the national need as determined by the majority, democracy is indeed
doomed.

A military force is by nature and practice undemocratic in
its rule. Orders must be unquestioningly obeyed; authority
descends from the top. Serving in it is a tough experience for
an individualist. But when, as on a ship in a storm or with
a party in the wilderness, survival demands submission to discipline, sensible democrats have always done so. This is as
truly a part of historic American life as is the New England
town meeting.

The real difference between democracy and its opposites,
when it comes to the military, has nothing to do with obedience
to the orders of a duly constituted superior. It does have to
do with the choice of that superior. Democracies can be betrayed by an autocratic military caste or even by individual officers subservient to anti-democratic groups. It is essential that
our armies be officered from those close to the people, by those
who believe in the cause they may have to fight for. And an
army composed of citizens, who return to civilian life as free
men, is not at all the same menace to democracy, either in war or
in peace, as a soldiery permanently dependent on the profession
of arms. If democrats control the government and compose

the army, neither preparedness nor war itself need endanger
our institutions as far as the military are concerned. . . .

FRENCH LABOR BATTALIONS [9]

For two days this week-end Vichy has been the center of
the first troop demonstration of the Labor Service for Youth,
which since the armistice has replaced the old obligatory military training for those who are 20 years old.

For eight months these young men have been under training
that is partly sporting and partly civil preparation under the
direction of demobilized officers of the old army. Half of
their time is devoted to work on public jobs.

Today Marshal Henri Philippe Pétain, appearing at the
municipal stadium, presented to the youth service its banner,
inscribed with the "Francisque," or battle axe, that the Marshal
has chosen for his emblem and with the motto of "Work,
Family and Country," which is that of the new French State.

A total of 2200 members of the labor group and delegates
from the six regional divisions of unoccupied France and from
North Africa participated in the ceremonies. They were dressed
in the new uniform of the service—dark green trousers and
jacket resembling ski costumes and berets like those of the
Chasseurs. The young men marched briskly in military formation, but without guns or tools. They were reviewed by Marshal Pétain, General Charles Huntziger, Minister of War, and
General de la Porte du Theil, who is the High Commissioner
of the service.

THE HEMISPHERE DEFENSE PROGRAM [10]

What *is* needed to make hemisphere defense a workable
military policy? . . .

[9] From "Labor Service Units Reviewed by Pétain." *New York Times.* June
30, 1941. p. 5. Reprinted by permission.
[10] By Hanson W. Baldwin, military and naval expert for *The New York Times.*
From "The Realities of Hemisphere Defense." *Reader's Digest.* 39:119-21. July,
1941. Reprinted by permission.

For the first time in our history we are facing enemies on both oceans, a hostile coalition of great powers—Germany, Italy, Japan, perhaps Russia. We must not underestimate their strength. But all of them collectively can muster no such strength as our own. *One* American steel company will this year turn out as much steel as all of Greater Germany combined. If we take the right measures this hemisphere can be defended and we need fear no evil. But we do have to take right measures. Our moats of oceans must be defended.

Hemisphere defense has four requirements: 1, sea power; 2, air power; 3, land power; 4, bases.

1. With completion of the present program we shall have ample sea power.

2. The plane is the weapon of the future. Our peculiar geographical conditions make the long-range bomber of vital importance to us. From our advanced bases, in Hawaii, Wake, Guam, Newfoundland, Bermuda, we must be able to bomb the enemy, his fleets and his bases consistently and persistently. As the years go on, the long-range bomber will tend to replace the fighting ship as our first line of defense; we must produce bombers of far longer range and greater bomb capacity than any other power needs. Fortunately we build the best; we must retain this lead in quality and we must materially increase the quantity. Our program has been revised in the past year to a scope which promises we shall eventually meet our needs for long-range planes, but not for rather a long time if we continue transferring the major part of our output to the British. . . .

3. Given the proper bases, ships and planes, hemisphere defense does not call for great manpower, but for highly trained and mobile forces ready for duty anywhere in the hemisphere. Part of this force should be organized as air infantry, with a spearhead of parachute troops. Another part should be especially equipped for amphibian operations, and like our newly reorganized Fleet Marine Force (sped to the scene of action by old but fast destroyers converted into transports), it should

be ready to move instantly to outlying parts of the western world. Still another part of this mobile force should be organized in armored divisions with considerable numbers of tanks. There should be specialists in winter warfare, in mountain, desert and jungle fighting. An army of 500,000 to 700,000 men would seem to provide all of these needs. But this army must be geared to the speedy tempo of modern war.

Indeed, navy, air force and army must be trained on the basis of speed. We must always be there first; we must never strike too late with too little. Our army still has this lesson to learn; we are still basing our ground defense too much on a slow-moving, mass-army concept.

4. The greatest weakness in our defenses is that we have no bases in South America which cover effectively the approaches to the bulge of Brazil. A large air and naval base on the shoulder of Brazil would complete our system of defense; with it we could certainly defend all that portion of South America that is important to our own security—the area from Recife, Brazil, northward—and it is probable we could defend all South America against any military assault. . . .

These, then, are the ingredients in a successful recipe for hemisphere defense.

WORLD EXPENDITURES FOR NATIONAL DEFENSE [11]
(*Figures in millions of dollars*)

	1933	1934	1935	1936	1937	1938	1939	1940
United States	540.3	710.0	911.7	964.9	992.1	1,065.6	1,162.6	1,800.2
Great Britain	455.5	480.6	595.6	846.9	1,263.1	1,693.3	1,817.1	2,300.0
France	678.8	582.7	623.8	834.4	909.2	731.5	1,800.2	1,800.0
Germany	299.5	381.5	2,600.0	3,600.0	4,000.0	4,400.0	4,500.1	6,000.0
Italy	241.2	263.7	778.1	916.1	573.4	526.0	873.4	1,000.0
U.S.S.R.	309.5	1,000.0	1,640.0	4,002.4	5,026.0	1,352.2	1,500.1	2,000.0
Japan	253.1	271.9	296.2	305.1	1,129.8	1,755.3	1,600.8	2,200.0
China	108.1	112.5	93.1	95.3	95.3	95.3	300.0	450.0

[11] From "National Defense Expenditures of the World." Table of figures from The Foreign Policy Association and other sources, as reprinted in *The World Almanac*, 1941. p. 104.

BIBLIOGRAPHY

An asterisk (*) preceding a reference indicates that the article or a part of it has been reprinted in this book.

ENCYCLOPEDIAS

Encyclopaedia Britannica. 6:282-6. 1937 edition. Conscription.

Basic information on the subject of conscription, with a discussion of its use in different periods in history.

Encyclopedia Americana. 7:544. 1940 edition. Conscription.

Historical materials are given with no attempt to analyze causes or results of compulsory service.

BIBLIOGRAPHIES

Matthews, M. Alice, comp. Conscription of men, material resources and wealth in time of war. 15p. mimeo. Carnegie Endowment for International Peace. Washington, D.C. 1940.

United States. Library of Congress, Division of Bibliography. List of speeches, addresses, etc., on national defense from Congressional Record, 1933-40. 39p. mimeo. Washington, D.C. 1940.

United States. Library of Congress, Division of Bibliography. Compulsory Military Training: a selected list of references. Ann Duncan Brown, comp. 25p. mimeo. Washington, D.C. 1940.

COMPILATIONS

Aly, Bower, comp. Military training: the fifteenth annual debate handbook. 2 v. 220p. ea. Artcraft Press. Columbia, Mo. 1941.

First volume contains analysis and interpretation of N.U.E.A. debate question, articles specially written for the handbook, and selected bibliography. Second volume includes reprints from current sources.

Johnsen, Julia E., comp. Compulsory military training. Reference Shelf, Vol. 14, no. 6. H. W. Wilson Co. New York. 1941.

Reprints of 25 articles on conscription, with brief and extensive bibliography.

BOOKS, PAMPHLETS AND DOCUMENTS

American Forum. Universal military training now. Yes! says James H. R. Cromwell; No! says Gerald P. Nye. Washington Daily News. 19p. June 29, 1940.

American Forum of the Air. v. 2. Shall we adopt compulsory selective military training and service now? Debate, June 30, 1940. 15p. Sen. Edward Burke, Arthur Capper and others. Ransdell, Inc. Washington, D.C. 1940.

American Forum of the Air. v. 2. Shall we conscript American manpower now? Debate. July 28, 1940. Sen. Arthur H. Vandenburg, Hon. James W. Wadsworth, Maj. Lewis B. Hershey, and others. Ransdell, Inc. Washington, D.C. 1940.

*American Legion. Why 18 to 21 universal military training? Publicity release by the American Legion Publicity Division, January 20, 1940.

A short history of the Legion fight for universal military training and a summarization of the current Legion attitude toward universal training.

Baldwin, Hanson W. United we stand! Whittlesey House publication. McGraw-Hill. New York. 364p. maps. 1941.

A comprehensive survey of the strength and weakness of the United States and an analysis of the military problems confronting the nation. Rated by reviewers as one of the best on the present national defense situation.

Baumer, William H. "21-35"; what the draft and army training mean to you. 143p. Prentice-Hall, Inc. New York. 1940.

Brooks, Robert Clarkson. Civic training in Switzerland, a study of the democratic life. 436p. Univ. of Chicago Press. Chicago. 1930.

Section devoted to Swiss military service, p. 142-70.

Capper, Sen. Arthur. Against peacetime conscription. Address over a National Broadcasting Company network, July 30, 1940.

An argument against conscription from the isolationist view, pointing out the hazard of such a course.

Cherne, L. M.   M-day and what it means to you. 103p. Simon
   & Schuster, Inc. New York. 1940.

   Questions and answers on the extent of government regulations to be expected
in wartime.

Compulsory military conscription.   7p. mimeo.   National Council
   of Jewish Women. New York. Ag. 1940.

Crowder, Maj. Gen. Enoch H.   The spirit of selective service.
   Century Co. New York. 1920.

   The selective service "bible"; one of the primary sources of information on
conscription and one of the most authentic.

De Gaulle, C. A. J. M.   The army of the future. 179p. Lippin-
   cott. New York. 1941.

   Originally published in 1934, this volume by the leader of the Free French
forces lists the principles of the new warfare by which the French did not act and
the Germans did.

Dickinson, John.   Builder of an army; a detailed account of
   legislation, administration and opinion in the United States,
   1915-20. 398p. Century Co. New York. 1922.

*Draper, Col. William H., jr.   Selective service in operation.
   An address before the Eighth Metropolitan Conference on
   Employment and Guidance, Park Central Hotel, New York
   City, November 16, 1940.   A press release of the national
   headquarters, Selective Service System.

   Discusses the origin of conscription in the U.S. and its workings at the
present time.   Points out that the major objective of present training is for
war, not for peace.

*Erskine, John.   Universal training for national defense. 15p.
   Pamphlet no. 27, issued by the Civilian Military Education
   Fund. Washington, D.C. 1940.

   Paper originally prepared as a report to General Pershing in 1919, lists suggestions for America based on A.E.F. experience in World War I and asks for a
year's training in camps for every man as an educational measure.

Fitzpatrick, Edward A.   Conscription and America; a study of
   conscription in a democracy. 153p. Richard Publishing Co.
   Milwaukee. 1940.

   Conscription from the historical and present day aspects, with analysis of its
effect on democracy.

Ford, H. S.   What the citizen should know about the army.
   230p. Norton & Co. New York. 1941.

   A consideration of the organization of the U. S. army, function of the general
staff, training of officers and men, the conduct of war.   Also includes the text of
the 1940 conscription bill.

French, Paul C. We won't murder. 189p. Hastings House. New York. 1940.

The case of the wartime conscientious objector and the history of religious pacifism. From the Quaker point of view.

Grafton, Samuel. All out! How democracy will defend America; based on the French failure, the English stand, and the American program. 104p. Simon & Schuster. New York. 1940.

Hagood, Gen. Johnson. We can defend America. 321p. Doubleday, Doran. Garden City, N.Y. 1937.

Contains sections on R.O.T.C., p. 227-39; C.M.T.C., p. 240-2; C.C.C., p. 242-6; and enlisted reserve, p. 246-8.

*Hershey, Brig. Gen. Lewis B. The present and future of selective service. An address made during the National Radio Forum, arranged by the Washington Evening Star and broadcast over the Blue network of the National Broadcasting Company, June 23, 1941. 5p. mimeo. Issued as an N.B.C. news release, June 23, 1941.

Hershey, Brig. Gen. Lewis B. The responsibilities of your generation. An address before the annual convention of the Junior Chamber of Commerce, Minneapolis, Minn., June 20, 1941. 9p. mimeo. Issued by the Selective Service System.

A plea for national unity in the defense program, stressing the need for youth in business to cooperate with labor and the government to build the nation's defenses.

Hershey, Brig. Gen. Lewis B. The selective service act and the college student. An address before the International Student Conference on National Defense, New Haven, Conn., April 5, 1941. 19p. mimeo. Issued by the Selective Service System.

James, George F. Eight years of the C.M.T.C.; a brief account of the Citizens' Military Training Camps, 1921-28. 23p. Military Training Camps Association of the U. S. Chicago. 1928.

Jauncey, Leslie C. Story of conscription in Australia. 365p. George Allen & Unwin. London. 1935.

Opening section shows the advancing trend toward compulsory military training, p. 1-35. Useful in contrasting public attitudes of both U.S. and Australia to a system to which both peoples have been traditionally opposed.

Johnson, Sveinbjorn. Military training as a factor in education. 19p. Pamphlet no. 25. Civilian Military Education Fund. Washington, D.C. 1938.

*Joint Army and Navy Selective Service Committee. American selective service. 35p. United States Government Printing Office. Washington, D.C. Oct. 1939.

A brief account of the historical background of selective service in America and its probable form in the future. Contains sections on military service in Great Britain and the United States and current plans (1939) for selective service and volunteering in wartime. Also includes a bibliography, the constitutional basis for conscription, and supreme court views on the subject.

Keenleyside, Hugh L., and Thomas, Andrew F. History of Japanese education and present educational system. 365p. The Hokuseido Press. Tokyo. 1937.

Section on military training, p. 199-201.

Keyhoe, Donald E. M-day; if war comes, what your government plans for you. 96p. Dutton. New York. 1940.

A popularized version of what will happen to citizens in every walk of life when war comes to America.

Military Training Camps Association of the U. S. National Emergency Committee. Why volunteer system is inadequate: facts and figures. 8p. The Association. New York. 1940.

Moore, Albert B. Conscription and conflict in the Confederacy. Macmillan. New York. 1924.

Nason, Leonard H. Approach to battle. 113p. Doubleday, Doran. New York. 1941.

Nickerson, Hoffman. The armed horde, 1793-1939. 384p. Putnam. New York. 1940.

The origin, growth, culmination and recent decline of the armed horde theory in modern warfare and the rise of the highly trained professional soldier instead of the raw draft legions.

*O'Kelliher, Lt. Col. Victor J. Selective service during and since the World War. A radio address made over station WOL, Washington, D. C., and the Mutual Broadcasting System. 5p. mimeo. Issued by the Selective Service System.

A brief analysis of selective service in World War I and its development up to the present time, with emphasis on the fairness and value of the system.

Palmer, John M. Statesmanship or war. 232p. Doubleday, Page. Garden City, N.Y. 1927.

"Switzerland has actually developed the type of armament proposed for us by the father of our country. Therefore in this book I have described the essential features of the Swiss military system and have explained how they can be adapted to American conditions on a purely voluntary basis"—Foreword.

Partridge, Alden. Educational value of military training. Pamphlet no. 20. Civilian Military Education Fund. Washington, D.C. 1936.

*Pershing, Gen. John J. Universal military training for youth. 8p. mimeo. Civilian Military Education Fund. Washington, D.C.

Partial text of statement before the committees on military affairs, U. S. Congress, Oct. 31, '19. Contains questions and answers relating to various problems of universal training, including length of training, character of training, training age and time limits, etc. Also includes quotations from other military leaders on universal training.

Public Affairs Committee, National Board of the Y.M.C.A. Conscription—the American way? 8p. Citizenship and Public Affairs Series, release no. 2. Aug. 1940. The Committee. New York. 1940.

States major issues: Is conscription necessary now; is the draft compatible with democracy; will it produce the kind of citizenship we want; and is it democratic; with pro and con arguments quoted from outside sources.

Rankin, E. R. comp. Universal military training; debate handbook. 102p. (Extension Bulletin. Vol. 20, no. 1) University of North Carolina. Chapel Hill. July 1940.

*Reilly, Brig. Gen. Henry J. Are our young men to have a chance? Blitzkrieg, its political and economic challenge. 24p. Pamphlet no. 29. Civilian Military Education Fund. Washington, D.C. 1940.

Develops history behind universal military training, the unfairness of the volunteer system, and includes sections on increased cost of national defense, the cost of unpreparedness, a comparison of the C.C.C. with the R.O.T.C. and suggests a plan for universal military training modeled after that of pre-war France.

Saerchinger, César. Compulsory service in the United States. 12p. mimeo. (Story Behind the Headlines, no. 35.) Columbia University Press. New York. June 30, 1940.

Schreiner, Albert. Hitler rearms. 336p. John Lane. The Bodley Head. London. 1934.

Contains sections on the new mass army and its value in modern warfare, p. 37-70; and on officer training under the new system, p. 71-106.

Stockton, Richard. Inevitable war. 806p. Perth. New York. 1932.

An analysis of the probable methods of enlistment, training, discipline, organization and equipment of the citizen army, p. 715-31.

Tansill, Charles C. Militarism. 31p. Digest Press. Washington, D.C. 1935.

Tobin, Harold J., and Bidwell, Percy W. Mobilizing civilian America. 276p. Council on Foreign Relations. New York. 1940.

A book on planned mobilizations as they stood in April, 1940. Contains sketches on government methods of regulation in wartime, its character and policies, army recruitment, civilian and military controls. A large part is devoted to a summary of experiences in World War I and the conclusions which may be drawn in relation to the future.

United States. Congress. House. Committee on Military Affairs. Compulsory military training and service. Hearings July 10-August 14, 1940, on H. R. 10132. 655p. 76th Cong. 3rd sess. Supt. of Doc. Washington, D.C. 1940.

United States. Congress. Senate. Committee on Military Affairs. Compulsory military training. Hearing June 2-4, 1936, on S. 3309. 297p. Supt. of Doc. Washington, D.C. 1936.

United States. Congress. Senate. Committee on Military Affairs. Compulsory military training and service. Hearings July 3-12, 1940, on S. 4164. 400p. 76th Cong. 3rd sess. Supt. of Doc. Washington, D.C. 1940.

United States. Congress. Senate. Committee on Military Affairs. Compulsory military training and service. Report on S. 4164, August 5, 1940. 13p. 76th Cong. 3rd sess. Rept. no. 2002. Supt. of Doc. Washington, D.C. 1940.

*United States. War Department. Bureau of Public Relations, radio branch. Educational bulletin no. 8. 3p. mimeo. July 7, 1941.

Paragraph 27 lists the strength of the United States Army as of July, 1940, as totalling 1,448,500 men.

Upton, Bvt. Maj. Gen. Emory. The military policy of the United States. War Department Document 290. Gov. Printing Office. Washington, D.C. 1904.

A guide to American military policy with historical information relating to past policies of recruiting, training, and universal service experiences prior to 1900. One of the most authoritative volumes available.

Werner, Max. The military strength of the powers. 324p. pa. Modern Age. New York. 1939.

Development of theme that since '32 a revolution in military technique has occurred and resulted in total war theory. The new developments analyzed include study of mobilization of entire war potential and the value to a nation of vast war materials reserves is emphasized. Author's conclusion aimed to show how potentially powerful the Soviet Union could be in wartime.

White, William Allen, ed. Defense for America. 205p. Macmillan. New York. 1940.

Woord, R. E. Our foreign policy. Address delivered Oct. 4, 1940, before the Chicago Council on Foreign Relations. 8p. mimeo.

An analysis of the interventionist and isolationist views on the war situation, with the conclusion that the only Nazi threat to America is economic warfare, but that aid to Britain is essential to protect our nation and to defeat Nazism.

PERIODICALS

Advertising and Selling. 33:22-4+. S. '40. Business effects of conscription. Paul T. Cherington.

American Bar Association Journal. 26:701-5. S. '40. Legal basis for conscription. Claude B. Mickelwait.

American Federationist. 48:3-4. O. '40. The draft: what it means to you and the nation.

American Historical Review. 21:100-3. O. '15. Conscription in the Civil War.

*American Magazine. 128:16-17+. D. '39. Uncle Sam's plans for you if war comes. Donald E. Keyhoe.

*American Magazine. 130:16-17+. S. '40. Every boy a soldier. Henry Cabot Lodge, jr.

American Magazine. 131:52-4. F. '41. Why not a universal draft? John Erskine.

*American Mercury. 51:295-302. N. '40. Legend of American invincibility. Willard K. Smith.

American Mercury. 52:558+. My. '41. Conscription hits the campus. Gaynor Maddox.

American School Board Journal. 102:28-9. F. '41. Military training in secondary schools. William P. Uhler, jr.

American School Board Journal. 102:43. Mr. '41. Waste of military training in high schools.

Annals of the American Academy. 66:173. Jl. '16. Democracy of universal military service. Franklin H. Gidding.

Annals of the American Academy. 204:49-53. Jl. '39. Defense of the Americas. George Fielding Eliot.

Atlantic Monthly. 166:1-7. Jl. '40. Hemisphere defense. Louis A. Johnson.

Atlantic Monthly. 166:138-44. Ag. '40. Army without arms. T. H. Thomas.

Bellman. 25:680. D. 21, '18. Universal military service.

Canadian Forum. 19:342-3. F. '40. Conscription in Canada.

Canadian Forum. 20:242-3. N. '40. Canada's democratic army. Miles Resartus.

*Chicago Sunday Tribune. Ap. 27, '41. Part I, p. 16. The conscripts.

*Chicago Sunday Tribune. Ap. 27, '41. Part I, p. 16. Britain's new army officers. Larry Rue.

Christian Century. 46:1459. N. 27, '29. Australia abolishes conscription.

Christian Century. 53:58-9. Ja. 8, '36. Enroll girls in Philippine army.

*Christian Century. 53:565-7. Ap. 15, '36. Army tries to teach. S. S. Sargent.

Christian Century. 54:107-9. Ja. 27, '37. Shall conscription come again?

*Christian Century. 57:845. Jl. 3, '40. Shall American youth be conscripted?

Christian Century. 57:894-5. Jl. 17, '40. No conscription.

Christian Century. 57:928. Jl. 24, '40. Conscription imminent, act now.

Christian Century. 57:949-51. Jl. 31, '40. This draft is despotism. Daniel Webster.

Christian Century. 57:988. Ag. 14, '40. Conscription—who wants it?

Christian Century. 57:994-5. Ag. 14, '40. If conscription comes.

Christian Century. 57:1074-6. S. 4, '40. Will colleges present arms?

Christian Century. 57:1126. S. 11, '40. Draft law means fascism wins.

Christian Century. 57:1165. S. 25, '40. Why did Mr. Roosevelt demand conscription?

Christian Century. 57:1220. O. 2, '40. Federal committee discusses the draft.

Christian Century. 57:1349. O. 30, '40. Training in Canada. Claris E. Silcox.

Collier's. 104:9-11+. N. 4, '39. They've picked your war job; this is how our lives will be changed when M-day dawns. Walter Davenport.

Collier's. 106:15+. Mr. 22, '41. We're in the army now. Gen. Hugh A. Drum.

Columbia Law Review. 40:1374. D. '40. Mobilization for defense.

Commonweal. 32:357-9. Ag. 23, '40. Against peacetime conscription. Philip Burnham; H. L. Binsse.

Congressional Digest. 17:68. Mr. '38. Roosevelt's message to Congress, Ja. 28, '38.

Congressional Digest. 17:71. Mr. '38. Policy of the United States army.

*Congressional Record. 86:15661. Ag. 13, '40. Selective service; senate discussion by Sen. Edward R. Burke of Nebraska.

*Congressional Record. 86:4231. Ag. 14, '40. Extension of remarks on the selective service bill by Hon. Butler B. Hare of South Carolina.

Congressional Record. 86:15771. Ag. 14, '40. Conscription laws of New Zealand and Australia, presented in Senate debate on the selective service bill by Sen. Burton K. Wheeler of Montana.

Congressional Record. 86:15964-5. Ag. 15, '40. Editorial from the Lawrence (Mass.) *Bee* on conscription, presented by Sen. Charles L. McNary of Oregon.

Congressional Record. 86:16125. Ag. 19, '40. Extension of remarks of Hon. Estes Kefauver of Tennessee on conscription.

*Congressional Record. 86:16144-6. Ag. 20, '40. Remarks on conscription by Sen. Elbert D. Thomas of Utah.

Congressional Record. 86:16420-1. Ag. 22, '40. Remarks on conscription by Sen. Rush D. Holt of West Virginia.

*Congressional Record. 86:16428-9. Ag. 22, '40. Statements of John L. Lewis and of heads of railroad brotherhoods on conscription.

*Congressional Record. 86:16441. Ag. 22, '40. Statement by C. Bruggmann, Minister of Switzerland, on the Swiss universal training system.

*Congressional Record. 86:16450. Ag. 22, '40. Remarks on conscription by Sen. William J. Bulow of South Dakota.

*Congressional Record. 86:16513. Ag. 23, '40. Radio comment on conscription by Fulton Lewis, jr.

*Congressional Record. 86:16518. Ag. 23, '40. Editorial from the Tulsa *Tribune* on conscription.

*Congressional Record. 86:16522. Ag. 23, '40. Editorial, "The Kids," from *PM,* by Ralph Ingersoll.

*Congressional Record. 86:16544. Ag. 23, '40. Remarks on conscription by Sen. Burton K. Wheeler of Montana.

Congressional Record. 86:17235. Ag. 30, '40. Article, "Machines, not men, are the country's most urgent need," by Maj. Al Williams.

*Congressional Record. 86:17308-9, 17311-12, 17318-19, 17334-5. S. 3, '40. House debate on the selective service bill, by Congressmen Johnson, Seccombe, Brown, Voorhis, Anderson.

Congressional Record. 86:17367. S. 4, '40. Remarks on selective service by Hon. Dewey Short of Missouri.

*Congressional Record. 86:17379. S. 4, '40. Remarks on selective service by Hon. Emanuel Celler of New York.

Congressional Record. 86:17548-9. S. 5, '40. Remarks on selective service by Hon. John J. Sparkman of Alabama.

Congressional Record. 86:19394. S. 9, '40. Remarks on peacetime conscription by Hon. John M. Vorys of Ohio.

Congressional Record. 86:21573-4. D. 18, '40. Article, "The American Legion and national defense," by Judge Warren H. Atherton.

Contemporary Review. 107:610-17. My. '15. Free service or conscription.

Current History. 48:43-5. My. '38. Schoolboys to officers. Edwin L. Stoll.

Current History. 49:43. Ja. '39. America's peace army. John L. Christian.

Current History. 49:54-5. Ja. '39. The life of a conscript. G. B. de Vilaines.

Current History. 51:22-6. N. '39. France goes to war. Robert Strausz-Hupe.

Current History & Forum. 51:16-19. Jl. '40. Arms for America. Basil C. Walker.

Current History & Forum. 51:32-6. Ag. '40. Mobilizing U.S. manpower. Robert Strausz-Hupe.

Current History & Forum. 52:51-3. My. '41. The first army. Gen. Hugh A. Drum.

Current History & Forum. 53:25-6. Je. '41. Army facts.

Current History Magazine of The New York Times. 5:446-9. D. '16. Australia's defeat of conscription.

Current History Magazine of The New York Times. 6:pt. 2: 292-3. Ag. '17. Canada to have conscription.

Debaters' Digest. 15:45-68. S. '41.
Analysis of terms, bibliography.

Economist (London). 135:294-5. My 6, '39. Issues of conscription.

Edinburgh Review. 230:43-59. Jl. '19. Conscript armies.

Editorial Research Reports. p. 71-84. Ag. 14, '40. Conscription in the U. S. Buel W. Patch.

Education. 41:152-8. N. '20. Training a citizen army.

*Education. 61:74-7. O. '40. CCC and defense of the nation. H. W. Oxley.

*Educational Record. 21:441-4. O. '40. Train conscripts for war and peace. John Erskine.

Events. 5:433-7. Je. '39. Conscription in Britain. Herbert Heaton.

Foreign Affairs. 18:35-54. O. '40. The new American army. Hanson W. Baldwin.

Foreign Affairs. 19:618-9. Ap. '41. The Mexican army. Virginia Prewett.

*Foreign Policy Reports. 16:220-7. D. 1, '41. The U. S. army in transition. David H. Popper.

Fortnightly. 103:1043-56. Je. '15. Conscription and democracy.

Fortnightly. 104:938. N. '15. Military preparation of young France.

Fortnightly. 106:55-65. Jl. '16. Democracy and universal military service.

Fortnightly. 150(ns144):549-58. N. '38. National service and a national register.

Fortnightly. 151(ns145):106-9. Ja. '39. Experiment in freedom. Stephen Gwynn.

Fortnightly. 151(ns145):527-33. My. '39. Democracy and compulsory service.

Fortnightly. 151(ns145):681-7. Je. '39. A Frenchman's military service.

*Fortune. 20:116. D. '39. Fortune survey: would you favor compulsory military service for all young men—18 or 19?

Fortune. 22:59-60+. S. '40. U. S. defense: the armed forces.

Forum. 75:375-7. Mr. '26. Universal service. Dwight Filley Davis.

Forum & Century. 94:131-2, 149-55. S. '35. Military training; a debate. Edwin C. Johnson.

Discussion. Forum & Century. 94:sup. 11. O. '35; 94:sup. 10-11. N. '35; 94:sup. 10-11. My. '36.

Forum & Century. 98:97-8. S. '37. Soldiers as educators.

Forum & Century. 103:282-7. My. '40. Future of CCC. C. S. Marsh.

Good Housekeeping. 111:4. N. '40. Insurance against war.

Harper's. 175:460-9. O. '37. Sons of the wolf.

Harper's. 182:1-13. D. '40. U. S. army.

Harvard Law Review. 54:278-92. D. '40. Mobilization for defense.

Independent. 85:183. F. 7, '16. British conscription.

Independent. 86:239. My. 15, '16. Draft act in England.

Independent. 90:41. Ap. 2, '17. Debate: should we adopt military service for everyone?

*Independent. 90:191-2. Ap. 28, '17. Conscription.

*Liberty. 18:20-1. Ag. 23, '41. Conscription and education. Robert Hutchins.

Life. 9:28-9. Ag. 26, '40. Senate debates conscription.

Life. 9:17-21. S. '30, '40. America answers Hitler with the draft.

Literary Digest. 55:25-6. Jl. 28, '17. Conscription splitting Canada.

Literary Digest. 57:21. Ap. 20, '18. Who caused the Quebec riots?

*Literary Digest. 90:14. S. 18, '26. Attack on draft armies.

Literary Digest. 95:10. N. 5, '27. Legion's conscription program.

Literary Digest. 109:8. My. 30, '31. U. S. peacetime plan for war.

Literary Digest. 123:10. Ja. 16, '37. Congressional controversy over militarism.

Living Age. 300:337-40. F. 8, '19. Was Lord Roberts right?

Living Age. 360:213. My. '41. Red army turns Prussian. V. Ossipev.

Nation. 101:402-3. S. 30, '15. Conscription: pro and con.

Nation. 102:510. My. 11, '16. Universal service.

Nation. 105:195-7. Ag. 23, '17. Canadian crisis.

Nation. 108:973. Je. 21, '19. American militarism waning.

Nation. 109:334-5. S. 6, '19. Framed in France—propaganda for universal military training.

Nation. 141:459-60. O. 23, '35. Take the army out of the CCC. R. G. Swing.

Nation. 144:236-8. F. 27, '37. Kill conscription.

Nation. 144:496. My. 1, '37. Blueprints for fascism.

Nation. 149:551-4. N. 18, '39. Canada's war election.

Nation. 149:602-4. D. 2, '39. The empire and the war. Albert Viton.

*Nation. 150:394. Mr. 23, '40. Report on military training at U. of C. Oswald Garrison Villard.

Nation. 150:525. Ap. 20, '40. Discussion.

Nation. 150:723-4. Je. 15, '40. Democratic program of defense. Freda Kirchwey.

*Nation. 151:85-8. Ag. 3, '40. There is no alternative. Freda Kirchwey.

*Nation. 151:86-8. Ag. 3, '40. Conscripting America. M. S. Stewart.

*Nation. 151:179. Ag. 31, '40. Youth and draft. David Burgess and Leonard Detweiler.

Nation. 151:184-5. S. 7, '40. Draft bill.

Nation. 151:200. S. 7, '40. Democracy and conscription.

New Republic. 6:205-7. Mr. 25, '16. The free man and the soldier. Ralph Barton Perry.

*New Republic. 6:266-8. Ap. 8, '16. Real implications of conscription. Norman Angell.

*New Republic. 6:309-10. Ap. 22, '16; 6:334-5. Ap. 29, '16. Universal service as education. John Dewey.

New Republic. 6:345-6. Ap. 29, '16. Relevance of conscription.

New Republic. 12:261-2. O. 6, '17. Future limitations of conscription.

New Republic. 12:274. O. 6, '17. Distorting the conscription issue.

*New Republic. 22:70-2. Mr. 17, '20. Universal training versus preparedness.

New Republic. 22:94. Mr. 17, '20. Military preparedness. Charles W. Whittlesey.

New Republic. 66:358. My. 13, '31. Breeding war.

New Republic. 85:47. N. 20, '35. Showing the military march.

*New Republic. 103:6-7. Jl. 1, '40. Universal military service.

*New Republic. 103:166-8. Jl. 29, '40. Political price of preparedness. George Soule.

New Republic. 103:206-7. Ag. 12, '40. Common sense on conscription.

New Republic. 103:231-2. Ag. 19, '40. Conscripting whom for what?

*New Republic. 103:294. S. 2, '40. Do we need conscription?

New Republic. 103:406-7. S. 23, '40. This man's army. Malcolm Cowley.

*New Republic. 104:364-6. Mr. 17, '41. Next four years: the citizen army. Jonathan Mitchell.

New York Times Magazine. 90:4-5 +. Je. 23, '40. How Hitler prepared: The rearming of the Reich. Otto D. Tolischus.

New York Times Magazine. 90:4-5. S. 22, '40. Call to arms, American style. L. H. Robbins.

*New York Times Magazine. 90:4-6. Ap. 6, '41. Trainee: four months later. Meyer Berger.

New York Times. 90:8. Je. 23, '41. German strength estimated. Hanson W. Baldwin.

New York Times. 90:8. Je. 23, '41. Soviet men in line put at 2,400,000.

*New York Times. 90:1. Je. 29, '41. Army is far short of war efficiency after year of effort. Hanson W. Baldwin.

*New York Times. 90:5. Je. 30, '41. Labor service units reviewed by Pètain.

*New York Times. 90:14. Jl. 1, '41. Emphasis in army swinging to speed. Hanson W. Baldwin.

New York Times. 90:3. Jl. 6, '41. Demand for draft reviewed in Canada. P. J. Philip.

*New York Times. 90:22. Jl. 6, '41. Lack of specialists disappointing to army.

New York Times. 90:23. Jl. 6, '41. Fifth division excels First in '17.

*New York World-Telegram. p. 1+. Ag. 25, '41. U.S. faces years of arming. W. P. Simms.

*Newsweek. 16:36+. N. 18, '40. Army expands military plant with eye to permanent setup.

*Newsweek. 17:24. Ap. 14, '41. Eight years of the CCC.

Newsweek. 17:40-1. Ap. 28, '41. Draft weathervanes.

Newsweek. 17:17. My. 5, '41. Democracy's front bolstered by expansion of naval patrol.

*Newsweek. 17:35-6. My. 19, '41. First year of defense effort spotlights vitality of nation.

Nineteenth Century. 81:468. F. '17. Compulsory service in Australia.

Nineteenth Century. 87:638-50. Ap. '20. Manpower in the next war.

Nineteenth Century. 88:679-98. O. '20. Nation in arms in Great War.

Nineteenth Century. 94:342. S. '23. Urgent need for compulsory service.

Nineteenth Century. 94:745. N. '23. National service.

Outlook. 115:688-9. Ap. 18, '17. Conscription and training.

*PM. p. 8. Jl. 29, '40. Editorial: The kids. Ralph Ingersoll.

Popular Mechanics. 75:8-13+. Ja. '41. Serving the U.S. for 12 months.

Popular Mechanics. 75:706-9. My. '41. American defenders on the firing line.

Printers' Ink. 192:123-5. S. 27, '40. How the 1940 draft will build new markets.

Reader's Digest. 35:23-7. Ag. '39. M-day and after. Cabell Phillips and J. D. Ratliff.

*Reader's Digest. 37:52-3. O. '40. American youth speaks up. George Gallup.

*Reader's Digest. 39:119-21. Jl. '41. The realities of hemisphere defense. Hanson W. Baldwin.

*Reserve Officer. Je. '41. Selective service. Maj. Ernest M. Culligan.
  Reprint issued by Selective Service System.

*Review of Reviews. 51:357-8. Mr. '15. English conscription and our Civil War draft.

Review of Reviews. 52:489. O. '15. Australasian military system.

Review of Reviews. 54:209. Ag. '16. Universal service.

Rotarian. 59:11-2. Jl. '41. Canada at war.

Saturday Evening Post. 213:27+. Je. 15, '40. Your son will not return—heil Hitler! John McCutcheon Raleigh.

Saturday Evening Post. 213:26. S. 28, '40. Conscription.

*Scholastic. 37:11+. S. 16, '40. Conscription issue: past and present. Henry Steele Commager.

Scholastic. 37:2. S. 23, '40. Conscription bill passed.

Scholastic. 37:38. O. 7, '40. Controversial issue.

Scholastic. 37:2. O. 21, '40. Conscription begins.

Scholastic. 38:16. Mr. 10, '41. Building a citizen army.

Scholastic. 38: .. O. 20, '41. Compulsory training—should all able-bodied men have one year of it before the age of 21? Thomas A. Rousse.

School and Society. 43:54-5. Ja. 11, '36. Committee on militarism in education.

School and Society. 46:524. O. 23, '37. Military education in Italy.

School and Society. 47:314-5. Mr. 5, '38. Militarization in Czech education. Joseph F. Roucek.

*School and Society. 51:261-8. Mr. 2, '40. School military training reconsidered. Edwin C. Johnson.

*School and Society. 51:725. Je. 8, '40. The new educational problems of national defense.

*School and Society. 52:366-7. O. 19, '40. Role of high school curriculum in national preparedness. Calvin P. Stone.

School and Society. 53:756-7. Je. 14, '41. Some arguments for reducing the draft age below 21. H. L. Kriner.

School Review. 25:177. Mr. '17. Principal military systems.

School Review. 47:723-4. D. '39. Timely opposition to militarization.

School Review. 48:481-3. S. '40. Declaration against military training.

*School Review. 49:195-205. Mr. '41. Retroactive experiments on effects of military training in high schools. Douglas E. Scates and Dale K. Spencer.

*Science News Letter. 37:172. Mr. 16, '40. Military training in college fails to change attitude.

Scientific Monthly. 9:15-17. Jl. '19. Eugenic aspect of selective conscription.

Scribner's Commentator. 10:102-3. Ja. '41. The cost of national defense. Frederick C. Smith.

Survey. 36:596+. S. 16, '16. Federal conscription act?

Survey. 37:492-3. Ja. 27, '17. Swiss and Russian views.

Survey. 42:859-60. S. 13, '19. Preparing for preparedness.

*Survey Mid-Monthly. 76:362. D. '40. Specific training for non-combatant defense service.

*Thought. 15:623-40. D. '40. Historical background of compulsory military training. C. C. Tansill.

This Week. (Syndicated feature) D. 8, '40. A year out of your life. Lyle M. Spencer.

Time. 27:27-8. Ap. 13, '36. For self-preservation.

*Time. 35:17. Je. 17, '40. Service for all.

Time. 36:12-13. S. 16, '40. Bitter end.

Time. 36:19-20. S. 23, '40. How the draft works.

Time. 37:32-5. Ja. 20, '41. Australia in arms.

*Time. 37:21-3. My. 19, '41. National defense: The U. S. effort, preparedness, 1941.

*Time. 37:69. My. 19, '41. The army goes to school.

U. S. News. p. 20. S. 27, '40. Conscription sentiments.

Virginia Quarterly Review. 17:no. 2:161-78. (Ap.) '41. Ivory towers into watch towers.

Vital Speeches. 4:267-9. F. 15, '39. Hatred on the rampage.

Vital Speeches. 6:629-31. Ag. 1, '40. Compulsory military training for what? Frederick C. Smith.

Vital Speeches. 6:647-8. Ag. 15, '40. Our duty is clear: compulsory service must be adopted. Henry L. Stimson.

Vital Speeches. 6:686-7. S. 1, '40. Crisis confronting nation; the country is being rushed pell-mell into military conscription. Harry Emerson Fosdick.

Vital Speeches. 6:712-14. S. 15, '40. We must prepare; address September 3, 1940. Franklin D. Roosevelt.

Vital Speeches. 6:729-30. S. 15, '40. Selective service right now. Hugh S. Johnson.

World Affairs. 103:128-30. S. '40. Selective service and training.

*World's Work. 33:16-24. N. '16. Shall we adopt universal service? Charles W. Eliot.

World's Work. 33:381. F. '17. Universal military service in Argentina.

*World's Work. 37:547-52. Mr. '19. What kind of military training? J. B. W. Gardiner.

World's Work. 37:705-8. Ap. '19. Universal training and officers.

*World's Work. 39:33-6, 200-4, 275-9, 380-4. N. '19-F. '20. Lest we forget—unpreparedness. Henry W. Lanier.

World's Work. 39:537-8. Ap. '20. A.B.C.'s of universal military training.

Yale Law Journal. 50:250-9. D. '40. Mobilization for defense.

University Debaters' Annuals

E. M. PHELPS, Ed. *Cloth. Price $2.25*

Series of year books, each a collection of representative intercollegiate debates on important questions of the day. Constructive and rebuttal speeches for both sides. Each debate is accompanied by selected bibliography and briefs.

Vol. XXVII. 1940-1941.

Industry Can Solve the Employment Problem; Conscription of Capital for Defense; Preservation of Democracy Through Decreased Government Control; Interstate Trade Barriers; Japanese Aggression; Union of United States and British Commonwealth of Nations; Regulation of the American Press; Compulsory Military Training; Strikes in Defense Industries; Western Hemisphere Defense.

Vol. XXVI. 1939-1940.

The Basis of a Lasting Peace; Shall the United States Enter the War?; Government Ownership and Operation of Railroads; Neutrality of the United States; Extension of Reciprocal Trade Agreements; The Third Term for President; Should the Roosevelt Administration Be Approved?; The Dies Committee; Civil Liberties; Labor; Foreign Affairs; Government and Business.

Vol. XXV. 1938-1939.

The Increase in the National Debt; The Anglo-American Alliance; Government Ownership and Operation of the Railroads; Alliance of United States, France and Great Britain Against Fascism; Have the Achievements of Science Brought Progress?; American Solidarity; The Problem of Unemployment; The American Newspaper; "Pump-priming" Should Cease; Government and Health.

Vol. XXIV. 1937-1938.

Democracy and Economic Prosperity; American Isolation from European Affairs; Protection of United States Citizens on Foreign Soil; Academic Freedom; Grades and Final Tests Subversive of the Aims of Higher Education; American League of Nations; Anglo-American Mutual Assistance Pact; N.L.R.A. and Arbitration of Industrial Disputes; Unicameral Legislatures; Uniform Marriage Laws; Regulation of Advertising.

Vol. XXIII. 1936-1937.

The Constitution a Menace; Government Ownership of Electric Utilities; Subsidizing College Athletes; Teachers' Oaths; Unicameral Legislatures; Economic Internationalism; Minimum Wages and Maximum Hours (two debates); Consumers' Cooperatives; The Present-day Family as a Social Institution; The Sit-down Strike.

Vol. XXII. 1935-1936.

A Written Constitution a Hindrance to Social Progress; State Medicine; Compulsory Military Training; Legalization of Sweepstakes; Admission of Negroes to State Universities; The Neutrality Policy of the United States; The Parole System; Admission of Hawaii as a State; Limitation of the Power of the Supreme Court (two debates).

Vol. XXI. 1934-1935.

Equalizing Educational Opportunity; An Evaluation of the New Deal; Social Services and Unemployment Relief; International Traffic in Arms and Munitions; Democratic Collectivism; The Agricultural Adjustment Administration; Collective Bargaining; Government Ownership and Operation of Public Utilities; Pacifism the Highest Form of Patriotism; Japan and Naval Parity.

Vol. XX. 1933-1934.

British System of Radio Control and Operations; Armed Intervention; Japanese Policy in the Far East; A Department of the Consumer in the President's Cabinet; University of Chicago Plan of Education; Economic Reconstruction; Increasing the Powers of the President; Socialized Medicine; Freer Trade; Problem of State Liquor Control.

Vol. XIX. 1932-1933.

Limitation by Law of Gifts, Incomes and Inheritance; Property Taxation for State and Local Revenue; British System of Radio Control; Safety-Responsibility Plan of Automobile Insurance; Voluntary Domestic Allotment Plan; Federal Regulation of Electric Power Utilities; Dictatorship Versus Democracy; Capitalism Has Broken Down; Peace Is Impossible Under Capitalism; Stimson Doctrine of Non-recognition of Territory Acquired Through Violation of Treaties.

Vol. XVIII. 1931-1932.

Russian and American Civilizations; Control of Production and Distribution in Major Basic Industries; Wage Cutting and Business Recovery; Capitalism on Trial; Intervention in the Caribbean; Industrialism vs. Agrarianism for the South; Recognition of Russia; Centralized Control of Industry; Cancellation of International War Debts (two debates).

Vols. XII-XVII available. Contents furnished on request.